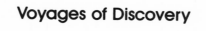

Voyages of Discovery

Voyages of Discovery

The Cinema of Frederick Wiseman

Barry Keith Grant

UNIVERSITY OF ILLINOIS PRESS
Urbana and Chicago

Library of Congress Cataloging-in-Publication Data

Grant, Barry Keith, 1947–
    Voyages of discovery : the cinema of Frederick Wiseman / Barry
Keith Grant.
        p.   cm.
    Filmography: p.
    Includes bibliographical references (p.   ) and index.
    ISBN 0-252-01844-3 (cl : alk. paper). — ISBN 0-252-06208-6 (pb :
alk. paper)
    1. Wiseman, Frederick—Criticism and interpretation.
2. Documentary films—History and criticism. I. Title.
PN1998.3.W57G73   1992
791.43′0233′092—dc20   91-16773
                                                                  CIP

for Zachery Blue and Gabrielle Amber

We make fables to hide the baldness of the fact and conform it, as we say, to the higher laws of the mind. But when the fact is seen under the lights of an idea, the gaudy fable fades and shrivels. We behold the real higher law. To the wise, therefore, a fact is true poetry, and the most beautiful of fables.

Ralph Waldo Emerson, *Nature*

God only knows, God makes his plan,
The information's unavailable to the mortal man.
We're workin' our jobs, collect our pay,
Believe we're really gliding down the highway
When in fact we're slip slidin' away.

Paul Simon, "Slip Slidin' Away"

Contents

Preface

The films of Frederick Wiseman constitute a densely intercon-
nected set of works, a situation that raises difficulties for the critic
who wants to discuss them in a manner that does justice to their
complexity without reducing them to mere demonstrations of particular theoretical models. Thus some initial remarks on the approach and organization of this book would seem necessary.

I quickly rejected as too mechanical the simplest approach of
discussing the films individually in the order of their release. Indeed, even the films themselves avoid a chronological structure.
But many other possibilities readily presented themselves. For example, *High School* and *Basic Training* could easily be discussed in
the same chapter, and several critics have already pointed out the
considerable connections between these two films. Then again,
High School could just as profitably be compared to the *Deaf and
Blind* films. *Canal Zone* and *Sinai Field Mission,* to take still another
example, might have been included in the chapter on military
films. For that matter, a category such as "military films" might
have been avoided altogether (on the grounds that such a heading
places undue emphasis on content) in favor of a stylistic rubric like
"self-reflexivity," a grouping that might include, for instance, *Manoeuvre, Welfare, Model,* and *The Store.* Yet other categories (psy-
chology, social work, foreign policy) are suggested by Wiseman's
own rental brochure. The groupings I finally settled upon seem to
me the best given the arguments I present, but this should in no
way be understood to preclude the possibility of other critical
schemas.

However one chooses to organize an analysis of these films,
what holds them together is their impressive richness as cinematic

texts. Although I do refer on occasion to Wiseman's comments about his work, whether my readings coincide with the film-maker's intentions has not been a concern. Their positioning of the spectator, mise-en-scène, and cinematic allusion is impressively controlled and powerfully expressive, rivaling the best fiction films. Also, it should be pointed out that this is primarily a book of film criticism rather than theory. In these pages, theory is employed in the service of criticism; my aim throughout is to provide readings of the films that demonstrate their richness as texts.

As I explain in the first chapter, Wiseman has referred to his films as "voyages of discovery." Since, as I argue, Wiseman's films depend to such a great extent on their address of the spectator, in writing this book I sought to become the kind of viewer that Dudley Andrew, in *Concepts in Film Theory,* calls "a new, or renewed spectator," understanding the films as signifying systems yet at the same time negotiating with them. Hence, the subtitle of this book refers to the cinema and not the films of Frederick Wiseman, for I treat these documentaries as works that exist in relation to the viewer rather than approach them simply as textual objects. My work as a critic has taken me on a similar journey; I have traveled with these documentaries and regard them as films that are of major importance. Certainly Wiseman's films are, in Roland Barthes' distinction, more writerly than readerly. They are about institutions, power, knowledge, religion, community, sexuality, technology, ideology, and cinema itself; and while no single voyage could claim to chart such vast seas, it is my hope that this book at least provides a useful map for subsequent exploration.

Finally, I would like to make two stylistic notes. First, while all the dialogue is taken from the Zipporah transcripts, I have not followed their terminology because of the apparent inconsistencies in designating scenes, sequences, and shots. Second, the introductory chapter has an exceptionally high number of footnotes so that the interested reader may determine where in the numerous interviews conducted Wiseman made a particular statement. The comments attributed to Wiseman for which sources are not provided are taken from a lengthy interview I conducted with the film-maker in his Cambridge studio in January 1989 and from several follow-up telephone conversations.

Acknowledgments

Several people provided me with invaluable assistance while working on this book. I am indebted to Ernest Callenbach, Terance Cox, Deborah Harrison, and Jeanette Sloniowsky for their careful readings of and insightful responses to early drafts of various parts of the manuscript. Bruce Jackson, director of the Center for Studies in Film, Mythology, and Folklore, SUNY Buffalo, offered me much practical advice. Dr. Cecil Abrahams, dean of humanities at Brock University, enthusiastically supported my work from the beginning. Barry Joe, professor of Germanic studies at Brock University, helped me to become semi–computer literate. Divino Mucciante produced the frame enlargements, for which permission was generously granted by Frederick Wiseman and Zipporah Films (with the unfortunate exception of *Titicut Follies*, because of legal restrictions that were rescinded only after this book was in production). Joyce DeForest, administrative assistant in the Department of Film Studies, Dramatic and Visual Arts, Brock University; Al Ciceran and his staff at Brock's language lab; and Karen Konicek and Bonnie Parsons Marxer of Zipporah Films all provided indispensable technical and clerical assistance. My former student Chris Byford also deserves mention for his help with the bibliography. Jim Welch, editor of *Film/Literature Quarterly*, allowed me to use passages from my essay "When Worlds Collide: *The Cool World*," which first appeared in vol. 18, no. 3 (1990) of that journal. The Social Sciences and Humanities Research Council of Canada provided the financial support without which this book would not have been possible. Ann Lowry, Theresa Sears, and Margaret Welsh at the University of Illinois

Press all gave the manuscript the careful editorial attention it required. And finally, I am grateful to Frederick Wiseman for his consistent accessibility and cooperation and for making the films that inspired my *Voyages of Discovery*.

CHAPTER 1

Man with a Movie Camera

Given the consistent production of documentaries in the history of film, their relative neglect within film criticism is surprising. In a sense, documentaries have been marginalized by scholarship in the same way they have been marginalized by the commercial cinema. Documentaries are almost always discussed *as documentaries* rather than closely read as film texts. And even if one accepts Alan Rosenthal's view that the last decade has witnessed a significant increase in theoretical writing on the documentary, it is nonetheless true, as Rosenthal himself goes on to note, that important critical and theoretical issues have been largely ignored or at best underexamined.[1] By contrast, the fiction film has been scrutinized by the full range of critical approaches—semiotics, psychoanalysis, structuralism, formalism, feminism, reception theory. Genres (the musical, the melodrama, film noir), styles (the classic Hollywood cinema, Soviet montage) and movements (the French *nouvelle vague,* New German cinema) have all been subjected to intense and repeated critical examination. And if film criticism seemed for a while to favor experimental or avant-garde cinema, the interest in narrative has been renewed in the last decade to the point that it virtually monopolizes the pages of the academic film journals.

The relatively little writing there is on the documentary tends to focus on historical, ethical, and political issues and to avoid close textual analysis of specific films. When documentaries are the subject, attention is all too frequently given to the conditions of production. The result is that technology, the physical apparatus, becomes unduly emphasized to the point that, as Annette Kuhn

has observed, it displaces the aesthetic dimension and becomes the
"determining feature of documentary film *texts*."[2] So, for example,
in their otherwise admirable study of American cinema verité,
Robert C. Allen and Douglas Gomery describe the aesthetics of
the form as consisting of "sync-sound location shooting of uncontrolled situations, minimal narration, [and] 'objectivity' of the
filmmaker in editing."[3]

As opposed to the case of classic auteurism, technology is so
privileged in the critical discourse on the documentary, that the
cameraperson (and even the editor) rather than the director is
sometimes seen as the shaping artist.[4] For example, because their
influence exceeded the technical, the cinematographer Richard
Leiterman is credited as codirector with Allan King of *A Married
Couple* (1969), while editor Charlotte Zwerin receives the same
credit with Albert and David Maysles for *Gimme Shelter* (1970).
Rosenthal suggests that for this reason "one could almost say
that the best documentaries are characterized by a multiple
authorship, as opposed to the lone *auteur* theory in commercial
features."[5]

Thus, one noteworthy symptom of this critical neglect is that
documentary filmmakers are seldom discussed as auteurs. Nowa-
days, of course, auteurism is critically unfashionable anyway, and
there are fewer such studies even of fiction film directors (yet
more than at first might be supposed). But the auteurist neglect
of documentary cinema predates the decline of auteurism and so
can hardly be explained simply as the result of a historical shift in
critical interest. It is possible that auteurist analyses of the documentary have been discouraged, at least in part, because documentaries are understood as seeking to capture a profilmic reality.
While this, of course, is not the result of naively viewing documentaries as "objective" or "neutral," consideration of style nevertheless tends to be deemphasized since it is often presumed that a
documentary maker's "vision" is, or should be, subservient to the
film's ethical purpose or to the integrity of profilmic events. But
this should account only for the cinematically unsophisticated
viewer's different responses to documentary and narrative films,
for only a naive empiricist sees the world as having objective
meaning and order and the camera as an unproblematical means
of photographing it. Certainly it is a commonplace of contempo-

rary film criticism that, because of such stylistic choices as camera position and movement, editing, and film stock, every documentary reveals a tension between profilmic reality and interpretation. As Raymond Carney succinctly puts it in his discussion of cinema verité, "its vérité is necessarily and inevitably arranged by its cinéma."[6]

Another problem in viewing the documentary director as auteur is embedded in the very articulation of classic auteurism. In 1962, even as observational cinema in America was developing with startling rapidity, Andrew Sarris attempted to give auteurism theoretical status by suggesting that the "interior meaning" of an auteur's work arises from the tension between the personal vision of the filmmaker and his or her material.[7] Earlier, André Bazin had asked, "auteur, yes, but what *of?*" Whether we understand them to mean subject ("little themes," in Claude Chabrol's sense), script, or generic tradition, neither Bazin's nor Sarris's formulation would seem inappropriate to the documentary because of the a priori existence of the profilmic events seen on the screen. The auteur becomes more difficult to discern in the documentary, since frequently there is no "script" and its traditions are much less clearly defined. Some critics do in fact vaguely refer to the documentary as a genre, while others see it as a form containing several genres—direct cinema, city symphony, ethnographic film, and so on. How, though, can a category of cinema that encompasses such disparate works as those of Robert Flaherty, Leni Riefenstahl, Stan Brakhage, and Peter Watkins be precisely defined in a manner similar to the fictional genres?

Already in 1950 Raymond Spottiswoode complained that definitions of documentary were "distressingly vague" (his own definition is hardly more satisfying),[8] and the situation has improved little since then. While most definitions have been clumsy and problematic, one that has remained useful, despite its vagueness, is John Grierson's "creative treatment of actuality." Lacking the cumbersome circumlocution of so many definitions of the documentary, it incorporates both the facts of the outside world ("actuality") and the filmmaker's inevitable influence ("creative treatment"). Documentary filmmakers themselves long ago noted this tension in their work: Jean Vigo described his first film, *A propos de Nice* (1930) as *"point de vue documenté,"* while Jean Rouch called his *Tourou et Bitti* (1967), in the film's voice-over commentary, "ethnographic cinema in the first person."

Serious critical attention has been given to the personal vision expressed in documentaries like *A propos de Nice*, but such work was encouraged because its director also made important fiction films. What, one wonders, would we think today of a film like *Las Hurdas* (Land without bread, 1932) if it did not have Luis Buñuel's name on it? Flaherty, of course, is the obvious exception that proves the rule. He is the only documentarian to have been granted pantheon status by Sarris in his influential book *The American Cinema* (1968) (although, tellingly, Sarris felt compelled to qualify his enthusiasm for a nonfiction filmmaker by declaring, "Actually, his films slip so easily into the stream of fictional cinema that they hardly seem like documentaries at all").[9] Much has been written about Flaherty's "romantic" Rousseauesque vision of exotic peoples triumphing over hostile environments. Riefenstahl seems to be recognized somewhat begrudgingly as an original voice in documentary, probably because of the politics of her films, while Dziga Vertov occupies his own visionary place in film history. Indeed, *The Man with a Movie Camera* (1929), the work for which he is best known, marks him as more of an experimental filmmaker than a documentarian; in fact, his theoretical writings have probably exerted more influence on the development of the documentary than his films have. In short, it is a lamentable fact of film criticism that while there are books on many minor Hollywood directors, there are none devoted to, for example, the cinema of Richard Leacock, D. A. Pennebaker, Arne Sucksdorff, Michael Rubbo, or the Maysles brothers. Yet each has produced a body of work rich enough to sustain such detailed analysis.

In the case of Frederick Wiseman, the relative absence of such criticism seems especially curious. His work is distinctively original, revealing a consistent style and attitude as immediately recognizable as that of any pantheon director. In conventional auteurist terms, his work clearly reveals the "stamp of the director's personality." Wiseman's films tend to emphasize the human face as dramatically and insistently as those of Ingmar Bergman, while his periodic insertion of hallway and street shots is a stylistic device as consistent, and as important, as Yasujiro Ozu's cutaways. Auteurists like to quote Jean Renoir's remark that a director al-

ways makes the same film; Wiseman, similarly, says his documentaries about institutions "are always the same film, by and large,"
and that they "are all one film that is 50 hours long."[10] Indeed, it
might be said that his films constitute individual sections of one
city-symphony work still in progress. In *Cinema Verite in America*,
Stephen Mamber concurs with Leacock's view that in these kinds
of documentaries the filmmaker cannot be said to function as a
director.[11] In the credits for all his documentaries, however, Wiseman explicitly identifies himself as "director" ("When you're signing the film, you are saying it's your film, this is the way you see it,"
he has said),[12] and in fact this term probably describes more accurately his creative shaping of the material.

    To insist that Wiseman, or any documentary filmmaker, is an
auteur is to run the risk of privileging the personal vision over the
film's historical contexts and "the documentary tradition" (to borrow the title of Lewis Jacobs's anthology). Indeed, this may help to
explain why this approach has been infrequent in documentary
criticism. In a critical discipline that is acutely conscious of both
the ideology of the texts under examination and the analytic
methodologies applied to them, no one wants to be accused of
minimizing the historical real at the expense of the aesthetic artifice. Concerning the historical contexts of Wiseman's films,
though, it is worthwhile to note that Wiseman claims to choose
subjects that interest him, that he has never picked a subject because of a historical event. That *Canal Zone* was filmed during the
American bicentennial and the negotiation of a new canal treaty
with Panama is, Wiseman says, simply coincidence. Given that
Wiseman has a list of potential subjects and that it takes a considerable amount of time to secure permission to film any of them,
historical connections may exist (as in the case of *Canal Zone*), but
they are not crucial to an understanding of the films themselves.

    As for the documentary tradition, it is obvious, I think, that
Wiseman's films exist not only within the tradition of the documentary generally but also in relation to other documentaries that
explore the same or similar subjects. Thus *Basic Training*, for example, might be compared to *Soldier Girls* (Nick Broomfield and
Joan Churchill, 1980); *Near Death* to *Dying* (Michael Roemer,
1985); and *Law and Order* and *Hospital* to, respectively, Brakhage's
Eyes (1970) and *Deus Ex* (1971), from his *Pittsburgh Trilogy*. But if

the aim of analysis is to demonstrate the films' stylistic strategies, such comparisons are fruitful only to the degree that one is interested in content. Additionally, as much in this chapter will make clear, Wiseman's work grows out of several other traditions in American art. If I emphasize the relationship of Wiseman's films to these other traditions as much as to the documentary, it is for the purpose of demonstrating in a detailed fashion their aesthetic qualities, to show that aesthetic pleasure is as crucial to a full understanding of the documentary as are history, technology, and ethics.

Certainly, as the following chapters demonstrate, some of Wiseman's films can be profitably discussed in terms of the tension between vision and generic material. For instance, *Titicut Follies* can be examined in relation to the musical, *Basic Training* and *Manoeuvre* can be compared to war films (even more specifically, as service comedies), and *Meat* can be viewed in relation to the western. Wiseman acknowledges that his documentaries exist in relationship to the dominant Hollywood cinema, noting that "they're all movies, and sometimes my movies play against the clichés of their movies, and sometimes it's quite deliberate." A humorous sequence in *Central Park* shows Francis Ford Coppola directing *Life without Zoe,* his contribution to the omnibus film *New York Stories* (1988), without ever rising from his seat. This suggests the true distinction between the typical Hollywood movie as passive entertainment and the Wiseman documentary as a work that actively engages the viewer. Wiseman has a love of film that dates from his youth,[13] and his knowledge of popular cinema shows in the ways he employs its conventions in his own work. Hollywood movies so dominate our perception of the world that people in Wiseman's films sometimes confuse cinema and reality. Hence the acting coach in *Model* describes a visual spectacle as being like "a flood by de Mille," while an officer in *Manoeuvre* refers to historical figures in an American history documentary as movie characters.

To date, Wiseman has directed twenty-three feature-length documentaries in as many years, and he has been involved in several fiction feature projects—a considerable oeuvre by any account. His documentary output, in fact, may be exceeded only by that of Rouch. Of the several American documentary filmmakers who came to prominence during the heady days of observational cinema in the 1960s, Wiseman is the only one who has consistently produced work of major significance. Moreover, his films probably have had a larger audience than any other group of documentaries (with the possible exception of Frank Capra's *Why We Fight* series, which was required viewing for GIs during World War II) because they were broadcast on television, "the ultimate medium for transmission of documentary communication" according to A. William Bluem.[14] It should be noted, though, that Wiseman claims to make films, not television programs, and he does not alter his style to suit the smaller screen of the electronic medium. Two successive five-year contracts with WNET, New York's Public Broadcast System (PBS) station, allowed him to make one film a year from 1971 to 1981 (beginning with *Essene*) without constraint as to subject matter or running time—although according to Wiseman he had to battle with network executives over sequences in *Law and Order* and *Hospital* and was forced to make cuts for the telecast of *Basic Training*.[15] Generally, the WNET showings have been followed by national PBS broadcasts, and with the exception of *Titicut Follies*, all of Wiseman's documentaries have been broadcast on PBS stations. As well, many have been shown on television in Germany, Sweden, Italy, Finland, Switzerland, Norway, Denmark, Great Britain, and the Netherlands.

Since the expiration of the second contract in 1981, Wiseman has used his MacArthur Foundation grant (a so-called genius award) of $250,000 to begin films for which he then obtains financing, in part from the Corporation for Public Broadcasting (CPB), on the basis of the rushes. These films have continued to be shown on PBS stations around the country, although Wiseman's relationship with the network is an uneasy one. The public television system in the United States is, in Wiseman's view, a "bloated and engorged bureaucracy" that, like the commercial networks and their policy of using only network-produced documentaries, discourages independent filmmakers. (To his great distress, Wiseman discovered only three days before the scheduled broadcast of the first of the four *Deaf and Blind* films that PBS planned to show them in a different order than he had intended. Fortunately, the proper sequence was restored after he protested, but the episode provided him with further evidence of American public television's bureaucratic insensitivity.) In a 1983 article in the *New York Times,* Wiseman attacked the administrative structure of both CPB and PBS, which brings together judges for the program fund who are unfamiliar with film as well as each other.[16] Since the expiration of the contract with WNET, Wiseman has been turned down eighteen times by CPB's program fund. Significantly, he has managed to maintain control over the distribution of his films by founding his own distribution company, Zipporah Films, in 1970.

Wiseman's work has won several major awards, including three Emmys. Many of his documentaries have been regarded as among the most important ever made in the United States, offering the most complete account of American institutional life to be found in any medium. Certainly critics have recognized the importance of Wiseman's cinema. He has been called "the most distinguished practitioner of cinéma vérité"; "the most interesting of American directors"; "our leading, our very best documentary film maker"; "the supreme documentary film maker of our time"; and "the most sophisticated intelligence in documentary."[17] However, despite such glowing encomiums and the publication over the years of several important interviews and critical essays in film and cultural journals, only one extended analysis of his work, Thomas W. Benson and Carolyn Anderson's *Reality Fictions: The Films of Frederick Wiseman,* has appeared prior to the present study.

Wiseman operates the tape recorder and not the camera during shooting (he was a court reporter during his stint in the army, "repeating everything that was said in a courtroom into a microphone for someone else to transcribe"),[18] but he directs the camerawork via hand signals worked out in advance with his cameraman or by leading the cameraman with the microphone. Doing the sound rather than looking through the viewfinder of the camera, Wiseman claims, gives him greater freedom to see what is around him and to choose those things that he considers to be of primary visual interest.[19] After using established ethnographic filmmaker John Marshall on *Titicut Follies* and Richard Leiterman, a major Canadian cinematographer, on *High School,* Wiseman has tended to work consistently with the same cameraman. William Brayne, chosen on Leiterman's recommendation and for his work on King's *Warrendale* (1967), has shot ten of Wiseman's films, and John Davey, who had years of experience as a documentary cameraman prior to working with Wiseman, has photographed twelve.

Thus, the communication between Wiseman and his camera operator has become particularly well established. Benson and Anderson have interviewed Wiseman's cinematographers, noting that their accounts of working methods differ from Wiseman's. They suggest, too, that the four cameramen "are not merely transparent windows for Wiseman's vision" and that each has a distinctive style,[20] although they fail to demonstrate this claim convincingly in their book. As the following chapters show, Wiseman is clearly the shaping influence in his films, for, I would argue, there is virtually no discernible visual difference from one to the next, regardless of the cinematographer.

While it is not an entirely accurate claim, Wiseman's films are generally described within the context of either direct cinema or cinema verité. Both documentary approaches involve the employment of lightweight portable cameras and sync-sound equipment, filming with a hand-held camera rather than a tripod, and capturing events as they happen (i.e., without a script). As well, they share the premise that capturing life in the "raw" (Siegfried Kracauer's term), or "life caught unawares" (Vertov), is not only inherently interesting but more revealing, more truthful to the complexities of experience than either fiction or documentary reconstruction. For champions of either method of filmmaking, life caught spontaneously by the motion picture camera yields a deeper truth. (Predictably, such grand claims have provoked equally intense critical antipathy, as in Bluem's rather overheated rejection of Leacock's *Children Were Watching* [1960].)[21]

Both Dia Vaughan and Colin Young use the term "observational cinema," conflating both the direct and verité approaches and avoiding the imprecision often attached to their use. While neither writer offers a definition that usefully applies to Wiseman's work,[22] observational cinema does foreground this characteristic feature of intense and spontaneous scrutiny of profilmic events. The observational filmmaker, perceiving not with the naked eye but with the kino eye, must enter what Rouch calls a "cine trance" and discover meaning as embodied in the surface of things, within the realm of visible phenomena. This is a crucial feature of Wiseman's cinema, both while the events are transpiring in front of the camera (the shot) and afterward, during the process of editing (the structure).

Elements of the observational style can be traced back to the beginnings of film history, to the Lumière *actualités,* and later to postwar Italian neorealism (Roberto Rossellini, Vittorio de Sica, Cesare Zavattini) and the British Free Cinema movement in the late 1950s (Lindsay Anderson, Karel Reisz, Tony Richardson). But it was with the development of portable sync-sound equipment around 1960 that this approach to the documentary began to appear almost simultaneously in several countries—most notably Canada, the United States, and France. In Canada, the form was pioneered by English and Quebecois filmmakers working for the National Film Board (NFB), founded by Grierson in 1939. In the NFB's Unit B, under executive producer Tom Daly, English-speaking directors Terence Macartney-Filgate, Roman Kroitor, and Wolf Koenig produced work for the Candid Eye series broadcast between 1958 and 1959 which clearly anticipated the style, despite the technological limitations that still existed at the time. In Quebec, Michel Brault (*Les Raquetteurs,* 1958, with Gilles Groulx) and Pierre Perrault (*Pour la suite du monde,* 1963, with Brault) used the observational style to give voice to their province's suppressed culture during the Quiet Revolution, even as they sought to fashion a personal approach to documentary filming.

In the United States, independent feature filmmakers began working with the new portable equipment. Among others, Lionel Rogosin (*On the Bowery,* 1956), Bert Stern (*Jazz on a Summer's Day,* 1959–60), John Cassavetes (*Shadows,* begun in 1959 but not released until 1961), and Morris Engel, apparently shooting with portable 35mm equipment of his own design (*The Little Fugitive,* 1953; *Weddings and Babies,* 1960), experimented with shooting synchronized sound on location in documentary and fictional contexts.[23] More importantly, a group of young documentary filmmakers organized by Robert Drew began making films for Time, Inc., in an attempt to transfer the style of magazine photojournalism to cinema. The group included D. A. Pennebaker, Albert Maysles, and Leacock (who had been the cameraman for Flaherty's last film, *Louisiana Story* [1948]). Together, they made a series of nineteen pioneering films for television, beginning in 1960 with *Primary,* about the Wisconsin presidential primary campaigns of John F. Kennedy and Hubert Humphrey, and ending with *Crisis: Behind a Presidential Commitment* in 1963. The Drew Associates sought to be invisible observers of events transpiring before the camera—like a "fly on the wall," as Leacock described it. They have frequently spoken about the exhilaration that resulted from being able to follow in one shot, for the first time, an action such as Kennedy entering and then crossing a crowded hall where he is to speak, climbing a narrow, more darkly lit stairwell, and taking his place on the stage.[24] According to Erik Barnouw, the technology of the portable equipment peaked with the Drew unit's *Eddie* (1961), about the racing car driver Eddie Sachs, with the camera, tape recorder, and microphone achieving independent mobility.[25] When the Drew unit disbanded, the individual filmmakers went on to make some of the most important American observational films.

In France the approach took a somewhat more assertive form. Jean Rouch, an anthropologist (credited as the first filmmaker to abandon the tripod completely), and Edgar Morin, a sociologist with an interest in film (his book on stardom in the cinema, *Les Stars,* was published in 1957), collaborated in 1961 to make the extremely influential *Chronique d'un été* (Chronicle of a summer), photographed by the French Canadian Brault. The filmmakers foregrounded their involvement in the film by appearing on-screen and prompting the Parisians they interviewed with questions. Later in the film they appear again, showing the footage to these people and talking with them about it. Two years later, Chris Marker made *Le Joli Mai* (The lovely May 1963), which also featured an assertive style of interviewing. Rouch and Morin subtitled their film "une experience de cinéma vérité," and although historical accounts variously ascribe the coinage of the term to one or the other of them (and film historian Georges Sadoul also claims to be first to use the term, in a 1948 translation of Vertov's "Kino-Pravda"),[26] it is clear that "cinema verité" was intended as an homage to Vertov and his idea of the "Kino Eye," a belief that the camera eye was capable of seeing better than the human eye. For Rouch, as for the revolutionary Soviet filmmaker before him, the camera is a catalyst that ignites sparks of truth from what it photographs.

According to Barnouw, "the direct cinema documentarist took his camera to a situation of tension and waited hopefully for a crisis; the Rouch version of *cinéma vérité* tried to precipitate one. The direct cinema artist aspired to invisibility; the Rouch *cinéma vérité* artist was often an avowed participant. The direct cinema artist played the role of uninvolved bystander; the *cinéma vérité* artist espoused that of provocateur."[27] Thus, for example, although both films deal with the same ostensible subject, the Holocaust, and even share some strikingly similar tracking shots, *Shoah* (Claude Lanzmann, 1986) is verité while *Nuit et brouillard* (Night and fog, Alain Resnais, 1955) is not. Yet to what extent this distinction is in fact accurate is a matter of debate, and Wiseman's films are not the only documentaries that refuse to fit comfortably into either category. Certainly the two terms are often used imprecisely and interchangeably, presumably because both relied for their development upon the technology of portable synch-sound equipment and eschewed the use of the heavy 35mm camera, that bulky, prominent apparatus that was for Renoir a "god" and for Leacock a "sort of monster" that commanded the center of attention.[28] The reflex (through-the-lens shooting) capability of the lightweight 16mm cameras meant that the camera no longer had to be the object of "worship," just as sound equipment was reduced in size and weight from approximately two hundred to twenty pounds.

Observational documentaries thus rely on conditions of production that are different from scripted documentaries and, consequently, have different aesthetic criteria (although, to return to my earlier point, it must be emphasized that while these aesthetic qualities in large part follow from the conditions of production, they are not one and the same). Since observational films are shot in uncontrolled situations, the camera must frequently adjust focus depth and lens aperture, compensating for changing light conditions and distance from the action. Camera movement is sometimes jerky and seemingly unmotivated, as the camera operator seeks out material of visual interest with varying degrees of success. The camera is not always in the ideal position to catch the action since it cannot anticipate what will happen or where. Sometimes its view is blocked by people moving in front of it, so that important action is missed or the camera must be repositioned. Thus, these films have developed a distinctive "look" that has come to signify "reality." So, for example, the scripted *Battle of Algiers* (Gillo Pontecorvo, 1966), which is shot in this manner, gains an impression of authenticity, as do the "furtive," shaky shots in the "News on the March" newsreel in *Citizen Kane* (Orson Welles,

1941), which show the reclusive Kane through the slats of a fence—even though the film predates observational cinema by more than a decade.

Further, sometimes the drama in observational documentaries resides as much in the camera's spontaneous search for points of visual interest as in the action of the profilmic events themselves. In Leacock's *A Happy Mother's Day* (1963), for example, while the camera is in the process of reframing Mr. Fisher, we momentarily glimpse Mrs. Fisher before the camera decides on a tighter framing of her husband. While the reframing likely was necessitated by the uncontrolled setup, the brief inclusion and then omission of Mrs. Fisher suggests how she has been consistently disregarded as the town attempts to exploit her quintuplets to promote tourism. Of course, such unforeseen situations are not always so expressive. Elsewhere in the same film the camera moves from the Fisher family obliging a photojournalist by driving their Model T Ford in circles to three ducks walking in a line, presumably making a point about the family's docile response to all the hoopla. But the ducks fail to do anything in particular, and the camera, as if reconciled to an unprofitable digression, wisely returns to the Fishers in their car.

For Rouch, instances of particularly concentrated observation in documentary filmmaking are privileged moments, which he defines as epiphanic flashes of insight, "those exceptional moments when . . . there's a revelation, a staggering revelation."[29] Such privileged moments are usually understood in the context of character revelation, when the camera pierces the truth behind a person's social facade. As early as 1949, Boris Kaufman (Vertov's brother), writing about his camerawork for Vigo's *A Propos de Nice*, claimed that the goal of what he called "social documentary" was for the camera to reveal "the hidden reason for a gesture," a person's "complete inner spirit through his purely external manifestations."[30] The moment when Jason Holiday's theatrical facade momentarily crumbles in Shirley Clarke's *Portrait of Jason* (1967) and tears roll down his cheeks; the final shot of Paul Anka in Koenig and Kroitor's *Lonely Boy* (1961), when the singer is at last offstage and his expression and body posture reveal his exhaustion; and the point where Paul Brennan questions his own ability in the Maysles brothers' *Salesman* (1967)—these are all powerful instances of privileged moments that yield deeper insight into the films' human subjects.

Whether and to what extent the presence of the camera affects the profilmic event—and how much this compromises the verité of the privileged moment—has been perhaps the most hotly debated issue concerning the observational documentary. For some critics, the presence of the camera makes people either self-conscious and inhibited or allows them an opportunity to perform, but in neither case are people acting naturally. For Rouch, though, the camera functions as a "psychological stimulant" that, while perhaps affecting behavior, allows people to do things they otherwise wouldn't, therefore revealing character. Paradoxically, Rouch sees the camera as adding an element of artifice to a situation that ultimately results in greater truth. As he puts it, the camera is for him less a brake than an accelerator.[31]

Wiseman believes that people do not significantly alter their behavior for the camera, that the camera therefore is capable of capturing truths of human character. In his view, if people are made self-conscious by the camera, then they will fall back on behavior that is comfortable "rather than increase the discomfort by trying out new roles. This means they will act in characteristic rather than new ways." Of course, in some sense all the world is a stage, and all of us, as Wiseman's fictional Seraphita observes, are actors, behaving (performing) in ways we assume are desirable or expected. Recent cultural and psychoanalytic theory have convincingly demonstrated the significant extent to which a subject's personality is constructed by ideology. Because of observational cinema's method of production, this is necessarily one of its great subjects. So if Wiseman feels that someone is altering his or her behavior for the camera, rather than out of social constraints (he calls this his "bullshit meter"), he will not use the footage.[32] He also feels that if someone he is filming acknowledges the camera, it breaks the viewer's suspension of disbelief (a dynamic of reception despite the qualification of "documentary") and allows him or her to escape the implications of Wiseman's cinematic construction. Wiseman prefers the term "magic moments," or, interestingly, "good scenes," since for him cinema ideally penetrates surface appearances.

One common criticism of observational filmmaking is that it tends merely to pile on details of surface reality, what Lewis Jacobs calls "the bric-a-brac of mere observation,"[33] in the hope that out of the sheer density of things some kind of truth will emerge. However, because this type of documentary is, like the classical narrative cinema, a system of visual signification complete with its own codes and conventions, the best of them do not merely accumulate visual facts but invest them with meaning. As with T. S. Eliot's notion of the "objective correlative," things can be invested with emotional or thematic significance through cinematic means, like iconography in genre films. Even Grierson, who strongly wished to avoid the "aestheticky" in documentary, acknowledged its symbolic potential. This is made clear in his attack on Flaherty's avoidance of social issues in *Nanook of the North* (1922): "When he draws your attention to the fact that Nanook's spear is grave in its upheld angle, and finely rigid in its down-pointing bravery, you may, with some justice, observe that no spear, held however bravely by the individual, will master *the crazy walrus of international finance.*"[34]

While it is possible for observational films to invest profilmic reality with symbolic significance, this aesthetic quality functions differently than it does in the fiction film. A crucial difference, of course, is that, unlike iconography, objects in observational films lack a priori symbolic significance. In these documentaries the physical elements of the mise-en-scène are found, not created. Metaphoric implications are discovered within the material rather than invented and imposed on it. Objects may begin as functionally present things in the world rather than as deliberately placed props within the diegesis, and people are real individuals rather than characters, but once captured by the camera and projected onto the screen, they become part of the imagery. As Allan King has remarked, in his film *A Married Couple,* Billy and Antoinette Edwards, the couple referred to in the title, are not real people but characters, images on celluloid.[35]

At the same time, because we know the events depicted in observational films "really happened," that is, documentary images reveal a greater degree of connection to the real world, it could be argued that the symbolism of observational cinema generates a greater power than similar imagery in fictional films, however convincing the verisimilitude. No matter how marvelous the special effects are in a fiction film, a death scene will never produce the same kind of horror as that generated by, say, actual footage of a Vietnamese bonze's self-immolation or the explosion of the space shuttle Challenger. It is exactly this ontological difference between real and fictional images that several years ago generated such controversy about what were dubbed "snuff films." Although violent death is depicted frequently and casually in fiction film, when it was thought that real death was being filmed for the sake of voyeuristic pleasure, many people protested vigorously. (In the end, it turned out to be a publicity hoax.)

Critics are quite aware of the experiential difference resulting from these two kinds of images, the fictional and the observational, but have yet to theorize adequately the implications of this difference. The usually insightful E. Ann Kaplan, for example, can only vaguely note, "While it is true that a documentary is a signifying practice and thus removed from lived experience, it seems to occupy a status differing in some measure from that of signs that are produced in a studio or in a fashion that assumes fiction-proper from the start."[36]

This point carries important aesthetic implications. Consider, for instance, James Wolcott's view that the final scene of Wiseman's *Welfare* is a serious aesthetic misjudgment because it is so obvious. The scene shows a frustrated man who, having been shuffled through the bureaucracy of the welfare system, addresses the ceiling and God, saying that he must be waiting for Godot. Wolcott confuses fiction and observation, basing his judgment on an implied equation of the two: "The guy seems to have wandered in from the set of a Cassavetes film," he declares.[37] Indeed. But what might make the scene simplistic in a fictional context is precisely what makes it extraordinary in a real one. As the novelist John Barth writes in *The Floating Opera:*

> Nature, coincidence, can often be a heavy-handed symbolizer. She seems at times fairly to club one over the head with significance. . . . One is constantly being confronted with a sun that bursts from behind the clouds just as the home team takes the ball; ominous rumblings of thunder when one is brooding desultorily at home; magnificent sunrises on days when one has re-

solved to mend one's ways; hurricanes that demolish a bad man's house and leave his good neighbor's untouched, or vice-versa; Race Streets marked slow; Cemetery Avenues marked ONE WAY. The man whose perceptions are not so rudimentary, whose palate is attuned to subtler dishes, can only smile uncomfortably and walk away, reminding himself, if he is wise, that good taste is, after all, only a human invention.[38]

In observational cinema, truth, no matter how obvious, can indeed be beauty. (For similar reasons André Bazin declares that the view revealed by a bronchioscope descending into the human body dwarfs constructed drama with its revelation of "supreme beauty.")[39] In the case of *Welfare,* because Wiseman did not invent the scene but happened upon it, he rightly included it at the end. As Dan Armstrong has convincingly shown, the entire film works as an extended analogy to Beckett's play.[40] The explicit reference at the film's conclusion nicely sums up much of what the film is about, and because one of the welfare clients says it, the filmmaker himself does not have to. As this example suggests, Wiseman is quite conscious of the different "status" of observational footage, and his films exploit this difference in a variety of ways to further complicate the viewer's response.

Certainly one of Wiseman's great skills as an observational filmmaker is that he knows where to look for and how to capture images on film that resonate with meaning despite the uncontrolled circumstances in which he shoots. His eye is less "innocent" (a term often used in reference to Flaherty) than it is disciplined. Wiseman has spoken of privileged moments of speech in his films as "found eloquence,"[41] but he could just as well have been describing his own art. Transcendentalists see the physical world as emblematic; Wiseman, like William Carlos Williams, knows how much depends upon observing a red wheelbarrow beside the white chickens glazed with rainwater. His images are charged with meaning beyond the literal to an extent that can only be called poetic, for he consistently seizes upon objects and physical details in the institutions he films and invests them with significance beyond their functional purposes.

The physical appearance of the school in *High School* (see p. 54) and the processed egg product in *Meat* are just two of the most obvious examples of how in his work physical space and objects,

(*High School*) The importance of body language in Wiseman's films is vividly shown by this close-up of the gynecologist's hand gesture.

respectively, function on a symbolic level. Hallways and exteriors especially are shown to embody the attitude of the institution under examination or to represent the attitude of the film toward it. Gesture and body language, often emphasized in close-up, frequently resonate with deeper meaning.[42] The zoom in to the wiggling finger of the sexist gynecologist talking to an assembly of boys in *High School* is an especially vivid instance of Wiseman's skill at reading body language symbolically. (He defends this particular part of the film with the claim that "it's not twisting what's going on to suit my point of view." By "twisting" he means imposing something that has not happened on the profilmic event.)[43] Hands especially tend to become expressive when shown in isolated close-ups (see, e.g., p. 151). In *The Store*, for example, there is an impressive sequence shot showing nothing but the hands of a jewelry salesman and customer as they discuss expensive rings. The *Deaf and Blind* films particularly rely on images of hands to express meaning. Finally, as for John Ford, ceremonies and rituals consistently assume additional significance, most prominently in such films as *High School, Canal Zone,* and *Sinai Field Mission.* In a sense,

Wiseman's vision is akin to that of the transcendentalists. For him, as for Emerson, "every natural fact is a symbol of some spiritual fact."[44]

Wiseman's films are full of close-ups of faces, revealing the startlingly expressive panoply of American visages. His ability to penetrate the surface of his subjects' countenances—to reveal the chaplain glancing at his watch during a conversation with a distraught soldier (*Basic Training*) or the repressed smiles on the faces of prospective models (*Model*), for example—is reminiscent of Walt Whitman's claim to "see neath the rims of your haggard and mean disguises."[45] People in Wiseman's films (for example, *Basic Training, Primate, Model, Blind*) are frequently shown putting on or taking off masks of one kind or another. As Seraphita notes, "many times the mask is different than what is underneath." Michael J. Arlen writes that Wiseman, like Vertov earlier had wished to do, looks at "men without masks." Indeed, his work fulfills what the film theoretician Béla Balázs saw as the ability of the cinema to reveal the "microphysiognomy" of human facial expression.[46] In *Primate* he achieves some of the most expressive close-ups of animal faces in all of cinema.

Wiseman's films treat sound in a similar manner. Most obviously, they capture the "barbaric yawps" (Whitman) and "primal warblings" (Emerson) of the American people, the rhythms of real speech that Louis Marcorelles has argued is so essential to the nature of direct cinema.[47] The authentic minimalist monologues of the arrested youth in *Law and Order* and the controller in *Manoeuvre* are examples of lived speech unmatched by even the most naturalistic dialogue in fiction films. The importance of language in Wiseman's work is amply demonstrated by Benson and Anderson, who tend (somewhat unfortunately) in their analysis to emphasize the films' verbal elements at the expense of the visual. Further, in the cinematic contexts established by Wiseman, dialogue frequently comes to resonate with meaning beyond that intended by the speaker. Lines like one scientist's wish to "let nature take its course" in *Primate,* or a worker's fear in *Meat* that "heads will roll" because of management policy accrue thematic weight hardly foreseen by the people who utter them. The occasionally muddy sound or dialogue drowned by ambient noise, especially in the more technically limited earlier films, can also work meaningfully.

In *High School,* for example, the viewer is unable to make sense of the lunchtime conversation in the teacher's cafeteria because of the din of clattering dishes and other background sounds. This suggests that their talk is in fact so much noise, as empty of significance as it is in the classroom. Similarly, the constant background noise in *Welfare* expresses the distance between the workers and clients during the seemingly interminable interviews.

Found music in particular almost always works symbolically in Wiseman, beginning with the first images in his first documentary, *Titicut Follies,* accompanied by an off-key performance of "Strike up the Band." Indeed, this first film shows a remarkable sensitivity to the textual implications of found music. When a guard talks about how they used to gas patients, making his eyes tear, a few notes of Erroll Garner's "Misty" are heard coming from the radio in the room. Such irony, however, is often more significant than simply comic. "Chicago Town," for instance, sung by Eddie and Willie, expresses the wish to be a child ("Oh, what a joy/to be only a boy") who delights in amusements ("I want to ride on the shoot-de-shoot/And the merry-go-round") of the big city ("That's where I long to be"). As Armstrong has pointed out, the patients of Bridgewater are in fact frequently treated like children,[48] yet it is also significant that the wish of the song contrasts sharply with the stultifying reality of the insitution. Most of the musical numbers feature lyrics about "elsewhere." Like the irony of "Chicago Town," the trombone rendition of "My Blue Heaven" in the yard contrasts pointedly with the purgatorial reality of people aimlessly milling about.

Further, in Wiseman's documentaries institutions themselves are treated symbolically. The films employ textual strategies that force the viewer to understand them as social microcosms, as interwoven parts of the larger social fabric. Wiseman says he is "interested in how institutions reflect the larger cultural hues." He refers to the process of filming institutions as a search for cultural spoors. He also likens it to tracking the abominable snowman—looking for the creature but finding only its traces.[49] Sarris once explained that the poetic nature of John Ford's films resulted from the director's ability to present "double images"—images that at once express both the concretely individual ("the twitches of life") and the generally social ("silhouettes of legend").[50] Wiseman's documentaries work in a similar way. In fact, sometimes his images, as in *Basic Training* and *Meat,* clearly evoke Ford's mise-en-scène (see pp. 80, 125). Metropolitan Hospital (*Hospital*), for example, comes to signify an illness in American society itself, while the world of Nieman-Marcus (*The Store*) metonymically embodies capitalist consciousness.

By framing the ordinary and familiar on the screen (Wiseman dabbled in still photography before making films), he provides a new "frame of reference" for the viewer and so creates what Vertov called "a fresh perception of the world."[51] Isolating and magnifying the familiar in his images, Wiseman affects a defamiliarization in the manner of the Russian formalists. As the following chapters show, Viktor Sklovskij's claim that "in order to render an object an artistic fact it must be extracted from among the facts of life . . . it must be torn out of its usual associations"[52] would seem to apply rather well to Wiseman's documentary practice.

Structure has been a particularly crucial issue in the aesthetic debate surrounding observational films. Its practitioners have insisted almost unanimously that the films must be structured chronologically in order to remain as faithful as possible to profilmic events. At the same time, as Mamber and others have pointed out, observational filmmakers have sought to combine conventional dramatic structures (protagonists overcoming obstacles to achieve goals) with chronology.[53] Leacock, who almost always structures his work chronologically, claims that the documentary filmmaker should avoid nonchronological editing "like the plague." The Maysles' work, similarly, with the exception of *Gimme Shelter* (1970), is consistently structured according to profilmic chronology. As Al Maysles declared, "in the long run what works best—and we find ourselves coming back to it—is having it happen just the way it happened."[54]

In contrast, Wiseman's films are clearly structured according to principles other than chronology. They are designed in a manner that Bill Nichols describes as a distinctive "mosaic" structure.[55] The chronology of profilmic events in his work is on occasion drastically altered. Sometimes even the temporal duration of specific events is violated, usually for thematic (rather than dramatic) purposes. From his first documentary, *Titicut Follies,* which begins and ends by showing parts of the same musical show, Wiseman has not hesitated to play with chronology and duration. Some films, such as *Meat,* reveal a relatively close fidelity to chronology because of the importance of the particular process (in this case, meat packing) to the function of the institution under examination. Sequences and shots are always connected by straight cuts rather than by fades, wipes, or dissolves so that temporal cues are not provided. These devices are seldom used in documentaries, probably because they call attention to the medium itself and so detract from a film's power as observation, but they do occasionally appear. In *Warrendale,* for example, major sequences are separated by dissolves. In *The Store* Wiseman humorously uses the opening and closing of elevator doors as the found equivalent of the wipe, but technically he relies, as always, on the cut. Wiseman seldom includes indications of temporal relations between sequences unless they happen to arise in dialogue, as when the chaplain in *Basic Training* mentions in his sermon that he has been speaking for five consecutive Sundays. Nor do Wiseman's films ever feature a narrator, either within profilmic events or as voice-over (except in one sequence in *Primate,* where a scientist explains the purpose of his experiments directly to the camera, his account continuing over shots of him at work).

Nevertheless, because Wiseman's films rely on the conventional techniques of narrative construction (establishing shot, cutaway to reaction shot, continuity editing) individual sequences in the films are relatively easy to comprehend. Wiseman's ability to construct individual sequences according to conventional narrative codes is indeed remarkable, given the fact that he films with only one camera. In the final sequence in *Primate,* following the scientists from the Yerkes Research Center to the air force jet, or the beginning of *Canal Zone* showing ships moving through the Panama Canal, Wiseman's camera seems able to move from one place to another, as does the omniscient camera of classical Hollywood cinema. As well, dialogue sequences are frequently constructed so as to appear seamless, revealing no apparent breaks in conversation or logic.

Nichols notes that while each film's individual sequences (the facets or "tesserae" of the mosaic) are organized by narrative codes of construction, the relations between these facets are rhetorical. It is at this level that the viewer must work to grasp the structural logic of Wiseman's films. Since sequences are arranged neither chronologically nor narratively, they actively engage the spectator, who must discover structural and thematic relationships between them. Sequences in Wiseman's films may relate in terms of comparison, contrast, parallelism, inversion, irony, analogy, metonymy, synecdoche, metaphor, or summation. Wiseman says he never pushes his point of view on the audience, for he abhors didacticism. Instead, his cinema is dialectical, asking the viewer to tease out meaning by discovering the structural logic at work. As might be expected, Wiseman's films have invited Marxist analyses, as much for their style as for their institutional subject matter.

It is in the process of editing, this "thinking through the material," where Wiseman engages in a kind of second order looking. It is while examining the material for less obvious significance that his films become profoundly observational. Wiseman readily admits the creative manipulation of his work when he describes his films as "reality dreams" or "reality fictions."[56] The most important aspect of this manipulation is, of course, his distinctively expressive editing. The individual shots themselves originate in the real world but, says Wiseman, "really they have no meaning except insofar as you impose a form on them."[57] In this editing process elements of profilmic reality are compressed, reordered, and omitted, resulting in the creation of an aesthetic construction, or what Vertov called a "film-object." While it is true that the profilmic events in Wiseman's films are always real, never staged, recreated, or rehearsed for the camera, the footage remains for him only a record of the events—meaningless until he structures it at the editing table. On occasion, he has acknowledged an analogy between his editing approach and the preparation of a legal brief. He has also referred to editing as a process of chipping away that which is extraneous to reveal the film, as Michelangelo sculpted.[58] Testimony in the *Titicut Follies* trial suggests that even before making his first film Wiseman was seeking to make documentaries that were both "poetic and true."[59]

Wiseman devotes a considerable amount of his time to editing. While he spends from four to six weeks shooting, he spends more time in the editing room sifting through and giving shape to the material. *High School* took him a relatively short four months to edit, *Primate* all of fourteen.[60] His shooting ratio is high, varying from ten to one for the lengthy *Near Death* to thirty to one for *Missile* and averaging about twenty to one. He admits to doing almost no sociological research in preparation for shooting in an institution; instead he reads novels relating to the subject. Shooting, he explains, is his research. He claims that he enters an institution with inevitable preconceptions and stereotypes but the experience of filming reveals to him a greater complexity about the institution.[61] He initially saw the making of *Law and Order,* for example, shot shortly after the 1968 Democratic convention in Chicago, as an opportunity to "get the pigs." After being out in patrol cars on a daily basis with the Kansas City police, however, Wiseman's attitude changed significantly.[62] What he discovered, he says—and indeed what a careful reading of the film reveals—is that "piggery is in no way limited to the police."

In editing, Wiseman works out a "theory," as he calls it, about events, which is then reflected in the film's structure, or the "web he spins." He sees the process as a "voyage of discovery" and the end result as "a report on what I've found."[63] (Only twice, with *Law and Order* and the *Deaf and Blind* series, did Wiseman return to an institution to shoot additional footage after beginning the editing process. In the first case, he found he didn't have enough material inside the precinct station, and in the second case it was "because it was difficult to keep in mind everything I'd need for four films.") The viewer in a sense repeats Wiseman's own process by discovering the structural logic to the films and exploring their implications. In Wiseman's words, viewers "have to fight the film, they have to say, 'What the hell's he trying to say with this?' . . . And they have to think through their own relationship to what they're seeing."[64] In a way, the films are examples of Kracauer's notion of "found stories," for with multiple viewings patterns begin to emerge from what initially might seem random, as when observing eddying waters in a river or lake.[65] Wiseman readily admits that his films are personal expressions, and, unlike the "phony baloney" rhetoric of direct cinema (an "incredibly pompous expression"),[66] he makes no pretentions about being objective. Still, Wiseman does insist that the views his films express are fair to the experience during the shoot.

Wiseman's style is thus a synthesis of realist and formative elements. He does not hesitate to manipulate the order of events or to break them up, and he has on occasion even "twisted" events, as he defines it. Sometimes, as in *Meat* and parts of *The Store,* he relies heavily on editing, building sequences of considerable length out of many brief shots. Wiseman's description of some of these sequences as "medleys" (as opposed to "montages") underscores his sense of their rhythmic and structural qualities. Yet his films also employ a good deal of camera movement and long takes, stylistic elements essential both to observational cinema and classic narrative realism. Nichols quotes Barry Salt's claim that the average shot length in classic Hollywood film is approximately nine to ten seconds and compares this to the average shot length for a third of *Hospital,* a considerably longer thirty-two seconds.[67] Just as the mosaic editing structure requires active participation on the part of the viewer, so do the long takes of the realist approach. Charles Barr has convincingly argued that when the filmmaker does not "signpost" his meaning through analytic editing, the viewer is forced to extract the meaning from the mise-en-scène. For this reason, as Roberto Rossellini puts it, "a realist film is precisely one which tries to make people think."[68]

It is possible, too, to view Wiseman's approach as a combination of observational documentary and the more traditional Griersonian documentary. His uncontrolled method of shooting, use of the portable camera (Eclair) and tape recorder (Nagra), and recording of wild sound all belong to the observational style. But such films have tended to focus on individuals (most of them, moreover, celebrities and stars such as Jane Fonda, Paul Anka, Bob Dylan, Joe Levine, Marlon Brando, and so on), but there are no true protagonists in Wiseman's films. The people he shows are generally average folks. A character may reappear within an individual film (and the notorious Miss Hightower from *Hospital,* who is not seen but is heard arguing with a doctor over the telephone, later appears in *Welfare*), but the mosaic structure encourages the viewer to focus on the logic of cinematic construction and institutional organization rather than to empathize or identify in any consistent fashion with specific individuals. The earnest Judge Turner in *Juvenile Court,* the postulant Richard and the Abbott in *Essene,* and the somewhat eccentric Dr. Weiss of *Near Death* (not to mention the four patients in this film) perhaps come closest to resembling recognizable protagonists in Wiseman's work. Even in these cases, though, the focus remains diffuse enough so that the possibility of sustained identification is thwarted. Rather, Wiseman says, the institutions are the stars of his films.[69]

The emphasis on institutions rather than individuals, of course, reflects the Griersonian concern with contemporary social issues. Wiseman sees his films together as presenting "a natural history of the way we live."[70] Just as the mandate of the National Film Board of Canada, founded by Grierson, was to interpret Canada to Canadians and the rest of the world, Wiseman shows the world genuine contemporary American life more consistently than any other filmmaker. Wiseman, observing his own culture as opposed to another, has created a series of ethnographic films that reveals how Americans really talk, dress, behave, and think.[71] Like certain great American photographers (Mathew Brady, Jacob Riis, Walker Evans), he has chronicled in pictures a period of national life. It is not insignificant that Wiseman chose an established enthnographic filmmaker, John Marshall (most notably, *The Hunters,* 1958), as cameraman for *Titicut Follies.* (Marshall himself, like Colin Young, emphasizes sequence shooting in ethnographic films but understands Wiseman's mosaic approach as appropriate to the abstract concept of an institution, even though personally he finds the style manipulative.)[72] Wiseman has defined an institution as "a place that has certain kinds of geographical limitations and where at least some of the people have well-established roles,"[73] although, as we shall see, his sense of what constitutes an institution has changed considerably over time.

Grierson's ideas about documentary, particularly his view of documentary as public education and propaganda, was greatly influenced by the social philosophy of Walter Lippmann, which he became acquainted with when he visited the United States in the 1920s. Lippmann believed that in contemporary democratic society it was becoming increasingly difficult for the individual to function as a responsible citizen directly and fully involved in the decision-making processes of government. This wish for responsible and direct participation in government recalls the idealist democracy of the nation's founding. Just as Thomas Jefferson once remarked that given a choice between government and newspapers he'd choose newspapers, so Grierson believed that "instead of propaganda being less necessary in a democracy, it is more necessary."[74] Wiseman himself suggests an analogy between documentaries and news and considers his films to be similarly protected by the First Amendment.[75] Like Peter Watkins, Wiseman sees one of the major functions of his work to be public education and awareness. When asked by Ted Koppel on ABC's *Nightline* (August 25, 1987) why he was opposed to a public screening of a censored version of *Titicut Follies,* Wiseman pointedly explained that "the censoring of *Titicut Follies* or any other film prevents people in a democracy from access to information which they might like to have in order to make up their minds about what kind of society they'd like to live in—it's as simple as that."[76] In short, as he has said elsewhere, "the public good outweighs any individual loss of privacy."[77]

Given their function as exposé, the films also belong to the muckraking tradition of American journalism. Like Ida M. Tarbell's *History of the Standard Oil Company* (1902) and Frank Norris's unfinished trilogy of novels, *The Epic of the Wheat* (including *The Pit* [1903], one of the sources for Griffith's *A Corner in Wheat* [1909]), Wiseman's documentaries reveal the underside of the American dream through its institutions. In a general sense, the camera's ability to document particulars recalls the muckrakers' uninhibited way of naming public figures and citing specific charges, an inherent aspect of observational filmmaking that Wiseman exploits vigorously. More specifically, Upton Sinclair's *The Jungle* (1906), although quite different in tone from Wiseman's *Meat,* focuses upon the same institution, the meat-packing industry. Where Sinclair exposes the unsanitary conditions of the Chicago stockyards and slaughterhouses, Wiseman shows the amazing efficiency of a streamlined Colorado packing firm; yet both wish to shed light on working conditions that for different reasons are deemed unwholesome.

Wiseman himself cites Pieter Brueghel (1525–69) and Jan Steen (1626–79), two painters of detailed social panoramas, as artists whose work anticipated his own. Wiseman's films, like their paintings, present a tapestry of the artist's social milieu. After making his first four documentaries, Wiseman declared that "he had directed four of the most depressing documentaries ever

made";[78] certainly in these films, as well as in some of the later
ones, Wiseman finds a kind of terrible beauty ("Even the corpse
hath its own beauty," said Emerson)[79] that suggests an affinity with
the imaginative worlds of Brueghel and Steen, as well as Hiero-
nymus Bosch. His work also has elements of American naturalism,
anticipated by painters like Thomas Eakins, whose depiction of
such then unlikely subjects as boxing matches (*Taking the Count*
[1898] and *Between Rounds* [1899]) set his work apart from contemporary salon painting. Eakins's startling depictions of surgery in
The Gross Clinic (1875) and *The Agnew Clinic* (1889) are reminiscent
of the opening of *Hospital*. The turn of the century "ash-can"
painters—John Sloan, William J. Glackens, and Everett Shinn (the
inspiration for Theodore Dreiser's *The Genius* [1915])—were followed in turn by the harsh leanness of Charles Sheeler and Edward Hopper. The work of all these painters reveals a certain
affinity with Wiseman's "depressing" documentaries.

There also are clear links between Wiseman's work and the literary realism of William Dean Howells, Hamlin Garland, Stephen
Crane (who took "snapshots" of bowery life in stories such as "The
Men in the Storm" and "An Experiment in Misery"), Theodore
Dreiser, John Dos Passos (whose style could be called, like Wiseman's, "mosaic") and Sinclair Lewis. Like Wiseman, these writers
often deemphasized the characterization of individuals to concentrate on the nature of institutional life and social forces. Dreiser's
description of the eponymous *Sister Carrie* (1900) as "a waif
amid forces," for example, could well describe many of the clients
of *Hospital* and *Welfare*, some of the accused youths of *Juvenile
Court*, the students of *High School*, the trainees in *Basic Training*,
and so on.

Wiseman began making films out of an urge for social reform.
Before becoming a filmmaker, he taught courses in criminal law,
family law, legal medicine, and psychiatry and the law at Boston
and Brandeis universities beginning in 1958. He got the idea for
his first documentary, *Titicut Follies*, from visits he made to the
Bridgewater, Massachusetts, Institute for the Criminally Insane,
where he took his law students to show them where they might be
sending convicted criminals. The film became the focus of a
lengthy legal battle that unfortunately displaced the institution itself as the subject of much media coverage. Wiseman's view is that

the appalling conditions at Bridgewater have not changed in any significant way.

As a result of this experience, Wiseman lost a good deal of faith in the ability of the cinema to affect social change. Sinclair's *The Jungle* may have been instrumental in initiating the legislative reform of the pure food laws, but Wiseman has remained skeptical. "I naively thought that all you had to do was show people how horrible a place was and something would be done about it," he explains. "I learned from *Titicut Follies* that this is not the case."[80] His early optimism had led also to his involvement from 1966 through 1970 in the Organization for Social and Technical Innovation (OSTI), which he described then as "a non-profit research and consulting corporation which works to bring about social and institutional change." Here, too, his experience was less than sanguine. Later he called it "a grand boondoggle" comprised of "middle-class professionals who were just sitting around in rooms, speculating about experiences they knew nothing about."[81] By 1984 Wiseman was claiming that there is no evidence that documentaries affect social change, and that "like plays, novels, poems, [they] are fictional forms that have no measurable social utility."[82] Wiseman recently reiterated this view, even as Randall Adams, an apparently innocent convict who spent years on death row in a Texas prison, was about to be released largely as a result of Errol Morris's stylish documentary *The Thin Blue Line* (1988).

Consequently, Wiseman's films have grown less didactic and more aesthetically complex, as indicated by their gradually increasing length. The first few documentaries have an approximate running time of an hour and a half; *Canal Zone* and *Central Park* are almost twice as long. *Deaf and Blind* became a series of four films, each approximately two hours in length, and the recent *Near Death* is just under six hours. (Wiseman claims not to consider external constraints, such as television programming slots, when editing his films but to work only according to the demands of the material. Indeed, at this point it would be premature to claim that there is a simple pattern where each film is longer than the ones that preceded it. *Missile,* for instance, is under two hours while the much earlier *Welfare* is almost three.) Rather than being motivated by the hope of social change, Wiseman now says he makes his films for himself first, to please his personal aesthetic sense.[83] Elsewhere he says that he intends his documentaries to be as structurally complex as a good novel.[84] Already by 1970, when asked if he considered himself a reporter, historian, or editorial writer, his reply was, significantly, "a filmmaker."[85]

A further difference between the earlier and later films is that the more recent work tends to focus on institutions that are working well rather than on those collapsing under the weight of bureaucracy or capitalist contradictions. In 1974 Wiseman observed that a recurrent theme in his work is the depiction of "a gap between the formal ideology and actual practice, between the rules and the way they are applied" in the different institutions he has filmed.[86] (Indeed, this may be a significant difference between important observational cinema in general and the earlier Griersonian documentary. Consider, for example, the mythic harmony between capitalist enterprise and worker envisioned by *Drifters* [Grierson, 1929], *Industrial Britain* [Grierson and Flaherty, 1933], and *Night Mail* [Basil Wright and Harry Watt, 1936].) Wiseman's first documentaries make these gaps obvious, throwing them into relatively sharp relief. The later films, which show institutions that appear to function seamlessly, reveal the gaps with more subtlety and analytical insight. For this reason, however, many critics have viewed Wiseman's more recent work as less powerful than his earlier films. Rosenthal voices this common view in his remark that Wiseman "seems to have lost some of his original brilliance. . . . his recent films . . . are somehow lacking."[87] However, as the following chapters demonstrate, these later films are no less incisive or critical but only less obvious, less animated by moral outrage and the tradition of exposé that had earned Wiseman the (misleading) title of "the Ralph Nader of documentary."[88]

These shifts in Wiseman's work suggest that his later films are closer in spirit to New Journalism than to the tradition of muckraking. Developed in the mid-sixties, this brand of journalism, as practiced by such writers as Tom Wolfe, Jimmy Breslin, Hunter S. Thompson, Truman Capote, and Norman Mailer, combined reportage with literary devices to present journalistic coverage in undisguised essay form. Capote's oxymoronic description of *In Cold Blood* (1965) as a "nonfiction novel" is similar to Wiseman's description of his films as "reality fictions." The tendency to use the narrative voice in New Journalism, either by writing in the first person or by writing about oneself in the third person, is perhaps analogous to Wiseman's establishment of authorial presence through his assertive editing strategies (although unlike, say, Rubbo, Michael Moore, or Ross McElwee, he never literally appears in his own work). According to Wolfe, Breslin's method was to arrive on a scene early and place himself firmly in the situation so that he could gather "novelistic" details—an approach that sounds quite similar to Wiseman's.[89] Furthermore, like Wiseman, the New Journalists tended to focus on institutions—for example, the military (John Sack's *M*, Mailer's *The Armies of the Night*), professional sports (George Plimpton's *Paper Lion*), and Wall Street (Adam Smith's *The Money Game*). Like Wiseman's sense of his films as "a natural history of the way we live," Wolfe saw the function of New Journalism to chronicle "the way people are living now." [90]

Despite the unflinching harshness of Wiseman's films, at the same time they are frequently very funny, again like much New Journalism. No account of Wiseman's work would be complete without mention of his sense of comedy. Often the comedy is rather dark, as in the case of *Primate* and *Missile*. Not infrequently the material is, frankly, humorous enough to make one laugh out loud. The sequence in *Basic Training* where recruits learn to brush their teeth in unison, the "drama" of the mortarboard tassel dangling on the valedictorian's glasses in *Canal Zone* as the lad gamely presses on with his vacuous speech, and the first couple's story in *Welfare,* which gets more ludicrous as it goes on, are three instances that come to mind immediately. At other times Wiseman simply presents quick shots of found material that is laughable for the irony of its context. Thus in *Canal Zone* we briefly see blank-faced Panamanians watching Kentucky Fried Chicken commercials on television, while in *Primate* a scientist swings on a trapeze to encourage a monkey to do likewise.

Wiseman describes the extended sequence in *Hospital* where the psychiatrist attempts to get welfare assistance for his patient from the improbably but appropriately named Miss Hightower as "an old Shelley Berman routine."[91] The material, says Wiseman, often has "situation comedy value" (as in the office of the vice-principal in *High School*), although his intention is not to make jokes at people's expense but rather to reveal the ironic quality of the gaps between an institution's stated goals and its practices. In the process he perhaps even reveals something of the comic element that informs the human condition. As the acting coach observes toward the end of *Model*, "tragedy and comedy are very close." This sentiment is shared by the model in *Seraphita's Diary*, who adds that "the world prefers to laugh than to cry." The strong comic element, perhaps most effectively revealed in *Primate*, presents the viewer with a complex blend of outrage, exposé, horror, and humor that complicates one's response and prevents one from making easy moral judgments.

Thus the comedy in Wiseman's films is "in the jugular vein" of dark humorists such as Terry Southern, Kurt Vonnegut, Vladimir Nabokov, Bruce Jay Friedman, and Joseph Heller and reminiscent of the absurdist drama of Samuel Beckett and Eugene Ionesco. (Wiseman has claimed that a collection of Ionesco's essays on playwriting was "the best book I ever read about filmmaking.")[92] In both traditions, contemporary life is seen as largely purposeless and illogical, engendering a metaphysical anguish that humor helps to contain. Friedman's observation that the *New York Times* "is the source and fountain and bible of black humor," and that "the satirist has had his ground usurped by the newspaper reporter"[93] would seem applicable to Wiseman's approach as well. Perhaps this kind of humor is in part a defense against the unsettling realities his camera records so boldly. It may seem counterproductive to the political nature of Wiseman's cinema, but as the following chapters demonstrate, the humor works to further involve, even to implicate, the viewer in the issues examined.

Structural complexities, shifts in tone, and the absence of the traditional Griersonian voice-over commentary in Wiseman's films heighten their ambiguity. Nichols claims that "observational documentary appears to leave the driving to us," and, therefore, the danger of observational cinema is that one can respond to it like a Rorschach test.[94] Some teachers, for example, have viewed *High School* as a positive depiction of public education, while others have seen it as an indictment. Some critics have dismissed Wiseman's films, contending that their structural subtleties drain them of clear positions and allow viewers to interpret them as they wish. Alan Westin, though he admires the films, refers to them as "a form of social Rorschach blot. The viewer can read into what he sees on the screen whatever judgment he holds about American society and its values." Richard Meran Barsam, too, uses the ink-blot metaphor, claiming that the meaning of Wiseman's films is determined by each viewer's stock responses and personal values.[95] Even Wiseman has said (although with characteristic understatement) that response to *High School* "is very much dependent on the values, attitudes and experience of the audience."[96] The sequences depicting Rorschach or similar psychological testing in *Juvenile Court* and *Canal Zone* may be seen as deliberate metaphors of viewer reception of the films themselves.

Despite his skepticism and acerbic humor, Wiseman remains a believer in the democratic system. "I have a horror of obvious, cliché-ridden political statements in films," he says. Instead, he believes that documentaries are suspect if they do not reveal ambiguity.[97] Wiseman's films have been attacked as politically soft, as vaguely liberal, since they take no immediately obvious political stand. Certainly Wiseman does not endear himself to leftist critics when he remarks that his politics are Marxist, but more Groucho than Karl.[98] Interestingly, in Thomas Waugh's anthology on the "committed" documentary, *Show Us Life*, Wiseman is treated disparagingly. This is curious, given that his work fulfills all of the requirements the book's contributors put forth as necessary for progressive political documentary filmmaking, including the absence of an authoritative narrator and dominant individual "stars," a sense of structure reflecting the complexity of events, and value as a catalyst for discussion.[99]

I believe Wiseman's style in fact constitutes a political cinema in the truest sense. Consistent with his democratic values, Wiseman refuses to condescend to the viewer by assuming an authorial superiority. Rather, he seeks to position spectators so that they have an experience similar to his own when filming. For Wiseman, "the true film lies halfway between the screen and the mind of the viewer."[100] Thus any serious analysis of Wiseman's work must take account of issues of audience address and reception, factors that, as Rosenthal has recently acknowledged, are glaringly absent from our understanding of documentary.[101] Wiseman's films seek, as he says, to eliminate the cinematic equivalent of the proscenium arch in theater[102] by engaging the viewer on a number of levels—rejecting narrative in favor of structural complexity and ambiguity, mobilizing generic expectations, making an unsettling mixture of tone and artistic traditions, and using periodic self-reflexive strategies. As D. W. Griffith had said, paraphrasing Walt Whitman, "to have great motion pictures, we must have good audiences, too."[103] Ultimately, it is these "good audiences" that Wiseman seeks to discover on his voyages.

NOTES

1. Alan Rosenthal, "Introduction to Part One," Alan Rosenthal, ed., *New Challenges for Documentary* (Berkeley: University of California Press, 1988), pp. 11–18.

2. Annette Kuhn, "The Camera I: Observations on Documentary," *Screen* 19, no. 2 (1978–79): 75.

3. Robert C. Allen and Douglas Gomery, "Case Study: The Beginnings of American Cinema Verité," in Robert C. Allen and Douglas Gomery, eds., *Film History: Theory and Practice* (New York: Knopf, 1985), p. 229.

4. Kuhn, "The Camera I," pp. 72, 76.

5. Alan Rosenthal, *The New Documentary in Action: A Casebook in Film Making* (Berkeley: University of California Press, 1972), p. 8.

6. Raymond Carney, *American Dreaming: The Films of John Cassavetes and the American Experience* (Berkeley: University of California Press, 1985), p. 16.

7. Andrew Sarris, "Notes on the Auteur Theory in 1962," *Film Culture* 27 (Winter 1962–63): 1–8; rptd. in Gerald Mast and Marshall Cohen, eds., *Film Theory and Criticism*, 2d ed. (New York: Oxford University Press, 1979), pp. 650–65; André Bazin, "La Politique des Auteurs," *Cahiers du Cinema* 70 (1957); trans. in Peter Graham, ed., *The New Wave* (Garden City, N.Y.: Doubleday, 1968), p. 155.

8. Raymond Spottiswoode, *A Grammar of the Film* (Berkeley: University of California Press, 1967), pp. 284, 289.

9. Andrew Sarris, *The American Cinema: Directors and Directions, 1929–1968* (New York: Dutton, 1968), p. 42.

10. Anon., "Viewpoints: Shooting the Institution," *Time*, December 9, 1974, p. 95; and Sherie Posesorski, "Social Trials Tracked through Institutions," *Broadcast Week*, June 18, 1988, p. 10. See also Ira Halberstadt, "An Interview with Fred Wiseman," *Filmmakers Newsletter* 7, no. 4 (February 1974): 24; and Christina Robb, "Focus on Life," *Boston Globe Magazine*, January 23, 1983, p. 33.

11. Stephen Mamber, *Cinema Verite in America: Studies in Uncontrolled Documentary* (Cambridge: MIT Press, 1974), p. 2; Richard Leacock, qtd.

in Louis Marcorelles, *Living Cinema: New Directions in Contemporary Film-making*, trans. Isabel Quigly (London: George Allen & Unwin, 1973), p. 53.

12. G. Roy Levin, *Documentary Explorations: 15 Interviews with Film-makers* (Garden City, N.Y.: Anchor Press, 1971), p. 321.

13. Robb, "Focus on Life," p. 17.

14. A. William Bluem, *Documentary in American Television* (New York: Hastings House, 1972), p. 16.

15. Thomas W. Benson and Carolyn Anderson, *Reality Fictions: The Films of Frederick Wiseman* (Carbondale: Southern Illinois University Press, 1989), pp. 351–52.

16. Glenn Rifkin, "Wiseman Looks at Affluent Texans," *New York Times,* December 11, 1983, p. 37; Frederick Wiseman, "What Public TV Needs: Less Bureaucracy," *New York Times,* November 27, 1988, pp. 35, 42. See also Vaughan, *Television Documentary Usage* (London: British Film Institute, 1976), chap. 3: "The Reign of Mannerism," for a discussion of how television discourages the development of distinctive and original documentary work.

17. Richard Shickel, "A Vérité View of High School," *Life,* September 12, 1969 (pagination varies by region); David Bromwich, "Documentary Now," *Dissent,* October 1971, p. 508; David R. Slavitt, "Basic Training," *Contempora* 2, no. 1 (September/February 1972): 11; Ken Gay, *"Primate,"* *Films and Filming* 21, no. 6 (March 1975): 38; and Pauline Kael, "The Current Cinema," *New Yorker,* October 18, 1969, p. 204.

18. Robb, "Focus on Life," p. 26.

19. Frederick Wiseman, qtd. in Eugenia Parry Janis and Wendy Mac-Neil, eds., *Photography within the Humanities* (Danbury, N.H.: Addison House, 1977), pp. 69–70; Halberstadt, "An Interview with Fred Wise-man," p. 19; Levin, *Documentary Explorations,* p. 318.

20. Benson and Anderson, *Reality Fictions,* p. 6.

21. Bluem, *Documentary in American Television,* pp. 128–31.

22. In *Television Documentary Usage,* pp. 22–23, Vaughan uses the term in a way indistinguishable from Rouch's approach to visual ethnography. Young is unnecessarily prescriptive in his description of observational cinema as a type of documentary that does not manipulate chronology through editing, where "the subject directs the filmmaker, rather than the other way around," where the director begins with a sympathetic attitude toward his or her subject, and where the presence of the camera is acknowledged, as in Rouch's notion of shared anthropology. See also "Observational Cinema," in Paul Hockings, ed., *Principles of Visual Anthropology* (The Hauge: Mouton, 1975), pp. 65–79.

23. For an early discussion of these filmmakers, see Jonas Mekas, "Notes on the New American Cinema," *Film Culture* 24 (Spring 1962): 6–16.

24. Critics have taken the same view. Cf. George Bluestone's comment about a sequence involving Humphrey in *Primary* that it "gives us more insight into the bone-crushing fatigue of a primary campaign than a thousand narrative assertions," in "The Intimate Television Documentary," *Television Quarterly* 4, no. 2 (Spring 1965): 52.

25. Erik Barnouw, *Documentary: A History of the Non-fiction Film* (New York: Oxford University Press, 1974), p. 236.

26. See Mamber, *Cinema Verite in America,* p. 5.

27. Barnouw, *Documentary: A History of the Non-fiction Film,* pp. 254–55.

28. Quoted in Ian Cameron and Mark Shivas, "Cinéma Vérité: A Survey Including Interviews," *Movie* 8 (April 1963): 13, 12.

29. See Mick Eaton, ed., *Anthropology—Reality—Cinema* (London: British Film Institute, 1979), p. 61; G. Roy Levin, *Documentary Explorations,* p. 137.

30. Boris Kaufman, "Jean Vigo's *A Propos de Nice,*" in Lewis Jacobs, ed., *The Documentary Tradition,* 2d ed. (New York: Norton, 1979), p. 78.

31. Levin, *Documentary Explorations,* p. 137; Rouch interviewed by Cameron and Shivas, "Cinéma Vérité: A Survey," p. 22.

32. Ira Halberstadt, "An Interview with Fred Wiseman," p. 20. See also Frederick Wiseman, "How Much Truth," in the column "TV Mailbag," *New York Times,* March 1, 1970, p. 22; Donald E. McWilliams, "Frederick Wiseman," *Film Quarterly* 24, no. 1 (Fall 1970): 25; and Levin, *Documentary Explorations,* pp. 318–19.

33. Lewis Jacobs, "Documentary Becomes Engaged and Vérité," in Jacobs, ed., *The Documentary Tradition,* p. 378.

34. John Grierson, "First Principles of Documentary," in Forsythe Hardy, ed., *Grierson on Documentary,* rev. ed. (Berkeley: University of California Press, 1966), p. 149 (emphasis mine).

35. Quoted in Alan Rosenthal, *The New Documentary in Action,* p. 32. Similarly, in their film *Letter to Jane* (1972), Jean-Luc Godard and Jean-Pierre Gorin specify on the soundtrack that they are not speaking about the person Jane Fonda, but "the function of Jane" as a star image.

36. E. Ann Kaplan, "Theory and Practice of the Realist Documentary Form in *Harlan County, U.S.A.,*" in Thomas Waugh, ed., *"Show Us Life": Toward a History and Aesthetics of the Committed Documentary* (Metuchen, N.J.: Scarecrow Press, 1984), p. 214. See also Michael Renov, "Rethinking Documentary: Toward a Taxonomy of Mediation," *Wide Angle* 8, nos. 3–4 (1986): 71–77.

37. James Wolcott, "*Welfare* Must Be Seen," *Village Voice*, September 29, 1975, p. 126.

38. John Barth, *The Floating Opera* (New York: Avon, 1967), pp. 116–17.

39. André Bazin, *Qu'est-ce que le cinéma* 1 (Paris: Editions du Cerf, 1959), p. 57, trans. by J. Dudley Andrew in *The Major Film Theories* (New York: Oxford, 1976), p. 144. Cf. Eric Rohmer's claim in "De la metaphore" that concrete reality on the screen is the stuff of poetry, in *Cahiers du Cinéma* 9, no. 51 (1955): 2–9, rptd. in Christopher Williams, ed., *Realism and the Cinema*, trans. Diana Matias (London: Routledge & Kegan Paul/British Film Institute, 1980), pp. 62–68.

40. Dan Armstrong, "Wiseman's Cinema of the Absurd: *Welfare*, or 'Waiting for the Dole,'" *Film Criticism* 12, no. 3 (Spring 1989): 2–19.

41. Wiseman used this phrase during the Editing Reality symposium at the State University of New York at Buffalo, September 24, 1988.

42. In an early essay published while a teaching fellow at Boston University's Law-Medicine Research Institute, Wiseman already revealed a sensitivity to the importance of body language and gesture as well as verbal intonation. "Lawyer-Client Interviews: Some Lessons from Psychiatry," *Boston University Law Review* 39, no. 2 (Spring 1959): 181–87.

43. Levin, *Documentary Explorations*, p. 323.

44. Ralph Waldo Emerson, *Nature*, ed. Warner Berthoff (San Francisco: Chandler, 1968), p. 33.

45. Walt Whitman, "Faces," *Leaves of Grass: A Facsimile of the First Edition* (San Francisco: Chandler, 1968), p. 83.

46. Michael J. Arlen, "The Air: Fred Wiseman's 'Kino Pravda,'" *New Yorker*, August 21, 1980, p. 94; Dziga Vertov, "The Birth of Kino-Eye," in Annette Michelson, ed., *Kino-Eye: The Writings of Dziga Vertov*, trans. Kevin O'Brien (Berkeley: University of California Press, 1984), p. 41; Bela Balazs, *Theory of the Film: Character and Growth of a New Art*, trans. Edith Bone (New York: Dover, 1970), chap. 8.

47. Marcorelles, *Living Cinema*.

48. Dan Armstrong, "Wiseman's Realm of Transgression: *Titicut Follies*, the Symbolic Father, and the Spectacle of Confinement," *Cinema Journal* 29, no. 1 (Fall 1989): 20–35.

49. McWilliams, "Frederick Wiseman," p. 17; Stephen Mamber, "The New Documentaries of Frederick Wiseman," *Cinema* 6, no. 1 (n.d.): 38; Mamber, *Cinema Verite in America*, p. 217; Anon., "Viewpoints," p. 95; and Janet Handelman, "An Interview with Frederick Wiseman," *Film Library Quarterly* 3, no. 3 (1970): 6.

50. Andrew Sarris, *The John Ford Movie Mystery* (Bloomington: Indiana University Press, 1975), p. 85.

51. Dziga Vertov, "Kinoks: A Revolution," *Kino-Eye: The Writings of Dziga Vertov*, p. 18.

52. Quoted in Peter Steiner, *Russian Formalism: A Metapoetics* (Ithaca and London: Cornell University Press, 1984), p. 50.

53. See Mamber, *Cinema Verite in America*, pp. 115–40.

54. James Blue, "Interview with Richard Leacock," *Film Comment* 3, no. 2 (Spring 1965): 17; James Blue, "Thoughts on Cinéma Vérité and a Discussion with the Maysles Brothers," *Film Comment* 2 (Fall 1965): 27.

55. Bill Nichols, "Fred Wiseman's Documentaries: Theory and Structure," *Film Quarterly* 31, no. 3 (Spring 1978): 15–28; and *Ideology and the Image* (Bloomington: Indiana University Press, 1981), chap. 7.

56. John Graham, "How Far Can You Go: A Conversation with Fred Wiseman," *Contempora* 1, no. 4 (October/November 1970): 32; Rosenthal, *The New Documentary in Action*, p. 72; and Anon., "Viewpoints," p. 95.

57. Graham, "How Far Can You Go," p. 32. See also Halberstadt, "An Interview with Fred Wiseman," p. 22; Frederick Wiseman, "A Film-maker's Choices," p. 30; Anon., "Viewpoints," p. 95; Janis and MacNeil, eds., *Photography within the Humanities*, p. 72; and Sylvia Feldman, "The Wiseman Documentary," *Human Behavior* 5 (February 1976): 65–66.

58. Philip and Elizabeth Nicholson, "Meet Lawyer-Filmmaker Frederick Wiseman," *American Bar Association Journal* 61, no. 3 (1975): 332; Hillary DeVries, "Fred Wiseman's Unblinking Camera Watches How Society Works," *Christian Science Monitor*, May 1, 1984, p. 27. Lindsay Anderson described Wiseman's cinema more accurately than his own work when he said it is "a form in which the elements that you use are the *actual* elements. It is the manipulation of the *actual* world into, as far as I am concerned, a poetic form—and that is documentary." Levin, *Documentary Explorations*, p. 66.

59. Benson and Anderson, *Reality Fictions*, p. 13.

60. Janis and MacNeil, eds., *Photography within the Humanities*, p. 71.

61. Alan Westin, " 'You Start Off with a Bromide': Conversation with Film Maker Frederick Wiseman," *Civil Liberties Review* 1, no. 2 (Winter/Spring 1974): 57.

62. Paul D. Zimmerman, "Shooting It Like It Is," *Newsweek*, March 17, 1969, p. 134; Mamber, "The New Documentaries of Frederick Wiseman," p. 39; Gary Arnold, *"Law and Order," Washington Post*, March 7, 1970, p. C6; and Frederick Wiseman, "Reminiscences of a Film Maker: Frederick Wiseman on *Law and Order*," *Police Chief* 36, no. 9 (September 1969): 32–35.

63. John Graham, "How Far Can You Go," p. 31; Halberstadt, "An Interview with Fred Wiseman," p. 22; McWilliams, "Frederick Wiseman," pp. 20, 22–23; Mamber, "The New Documentaries of Frederick Wise-

man," pp. 38–39; Allan T. Sutherland, "Wiseman on Polemic," *Sight and Sound* 47, no. 2 (Spring 1978): 82; Rosenthal, *The New Documentary in Action*, p. 72; Levin, *Documentary Explorations*, pp. 316–18; Janis and Mac-Neil, eds., *Photography within the Humanities,* p. 72; Philip and Elizabeth Nicholson, "Meet Lawyer-Filmmaker Frederick Wiseman," p. 329. In his taxonomy of documentary genres, Bruce E. Gronbeck specifically cites *High School* as an example of "the report." "Celluloid Rhetoric: On Genres of Documentary," Karlyn Kohrs Campbell and Kathleen Hall Jamieson, eds., in *Form and Genre: Shaping Rhetorical Action* (Falls Church, Va.: The Speech Communication Association, n.d.), pp. 139–61.

64. Graham, "How Far Can You Go," p. 33. See also Halberstadt, "An Interview with Fred Wiseman," p. 20; and Janis and MacNeil, eds., *Photography within the Humanities,* p. 75.

65. Siegfried Kracauer, *Theory of Film: The Redemption of Physical Reality* (New York: Oxford, 1965), pp. 245–46.

66. Robb, "Focus on Life," p. 28; Berg, "'I Was Fed Up with Hollywood Fantasies,'" *New York Times*, February 1, 1970, sec. 2, p. 26. See also Levin, *Documentary Explorations*, p. 318.

67. Nichols, *Ideology and the Image*, pp. 210–11.

68. Charles Barr, "Cinemascope: Before and After," in Gerald Mast and Marshall Cohen, eds., *Film Theory and Criticism*, 2d ed. (New York: Oxford University Press, 1979), pp. 140–68; Roberto Rossellini, "A Discussion of Neo-Realism—Rossellini Interviewed by Mario Verdone," *Screen* 14, no. 4 (Winter 1973/74): 71.

69. Berg, "'I Was Fed Up with Hollywood Fantasies,'" p. 26; Rosenthal, *The New Documentary in Action,* p. 69; Mamber, "The New Documentaries of Frederick Wiseman," p. 39; and Janis and MacNeil, eds., *Photography within the Humanities,* p. 67.

70. David Eames, "Watching Wiseman Watch," *New York Times Magazine,* October 2, 1977, p. 97.

71. In his important article on this type of documentary film, "Prospects of the Ethnographic Film," *Film Quarterly* 23, no. 2 (Winter 1969/70): 16–30, David MacDougall includes *Titicut Follies* in his list of ethnographic films about industrialized societies.

72. John Marshall and Emile de Brigard, "Idea and Event in Urban Film," in Hockings, ed., *Principles of Visual Anthropology,* p. 138.

73. Janis and MacNeil, eds., *Photography within the Humanities*, p. 67. See also Rosenthal, *The New Documentary in Action,* p. 69.

74. Thomas Jefferson, *The Papers of Thomas Jefferson,* 17 vols., ed. Julian P. Boyd (Princeton: Princeton University Press, 1955), II:49; John Grierson, "The Nature of Propaganda," in Richard Meran Barsam, ed., *Nonfiction Film: Theory and Criticism* (New York: Dutton, 1976), p. 39.

75. Westin, "'You Start Off with a Bromide,'" p. 64; Levin, *Documentary Explorations*, p. 319.

76. See also Frederick Wiseman, "A Filmmaker's Choices," p. 30; Sutherland, "Wiseman on Polemic," p. 82.

77. Quoted in Mamber, "The New Documentaries of Frederick Wiseman," p. 40. The ethical implications of this view are explored by Calvin Pryluck in his essay, "Ultimately We Are All Outsiders: The Ethics of Documentary Filming," *Journal of the University Film Association* 28, no. 1 (Winter 1976): 21–29.

78. Berg, "'I Was Fed Up with Hollywood Fantasies,'" p. 25.

79. Emerson, *Nature*, p. 20.

80. Quoted in Sutherland, "Wiseman on Polemic," p. 82. See also McWilliams, "Frederick Wiseman," p. 19; Westin, "'You Start Off with a Bromide,'" pp. 61–62; Anon., "Viewpoints: Shooting the Institution," p. 96; and Janis and MacNeil, eds., *Photography within the Humanities*, p. 77.

81. McWilliams, "Frederick Wiseman," p. 19; Westin, "'You Start Off with a Bromide,'" p. 62.

82. Wiseman, "A Filmmaker's Choices," p. 30.

83. Rosenthal, *The New Documentary in Action*, p. 74. See also Levin, *Documentary Explorations*, p. 326.

84. Eames, "Watching Wiseman Watch," p. 98.

85. Graham, "How Far Can You Go," p. 31. See also Halberstadt, "An Interview with Fred Wiseman," p. 22.

86. Westin, "'You Start Off with a Bromide,'" p. 60. See also Rosenthal, *The New Documentary in Action*, p. 72.

87. Alan Rosenthal, ed., "Introduction," in *The Documentary Conscience: A Casebook in Film Making* (Berkeley: University of California Press, 1980), p. 9.

88. Harry M. Geduld, "Garbage Cans and Institutions: The Films of Frederick Wiseman," *The Humanist* 31, no. 5 (September/October 1971): 36.

89. Wolfe, "The New Journalism," in Tom Wolfe and E. W. Johnson, eds., *The New Journalism* (New York: Harper & Row, 1973), p. 14.

90. Ibid., p. 28.

91. Janis and MacNeil, *Photography within the Humanities*, p. 69; Mamber, "The New Documentaries of Frederick Wiseman," p. 39.

92. Robb, "Focus on Life," p. 28.

93. Bruce Jay Friedman, "Forward," Bruce Jay Friedman, ed. *Black Humor* (New York: Bantam Books, 1965), pp. viii, x.

94. Bill Nichols, "The Voice of Documentary," *Film Quarterly* 36, no. 3 (Spring 1983): 20, 21.

95. Westin, "'You Start Off with a Bromide,'" pp. 54–55; Richard Meran Barsam, *Nonfiction Film: A Critical History* (New York: Dutton, 1973), p. 272. See also Cristine Russell, "Science on Film: The *Primate Controversy*," *Bioscience* 25, no. 3 (March 1976): 151. Benson and Anderson are the only critics who invoke the metaphor to disagree with it: "Are the films merely inkblots? We think not," *Reality Fictions*, p. 6.

96. Rosenthal, *The New Documentary in Action*, p. 75. See also Mamber, "The New Documentaries of Frederick Wiseman," p. 39; Levin, *Documentary Explorations*, p. 323; and Graham, "How Far Can You Go," p. 33.

97. McWilliams, "Frederick Wiseman," p. 23.

98. Westin, "'You Start Off with a Bromide,'" p. 55.

99. Waugh, *"Show Us Life."* See especially the essays by Chuck Kleinhans, "Forms, Politics, Makers and Contexts: Basic Issues for a Theory of Radical Political Documentary," pp. 318–42; and Julianne Burton, "Democratizing Documentary: Modes of Address in the Latin American Cinema, 1858–72," pp. 344–83.

100. Quoted in Anon., "The Talk of the Town," *New Yorker,* October 24, 1988, p. 32. See also John Graham, "'There Are No Simple Solutions': Wiseman on Film Making and Viewing," in Thomas R. Atkins, ed., *Frederick Wiseman* (New York: Simon & Schuster, 1976), pp. 44–45.

101. Rosenthal, "Introduction," *New Challenges to Documentary*, p. 15.

102. Graham, "'There are No Simple Solutions,'" pp. 44–45.

103. D. W. Griffith, from "Motion Pictures: The Miracle of Modern Photography," in Harry M. Geduld, ed., *Focus on D. W. Griffith* (Englewood Cliffs, N.J.: Prentice-Hall, 1971), p. 57.

CHAPTER 2

American Madness

Titicut Follies (1967) • *High School* (1968) • *Law and Order* (1969)
Hospital (1970) • *Juvenile Court* (1974) • *Welfare* (1975)

In 1835, Alexis de Tocqueville, perhaps the most perceptive of the many Europeans to visit the United States in the first half of the nineteenth century, observed that social mobility and the lack of a true aristocracy in America broke the social chain of being that had characterized European society and freed the individual "links." He found democracy therefore paradoxical and prone to instability, with the individual subsequently rendered "puny" even as he or she was empowered politically. De Tocqueville attributed the amazing preponderance of institutions and organizations he had discovered in America to an attempt to counter the individual's reduced sense of social cohesion and importance.[1]

Wiseman's cinema examines these institutional and organizational structures and how, ironically, they have made us all feel "puny," both individually and collectively. "Each film," Wiseman has said, "explores a different aspect of the relationship of the individual to the state in a democratic society."[2] From the disempowered black youths struggling to survive in the ghetto in *The Cool World* to the medical staff, patients, and families grappling with the ethical choices that arise as a result of technology in *Near Death*, people in Wiseman's films are presented as reduced in a variety of ways, made one-dimensional by contemporary American culture. The recurrent images of people forcibly shaved, as in *Titicut Follies*, *Basic Training*, and *Hospital*, as well as the monkeys shaved for experiments in *Primate* and the sheared sheep in *Meat*, express this diminished autonomy of the individual. Shots of files and dossiers, computer cards and tape, punctuate the films, suggesting how people have been reduced to statistics. A former student in *High School,* about to be dropped behind the DMZ in Vietnam, defines himself as "only a body doing a job." This phrase reverberates tellingly throughout Wiseman's *oeuvre.*

Six of the early documentaries share a common focus on public, tax-supported institutions. Wiseman approaches these institutions as, in his words, cultural "spoors" or social microcosms. In *Primary,* the Drew filmmakers want us to view the campaigns of Hubert Humphrey and John F. Kennedy as emblematic of the American political process and its debasement by the mass media. Yet the film finds no textual strategies for representing its profilmic material in this way and so must fall back on the narrator's assertion that what happened in Wisconsin in 1960 could happen anywhere, anytime. Wiseman's films, by contrast, while viewing their subjects with the concrete force that observational cinema is ideally suitable for, encourage a wider reading of the specific institution as a reflection of American society itself. This wider view is animated by a sense of outrage, a strongly negative vision of institutions. Because of this moral concern, Wiseman refuses to provide a comfortable position for viewers, offering instead textual ambiguity. These six films inaugurate Wiseman's search for an aesthetically satisfying form for his concept of "reality fiction," establishing the basic method and style that characterize his subsequent, aesthetically richer, work.

From the outset, the effect is provocative. The wryly ironic opening of Wiseman's first documentary, *Titicut Follies,* about the Bridgewater, Massachusetts Hospital for the Criminally Insane, presents some darkened, at first indistinct faces. The camera pans from one face to the next, momentarily bringing each out of the engulfing darkness into the light, only to make them disappear into darkness again. The light itself is ghastly, emanating from harsh footlights below, as in an old Hollywood horror film. Wilfred Sheed's description of the production as "a travesty of the latest Ziegfeld, as interpreted by Trappist monks"[3] only begins to capture its eerie quality. These sickly faces sing the Gershwins' "Strike Up the Band" as if marking the initiation of Wiseman's entire institutional series.

This opening sequence, at the inmates' annual musical revue from which the film gets its title, inaugurates a reflexive examination of observational cinema that Wiseman has continued throughout his work. It immediately establishes the filmmaker's awareness of his chosen medium and the viewer's position as active participant.[4] Because it depicts a performance, the sequence addresses the debate about how the camera affects the profilmic event and to what extent people perform for the camera. The implication is that people indeed may perform, and sometimes do, but as Wiseman (like Rouch) has said, this does not necessarily invalidate the observational method, for out of it insights may nevertheless emerge. As a teacher tells a parent in *High School,* "we can only judge on the basis of performance."

The camera views the performance from the audience's vantage point, as if the performance is put on for the film viewer. One is reminded of Norman Bates's attack on Marian Crane in *Psycho* (Alfred Hitchcock, 1960) when she suggests he send his mother to an institution; his description of the place with "the cruel eyes studying you" suddenly makes us, along with Marion, feel ashamed. We are made to respond similarly in *Titicut Follies.* This is one of *our* institutions, after all (Barsam notes that *"Titicut Follies* exposes more about us than it does about Bridgewater"),[5] and so attention must be paid. Wiseman says that "the ideas of the movie came out of the absolute sense of shock about what Bridgewater was about."[6] This feeling is, in turn, conveyed to the viewer, who is not allowed to maintain the comfortable position of voyeur. A position as the invisible, unacknowledged spectator that Leacock calls "the fly on the wall" is one that can rarely be assumed in Wiseman's cinema for any length of time, despite first impressions based on his generally unacknowledged camera.

This undercutting of voyeuristic invisibility is reinforced at several points in the film when the camera's gaze is returned by patients. The most powerful example of this occurs when the camera follows the naked ex-schoolteacher Jim into his cell, where he huddles in a corner trying to cover his genitals with his hands. Jim's futile attempt at modesty signals his awareness of the camera's presence, as does his direct return of the camera's gaze. Momentarily he halts in his action, as if sizing up the camera's focus on him. Inevitably, we become painfully aware of the camera's (and of our) intrusive presence.

Further, performance is thematically central to the film since the inmates are forever "on stage," always under observation by the staff. As Michel Foucault has shown, the mental institution is a place where the behavior of people labeled insane is always being observed and judged by those in control, "a sort of invisible tribunal in permanent session."[7] The film shows inmates in a variety of performances, some overt, others more subtle. As in Samuel Fuller's *Shock Corridor* (1963), sanity at Bridgewater is defined as a "convincing performance."

Vladimir, trying too hard to convince the staff that he is sane and should be sent back to prison, overplays his role such that his request is denied. Even Eddie, one of the guards, seems to define himself more as a performer (he acts as emcee of the follies revue and sings several other times in the film) than a guard. After his song in the party sequence, he does an encore and exits with a theatrical flourish. The film ends with another song from the revue, the finale ("We've had our show / The best that we coud do / To make your hearts aglow"). Like a musical, the entire film is framed within the context of a show, demonstrating the work's awareness of its performance aspect. In contrast to the classical musical's vision of a harmonious, utopian community,[8] however, *Titicut Follies* presents a dystopian collection of alienated individuals.

Along with *Essene*, the title *Titicut Follies* is for Wiseman's work uniquely nondescriptive. It gives us no indication of its subject, and its significance is never explained within the film. Even if we happen to possess this information in advance, the opening performance is still confusing because it is impossible to know with any degree of certainty the status of some of the people we are shown. Are these all inmates, or are some of the men guards? We do not discover that Eddie is in fact a guard until he is glimpsed walking by the camera in his uniform in a later sequence. Critic Robert Hatch complained that the film was inept because it raised but failed to answer so many questions: "Is the show a part of their therapy, how does the audience respond (there is not a single shot into the house), is this a regular feature of the hospital life?"[9] But, of course, this is quite to the point, for the sequence attacks our

comfortable position as spectators from several flanks at once. After the finale, Eddie, as emcee, asks with unintentional irony,
"weren't they terrific?" These are the film's last words, leaving us
to determine our responses to and judgments about the inmates,
their "performance," and their situation.

The black humor (Eddie declares, "And it keeps getting better
and better"), the found symbolism, the importance of social functions and rituals, the problematized relationship of the spectator
to the text, and the reflexive implications about observational cinema itself are all significant elements of this opening sequence.
Thus begins Wiseman's work in documentary filmmaking, a pre-
scient sequence that adumbrates various aspects of his style.

At the same time as the film forcefully confronts us with particular people in a specific institution, we are invited by the text to
view Bridgewater metaphorically. One patient (identified in the
transcript as Kaminsky) delivers a delirious monologue that explicitly makes an analogy between Bridgewater and America itself.
The country's military aggression is, he says, a result of frustration, of being "sex crazy," the same opinion Dr. Ross holds of the
sex offender Mitch. Several contemporary reivews of *Titicut Follies*
compared the film to Peter Weiss's play *Marat/Sade*, made into a
successful film by Peter Brook in 1966 and shot in a pseudo-direct
cinema style.[10] Both films are set in mental institutions, both feature aspects of performance within the text, both make important
use of music, and both explore the nature of madness in the context of politics and the state.

However, more resonant connections can be discerned with Ken
Kesey's novel *One Flew Over the Cuckoo's Nest* (1962), although they
seem to have been overlooked, at least by reviewers. The work of
Kesey and Wiseman shares a view of the mental institution as a
metaphor for what Wiseman calls the "larger cultural hues" of
America. (It is probably for this reason that Wiseman inserts a shot
of a cinema marquee advertising Milos Forman's 1975 film version of Kesey's novel in *Canal Zone*. Benson and Anderson report
that, according to Wiseman, Forman's cast and crew watched *Titicut Follies* repeatedly before beginning production.[11]) The book's
self-conscious "American theme" is suggested by Kesey's narrator,
a mute Native American, just as Wiseman's "Titicut" is the Native
American name for the Bridgewater area. *Welfare*, tellingly, begins

with a displaced Native American protesting that he is "a person." The man's description of the reservation as a concentration camp echoes Chief Bromden's fantasy in Kesey's novel about the military-industrial compex that he calls "the combine" (the same phrase that is used by Governor Parfitt to describe the political economic control of zonian life in *Canal Zone*). *Titicut Follies* and *Cuckoo's Nest* both focus on issues of emasculation through medication (in *Titicut Follies*, one patient imagines that the doctors are going to remove his testicles) and other severe forms of treatment as a way of maintaining social control. (In this sense, the film anticipates *Primate*.)

Finally, both works question the definition of madness and sanity. In *Titicut Follies*, Dr. Ross and the patient Vladimir have a discussion in the yard. Dr. Ross predicts that if released Vladimir will return to the asylum immediately. Then, strangely, Dr. Ross tells Vladimir that if the prediction is wrong "you can spit on my face." Obviously as taken aback as the viewer, Vladimir responds with the sensible question, "Why should I do that?" At this moment the doctor, like Kesey's Nurse Ratched, seems to be the mad one. Similarly, the behavior of some of the guards may also seem "crazy." In *Titicut Follies*, however, insanity is less the seething, controlled hostility of a big nurse than the banality of common callousness, as when Jim is taunted about his dirty room and Albert is teased in the bathtub.

Yet there is a crucial difference between the two works. In Wiseman's vision of the American snake pit there is not boisterous embodiment of the life principle to equal Kesey's robust Randall Patrick McMurphy. Vladimir, like the novel's Billy Bibbitt, can mount only a weak protest, the response to which is increased medication. His inescapable position is represented by the brick wall in the yard behind him where he talks with Dr. Ross. In Kesey's book, McMurphy's lobotomy serves as a sacrificial act that redeems the Chief from his muteness. In the end, Bromden escapes the institution to return to his land ("I been away a long time," he says). But the vision of *Titicut Follies* is darker, for it seems that the only way out is through death. Vladimir wants to leave, but cannot, while, as far as we are shown, only a corpse is allowed to depart. In the film Vladimir may resist, but it helps neither him nor anyone else.

The film refuses to allow the viewer a comfortable experience because of its strong sense of moral indignation—a point of view clearly signaled by the word "Follies" in the film's title. Indeed, in *Titicut Follies* Wiseman criticizes the conditions at Bridgewater with editing that, like Sergei Eisenstein's notion of the "Kino-fist," is far from subtle. Immediately after the opening performance, there is a quick shot of a guard ordering an inmate to get his clothes. This is followed by Mitch's interview with Dr. Ross, who questions him in a blunt way that, while likely necessary, nevertheless seems unduly callous. As the interview proceeds, Wiseman cuts suddenly to some guards strip-searching newly arrived inmates. The film then returns to the interview, where Dr. Ross's questions become more aggressive, perhaps even tinged with cruelty. (Arthur Knight describes him as "a German-accented doctor who licks his lips over every sex question," while Amos Vogel calls him a "Dr. Strangelove psychiatrist.")[12] Viewer sympathy here is more likely to align itself with the patient, who admits his problems and seeks help, than with the doctor, who says weakly, perhaps even begrudgingly, "you'll get it here, I guess." The inserted shot of the stripping of the inmates offers an obvious comparison between the two procedures; Dr. Ross' interview with Mitch is a psychological stripping, a cold, incompassionate prodding that offers little warmth or comfort. As Foucault said of the science of psychiatry as it developed in the institution of the asylum, it would always be observation and classification, never a dialogue.[13]

Similar in tone is Wiseman's presentation of the emaciated Malinowsky, the inmate who is force-fed because he has refused to eat. Like the inmates in the earlier strip-search sequence, the man is naked, a sign of his vulnerability and powerlessness. As the tube is lubricated and pushed through one of Malinowski's nostrils (on a wall behind the doctor hangs a calendar with an advertisement for "Perfection Oil"), Wiseman inserts several quick shots of the same man being prepared for his funeral at a later date. The shaving of the corpse connects the treatment of Malinowski to the earlier rough shaving of Jim's face, which causes blood to trickle down his chin and, as Stephen Mamber notes, ironically suggests that Malinowski received more attention in death than he did when alive.[14] Moreover, the inserted shots draw precise ironic parallels between the two procedures. When the tube is put into his nose, a shot is inserted of the dead Malinowsky being shaved; when Wiseman's camera pans to the watching eyes of the guards holding him down, there follows a shot of the dead man's eyes being stuffed with cotton; after Ross removes the tube from Malinowsky's nose, there is a shot of the shaving process completed; and after Malinowsky is led away, there is a shot of the body being stored on a sliding tray in the morgue. The contrast between these two events is emphasized even further by the soundtrack, for the feeding procedure is accompanied by a clutter of ambient noise and voices while each of the embalming shots is starkly silent. Finally, while forcefeeding the inmate, Dr. Ross smokes a cigarette, its long ash hanging precipitously over the funnel through which the patient is receiving his food. Like the cigarette and ruler in the hand of the coroner at the end of Stan Brakhage's *The Act of Seeing with One's Own Eyes* (1971), the image is a powerful objective correlative of institutional indifference.

The stark, unsettling power of *Titicut Follies* embroiled Wiseman in a complex legal battle that was not resolved until July 1991, when Judge Andrew Gil Meyer of the Massachusetts Superior Court reversed the earlier ruling.[15] Before the court's decision to restrict the film, *Titicut Follies* was screened as part of the "Social Change in America" program of the New York Film Festival in the fall of 1967 and then had a six-day commercial run. With the exception of reviews by the more perceptive Robert Coles and Richard Schickel, the film was not particularly well received. Wilfred Sheed, for example, saw the film as exploiting the inmates ("offering a vulture's-eye-view"), while Arthur Knight thought it violated "common decency" and even accused Wiseman of shooting with hidden cameras. Brendan Gill claimed it "was a sickening film from start to finish," and that it "has no justification for existing except to the extent that it is intended to have legislative and other non-aesthetic consequences." Vincent Canby, not knowing exactly what to say about it, described the film as "occasionally awkward and always compelling."[16]

The result of the extended legal battle, dubbed by Charles Taylor "The *Titicut Follies* Follies,"[17] was that the film itself became the focus of attention rather than the conditions at Bridgewater. The much-publicized litigation may have gained Wiseman some notoriety early in his career, but it did little to improve conditions at

the institution. It was reported by the press in the Spring of 1987,
twenty years after Wiseman's film, that five inmates had died that
year alone at Bridgewater, three of them by suicide. The institution was the subject of ABC's *Nightline* on August 25th that year,
with Wiseman as one of the guests. The *Titicut Follies* experience
taught Wiseman that social change is not easily achieved. This lesson, it would seem, significantly affected his filmmaking practice,
for not only did Wiseman become more careful of legal concerns
but his style became less didactic in manner, more subtle in its social criticism.

High School, Wiseman's second film, already reveals such aesthetic growth. Indicative of this was his decision to film in an institution that seemed to be working relatively well. The film was
shot at Philadelphia's Northeast High School, a relatively "good"
school in the system (unlike Bridgewater, neither underfunded
nor understaffed) chosen because Wiseman felt an inner city
school would be too easy a target.[18] The film demonstrates a remarkable advance in Wiseman's sense of structure. From the
sledgehammer Kino-fist style of *Titicut Follies,* he begins in this
film to explore a more complex dialectical form of montage,
establishing more resonant relationships between sequences that
are themselves embedded within a more carefully organized
structure.

Elements of the film's style, it is true, particularly the numerous
close-ups, retain the heavily didactic quality of *Titicut Follies* and
obviously portray the teachers at Northeast negatively. *High School*
relies on these close-ups to a greater extent than any of Wiseman's
other films, with the exception of *Essene,* where they function differently. In *High School,* the close-ups appear consistently, beginning with the first teacher who announces the "thought for the
day." With few exceptions they are of teachers' faces rather than
students'. When the vice-principal (identified as the dean of discipline in the transcript) speaks to a boy who does not want to take
gym, for example, the camera zooms in to a big close-up of his
mouth. The image of the mouth, isolated from the rest of his face
and magnified in close-up, implies that he is talking at rather than
to the boy. Moreover, the mouth's unnatural bigness on the screen
gives it a menacing quality wholly appropriate in context; the camera zooms out, as if recoiling, when the vice-principal rises from

(*High School*) This big close-up of the vice-principal graphically expresses the teachers' dominance over the students.

his chair and ominously approaches the boy. By contrast, close-ups of students' faces are almost always accompanied on the sound-track by a teacher's voice, and so tend to suggest passivity. As in *Titicut Follies*, there is very little real dialogue in the film; we almost never see the kids communicate with each other, as the students frequently do in the *Deaf and Blind* films. Twice teachers ask, "Any questions?" but there are none, and we see nothing of the prom-ised discussion of Simon and Garfunkel's appropriate "The Dan-gling Conversation." As the vice-principal so aptly puts it to the boy who does not want to participate in gym: "Don't you talk and you just listen!"

Some critics have reacted to this aspect of the film's style as heavy-handed manipulation, perceiving the close-ups as "cheap shots." "Take the scene with the counselor, an older woman with bottle-glasses. Those extreme close-ups of the woman make her look grotesque, which prejudices us against her in a certain way," objected G. Roy Levin, for example. Like Gulliver's response to the Brobdignaggians, some viewers are inevitably repulsed by the de-tails of common faces with all their blemishes magnified on the

(*High School*) This teacher's thick glasses serve as an image of the school administration's myopic approach to education.

movie screen. Close-ups of the teacher with the thick glasses or the guidance counselor with extremely puffy eyelids are perceived as degrading images rather than as ironic expressions of the school's narrow, myopic vision. Wiseman countered Levin's interpretation by claiming that it is one conditioned by Hollywood's reliance on beautiful stars and that the shots are thematically motivated.[19] His assertion that their significance can only be understood in context suggests the extent to which Wiseman is already approaching his material in cinematic terms.

The film's editing, though, is on occasion heavy-handed in its irony, as, for example, when an English teacher's painful reading of Ernest Thayer's "Casey at the Bat" (the last line is "Mighty Casey has struck out") is followed by girls swinging at baseballs in gym class. Somewhat more subtle is the placement of the sequence with the vice-principal and the boy who is avoiding gym. Wiseman edited it in between classroom scenes of foreign languages, an ironic suggestion about the remote relationship between teachers and students. As far as the student who wants to be excused from gym is concerned, it is as if he and the vice-principal are speaking two different languages since it is only after he agrees to put on his gym outfit that he is suspended. Such moments of playful or ironic montage construction, however, may obscure the film's more thoughtful design wherein, as the English teacher says of the Simon and Garfunkel song, "all the various poetic devices reinforce the theme." Ultimately, these more subtle structural relations demonstrate the potential of Wiseman's observational cinema to probe events for meaning beyond the visibly apparent.

High School is structured according to two organizing principles. The first is the conventional "day in the life of" approach. Thus the film opens with the camera riding in a car, presumably on the way to school in the morning. The first classroom shots contain announcements and the "thought for the day" that clearly mark it as the beginning of the school day, and about midway through the film there is a sequence of teachers having lunch. The second aspect of the film's organization, frequently mentioned by Wiseman in interviews, is his presentation of school as being similar to a manufacturing process (indeed, there are several links between this film and, for example, *Meat*). Wiseman has said that when he first saw the school, he was struck by how much it resembled a factory, like a General Motors plant, and so he integrated this perception into the film's structure.[20] Shown in the opening sequence from the car, the exterior of the building, with its smokestack and fences, looks at least as much like a factory as it does a school. The idea of the school experience as a factory-like process, with the students becoming socialized "products," informs a more complex thematic structure than the day-in-the-life format and gradually subsumes it.

After the opening shots in the car, the camera stays inside the school until the third from last sequence in which the returning Vietnam veteran talks with the gym coach in the schoolyard. The initial movement from exterior to interior space suggests, as in the beginnings of *Hospital* and *Canal Zone,* that the film will take a penetrating look *into* this institution rather than merely observe (from the outside) its surface phenomena. The first words spoken in the film, a teacher's "thought for the day," is, on this level, an appropriate aphorism: "Life is cause and effect. One creates his tomorrow at every moment by his motives, thoughts, and deeds of today." This sentiment is echoed by the teacher in the girls sex

(*High School*) Northeast's architectural resemblance to a factory reinforces the film's view of education as an impersonal process.

education lecture, who says that boys "never connect what they are doing today with what happens tomorrow," and by the counselor, who remarks that "the only thing that you can do is try to do better in the present so that the future will be better." All three comments emphasize the relation between present and future, between earlier sequences and later ones, and how film sequences are read in terms of their context, their position within the text.

This idea is borne out by the dialectical manner in which the sequences are ordered. Individually, most of them are stylistically "neutral," offering little textual evidence for a negative reading of the institution. After the homeroom announcements, the first lesson shown is the Spanish class discussing existentialism. Here Wiseman immediately establishes the film's attitude by beginning with a lesson about a philosophical worldview that champions individualism, that claims "existence precedes essence." The content of the lesson is ironic in the context of its presentation, for the teacher's approach is to have the entire class drone in unison everything she says. Individual response is not permitted and, like society's containment of Albert Camus' Mersault, we see later that the school safely contains its *etrangers*—those who have not wholeheartedly accepted the school's values—in an isolated discussion group. The Spanish lesson scene is significant because of its placement as the first class shown and because Wiseman cuts from it to a percussion lesson, with the music teacher's conducting hand, emphasized by the framing of the shot, keeping the beat for the students. Here, as in the Spanish class and everywhere else in the film, there is no room for a different drummer.

The school's claim for the importance of individualism, consistently denied in practice, is only one instance of the institution's contradictory messages, what Thomas Benson, citing Gregory Bateson, calls "the double bind."[21] On a formal level, these double binds are expressed by a motif of paired sequences; there are two language classes, two English classes, and two scenes with Rona's parents (one profilmic event separated by editing). Frequently, these pairs relate in terms of strong contrast, further emphasizing the double bind. One of the English classes, for example, features the stiff recital of "Casey at the Bat," while the other contains the more contemporary Simon and Garfunkel song (a "rock with Shakespeare" display is visible on the back wall of this classroom).

As many commentators have noted, most of the film's sequences in one way or another emphasize depersonalization and ideological indoctrination. ("You have had practice in controlling your impulses and feelings ever since you have been a baby. . . . You have learned by now that it's part of being human, that you can't have what you want when you want it," the teacher in the girls sex education lecture declares.) The similarity of the row houses glimpsed in the opening drive to school foreshadows the impersonal conformism that dominates the school's activities and approach to education. The girls in the fashion class are identified by number, as are the three "astronauts." In the girls gym class the camera focuses not on their faces but on their bodies, clad in identical uniforms, their group calisthenics anticipating similar scenes of regimented exercise in *Basic Training* and *Juvenile Court*. One teacher explains to a girl who wants to wear a short dress to the school prom that "it's nice to be individualistic, but there are certain places to be individualistic" (although we see no such places in the film), and the girl is forced to apologize ("I didn't mean to be individualistic"). Bob Walters, a former student and author of the

(*High School*) The "Penn Maid" logo in the opening sequence is a visual pun that initiates the film's examination of sexual conditioning and gender definition.

letter read by the principal in the last sequence, describes himself as "only a body doing a job." For Wiseman, he is the logical end of the process, the final product of the assembly plant, an unquestioning, obedient person, the "Chevrolet rolling off the GM line."[22]

The school lessons and activities tend to focus particularly on issues of sexual identity and gender definition. Wiseman refers to the film's emphasis on sexual issues as its "unisex theme,"[23] although it is more accurate to describe it as the learning of sexual difference according to dominant ideology. On the back of the dairy truck in the opening sequence we see a "Penn Maid" logo accompanied by a caricatured contented cow featuring prominent painted lips and a fulsome, pendulous udder. The image puns in two ways. "Penn Maid Products," as Benson has noticed,[24] refers to the students as products of this Pennsylvania school and as prison inmates. The cartoon image also graphically expresses the simplistic yet strong sexist attitude that pervades the school and which is one of *High School*'s dominant motifs (as made clear in the rally scene where boys dress as cheerleaders complete with large breasts).

The film's final sequences draw this view to a logical conclusion, suggesting the implications of this specific school's process of socialization by progressively connecting it to another national institution, the military (which had particular significance for students in 1968). Wiseman's strategy of pursuing the larger implications of Northeast's ideology follows from the vice-principal's definition early in the film of manhood as being the ability to take orders, and several critics have noted the strong connections between *High School* and *Basic Training*.[25] The first major sequence after the former student on leave from duty in Vietnam visits the gym teacher involves the simulated landing of the three student astronauts as part of Project SPARC, an activity endorsed by NASA. The teacher reads a letter of congratulations from real astronaut L. Gordon Cooper. The next and last sequence is the reading of the letter from Bob Walters, who at the time of writing was waiting to be dropped behind the DMZ. The order of the sequences reminds the viewer that space research exists in a military context, much as the scientists' idea of "pure research" in *Primate* is undercut by the subsequent experiment aboard a U.S. air force jet. Even the short sequence shot positioned between these last two important sequences, showing the school color guard carrying the flag and dummy rifles, possesses a pronounced militaristic quality.

In the scene where the boy who has not dressed for gym is suspended, a photograph of an American flag on the wall behind the vice-principal recalls that the teacher's attitude reflects national ideology and thus that the school is a representative social microcosm. In the second sequence in the office, where Michael is forced to take a detention against his principles, the flag photo is again featured prominently in the frame directly above the vice-principal's head. Later, the vice-principal himself unintentionally contextualizes his own role in the larger social fabric when, teaching a lesson on the history of organized labor in America, he explains that workers felt it necessary to unionize because there was a lack of communication between employers and employees.

Over the opening car ride sequence, Otis Redding's "(Sittin' On) The Dock of the Bay" is heard on the soundtrack. The song does not emanate from the car radio, but was added to the soundtrack. This is a rare instance of Wiseman's "twisting" of the material, which he defends as observationally true to the experience since he in fact did hear the song every morning during the shoot

(*High School*) The image of the American flag is used to acknowledge the film's examination of the school as a "cultural spoor."

while driving to the school. Wiseman has interpreted the song's thematic significance as being about the death of the American dream, for its narrator has removed himself from the world by turning away from civilization: "It's about a guy who has left Georgia and gone to California in search of America. . . . He's at the end of the continent. He's traveled all over and it doesn't mean a thing to him!"[26] Like Huck Finn, he has lit out for the territory, and so from the very beginning the viewer is encouraged to read the film for its larger social implications.

The principal's remark after reading Bob Walters's letter, while grammatically a declarative statement, functions like a rhetorical question, addressed as much to the viewer as to the assembled teachers. "Now when you get a letter like this," she says, "to me it means that we are very successful at Northeast High School. I think you will agree with me." The fact that the film ends abruptly as she concludes her reading leaves the viewer to contemplate the extent to which one agrees with her assessment of the letter. Like Eddie's evaluation of the inmates' performance at the end of *Titicut Follies,* phrased as a question, the viewer is left to consider the implications and consequences of the high school experience as depicted in the film.

After the gynecologist's lecture comes a sequence from a sex education film that the students are also watching. The narrator discusses gonorrhea and its effect on pregnant women, concluding with the statement that "when the baby is ready to be born there is danger that she may transmit the disease to the child when it passes out of her body." The transmission of disease to the young who emerge into the world in this context acquires a social meaning for students who graduate and enter the world of adulthood, especially since Wiseman follows this sequence with the soldier visiting the gym coach.

Hospital, Wiseman's fourth film, picks up on this metaphor, examining New York's Metropolitan Hospital as a symptom of larger social ills. One doctor's remark that "man is not born with disease. He acquires these disorders when he tries to adapt to a certain level of civilization," articulates the film's thesis. In *Hospital,* Wiseman, so to speak, performs a cinematic exploratory—the cut of the scalpel analogous to his work as film editor. The malignancies he finds are unpleasant truths. In order for us to understand the hospital itself as a symptom, along with Wiseman we must look intently, like the interns who unflinchingly examine the brains of deceased patients. As in *Titicut Follies,* with *Hospital's* very first image—a high angle shot of an anaesthetized patient—Wiseman seeks to grab viewers and shake them out of a voyeuristic complacency by moving beyond, as it were, a "gut response." *Hospital* is a clear example of what Nichols has called Wiseman's "tactlessness,"[27] for in the surgery images or the lengthy sequence of the induced vomiting of a young man who had taken mescaline, the film deliberately violates "good taste." The psychiatrist's appeal to the camera (actually he speaks to a resident in the room who is kept out of frame) that Miss Hightower at the welfare office "hung up on me" directly connects the viewer to the film. ("Let us go then, You and I," the beginning of Eliot's "The Love Song of J. Alfred Prufrock," is evoked by the opening image of the patient etherized upon a table.)

Its structure, too, works to grab and hold the viewer's attention. As Brian Winston has noted, *Hospital* "is structured around sequences of normal, emotionally uncharged activities crosscut with

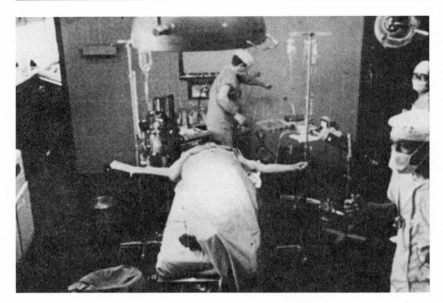

(*Hospital*) The opening shot, with its Christian overtone, introduces the film's examination of both physical and spiritual illness.

sequences of distress, whereby the former become shorter and the latter longer and more distressful as the film progresses."[28] Despite the many unpleasant sights in the film, *Hospital* in fact generally avoids a sensationalistic approach. Most importantly, the film does not condemn the staff of Metropolitan Hospital by showing them brutalizing patients in the manner of *Titicut Follies*. Indeed, one doctor who has commented on the film asserts that if any criticism is to be leveled at *Hospital*, it is that the staff is depicted as impossibly positive.[29]

The biggest gap revealed in *Hospital* is not between the ideology of the institution and its practice, but rather, as Harry M. Geduld notes, between the rich and poor.[30] The film emphasizes that this economic disparity—what one of the teachers in *High School* calls, after Michael Harrington, "the other America"—is but a symptom of social illness. Indeed, there is a gross irony in the fact that the horses in *Racetrack* receive better medical attention than many of the human patients in *Hospital*. Unlike *High School*, which Wiseman chose to film in a "good" school, *Hospital* was filmed in a large, overburdened public health facility located near Harlem and Spanish Harlem. The film concentrates almost exclusively on the hospital's emergency room, where the need for immediate medical attention heightens the sense of the place itself as a site of crisis. Many of the patients suffer from drug related problems, injuries received in fights, or from family or social neglect—problems not restricted to a particular class but certainly more prevalent among the economically underprivileged. Economic issues are therefore inevitably foreshadowed, since these patients are obtaining medical service at this hospital not by choice but because of economic necessity. Wiseman himself says that the film is not a critique of this particular institution.

> It's too much of a liberal's thing to say, "If only we had more doctors, if only we had more nurses, the situation would be different." The problems are so much more complicated, so much more interesting. You see people who have never been to doctors in thirty years, who can't read or write, who live in crappy houses, who don't have jobs, are recent immigrants either from other countries or from rural or urban areas. And you see the staff trying to deal with them as best they can—but they can't correct the conditions that led to these people walking through the hospital door in the first place.[31]

Toward the beginning of the film, Dr. Schwartz calls another hospital that has just transferred a female patient to Metropolitan. He complains about the sloppiness of the procedure; no information was sent with her or in advance, even though her condition may require emergency surgery. It is as if she had been regarded as so much baggage, a situation that is apparently all too common. With stoic resignation in his voice, Dr. Schwartz concludes his phone call by saying, "this is the sort of thing that we see all the time, and whenever it happens, I make it a habit of calling the administrator and voicing my complaint." Near the end of the film, similarly, an ambulance driver and a policeman discuss a woman just brought into the hospital. The driver had searched several hours without success for a hospital to admit her. He says repeatedly that "it don't make sense" (a phrase also used earlier to describe a situation in which a neglected boy who has fallen out of an apartment window cannot be kept in the hospital overnight until social services investigates), but the policeman diagnoses the problem as an economic one: "I guess that's what happens when you

(*Hospital*) A graphic representation of "The Other America" that suggests the film's understanding of Metropolitan Hospital itself as a symptom of illness.

don't have no money at all. You have to take what comes." These two sequences bracket most of the medical procedures in the film, lending them all a sense of economic constraint.

Perhaps the film's most visually striking instance of this theme is the sequence of a psychiatrist's interview with a young, gay black man. Throughout the interview the man is seated against a wall, while the camera pulls back slightly to incorporate within the frame a picture of then-mayor of New York John V. Lindsay hanging above him. The picture, originally a cover from *Life* magazine, features the caption, "The Lindsay Style." The gay man and the image of Lindsay within the film's image offer a striking contrast: one is black, the other white; one is poor, "freakish," and disempowered, unable to obtain welfare assistance and rejected even by his mother; the other is wealthy, glamorous and politically influential. The gay man describes himself as "not a normal human being," while the specter of Lindsay hovering above him expresses much of society's masculine ideals. The contrast between them is amplified by the fact that the gay man's body, arm, and head are arranged in a manner almost identical to Lindsay's pose in the

(*Hospital*) The reverse zoom that concludes the film is a forceful comment on contemporary alienation and indifference.

photograph. These two nevertheless radically different male images graphically express the examining psychiatrist's diagnosis of the man as a schizophrenic. He can never attain the cultural ideal literally hanging over his head in this scene, because of his skin color, economic status, and sexual orientation.

The film extends its social criticism to the viewer as well, particularly in the conclusion, one of the most powerful moments in all of Wiseman's work. The last sequence of the film shows patients praying in the hospital's chapel. There is a cut to a long shot of the hospital building taken from a nearby highway. The hospital seems to recede with the slow reverse zoom of the camera while cars traveling on the highway enter the frame and then fill it, moving across the image between the camera and the hospital. The voices of the patients singing a hymn in the chapel can still be heard, but they gradually diminish in volume and are replaced by the "whooshing" of the automobiles driving past the camera. The moving cars express the peripatetic rush of contemporary life. Their growing domination of the image visually (filling the foreground of the frame) and aurally (their sounds replacing the hymn on the soundtrack) suggest how, in Wordsworth's famous phrase, the world is too much with us. In the immediate concerns of everyday experience we forget spiritual values, just as when we are healthy we prefer not to think about illness—whether physical or social. The position of the patient's body on the operating table in the film's opening image evokes not only Eliot's "Prufrock" but also the crucifixion (as does the force-feeding of Malinowsky in *Titicut Follies*),[32] and connects to the final highway shot by suggesting it is "our sins" that are depicted here. While it is true that the soundtrack is here manipulated beyond the limitations of synchronization, like Wiseman's use of the Otis Redding song in *High School*, the effect is consistent with the film's point of view and provides an effective summation of its social concerns.

Both *Law and Order* and *Juvenile Court* also deflect their social criticism back to the spectator by presenting a deliberately shifting view of institutional authority, although neither film reveals the observational innovations of *Titicut Follies* or *High School*. Both employ a similar symmetrical design, but to different ends. *Law and Order* avoids a simplistically negative treatment of the Kansas City police by showing them from a double perspective. The sequence where one policeman becomes a father figure to a lost little girl, bringing her to the station and giving her candy, may be, as Mamber asserts, the most annoying scene in all of Wiseman's work because it is both obvious and cloying.[33] But it functions as only one instance in a series of sequences that systematically presents the police as alternately kind and cruel. The policeman himself provides the perfect emblem of his "parental" position by taking out a pipe and smoking it as he drives the patrol car with one arm wrapped protectively around the child, and Wiseman clearly encourages this view of him by shooting the policeman from a low angle. But elsewhere in the film we see events that are likely to make us angry, such as the scene where a detective seems excessively violent to a prostitute, choking her even as he denies doing so. For every scene in which a policeman does something like find a lost purse for an elderly woman, there is another such as the one in which a detective seems inexplicably to ignore a man who wants to report someone with a gun.

Thus viewers are placed in a double position in relation to the police, their torn response analogous to the position of the police themselves. The film suggests that the sometimes inadequate or excessive responses of the police are, in turn, symptomatic of the impossible demands—as in *High School,* a double bind—made upon them as a result of larger social problems. The police can neither solve domestic crime nor prevent it. Often, all they can do is inform people that "there's nothing we can do about it," the response they give in both the opening and closing sequences. Indeed, most of the police force's activities in the film involve handling drunks, accident victims, and domestic conflicts. The domestic emphasis of routine police work is expressed by the number of sequences in the film that refer to family and social tensions. In addition to the two domestic arguments that bracket the film, there are also, among others, a man charged with molesting a boy, a man who threatens to kill another man for molesting his niece, and a runaway boy. As well, the fear of a recent race riot permeates the dialogue, and racial tension is evident throughout the film. A white woman who has been arrested makes a point of specifying the racial identity of the arresting officers, for example, while black youths arrested in a clothing store blame their fate on racial prejudice. Richard Nixon's campaign speech near the end of *Law and Order,* in which he says voters are faced with a clear choice between rising crime and reestablishment of "respect for law and order in this country," makes explicit the social tensions that infuse the film. Society itself is torn by racial hate and fear, just like the police and the viewer are torn. And just as Wiseman, as explained in the previous chapter, developed a more complex view of police work during the shoot, so the viewer is challenged to do so as well.

The film is bracketed by scenes of family arguments that the police attempt to mediate. Wiseman has described the film's design as circular, saying that when the "guy runs off at the end of the film he's running off to the beginning of the film."[34] *Law and Order* is "circular" in the sense that it differs from the structure of, say, *Titicut Follies* and *High School,* both of which can be seen as "linear" (to the extent that this is possible within the overall mosaic structure) since both show beginnings and ends to their respective institutional processes. By contrast, *Law and Order* presents an accumulation of events, an ongoing process, and so is closer in this sense to *Juvenile Court* and *Welfare* as well as *Hospital.* This structure is appropriate, given the film's view of police work as a combination of routine and danger, a situation that Wiseman has described as being "like a taxi driver playing Russian roulette."[35] Both aspects of police work are shown at once in the sequence of Howard Gilbert's arrest for auto theft. The camera waits with the youth and the arresting officers, who must listen to his string of racist insults for over five minutes of screen time until the paddy wagon arrives. Later, we hear two references to the fact that Gilbert has been released because he is a youthful offender. Thus the film's structural symmetry suggests futility rather than closure; indeed, over the final credits, a voice from the police radio speaks of yet another dangerous suspect in a seemingly endless parade.

Juvenile Court examines the legal process for youthful offenders, in a sense picking up where *Law and Order* leaves off, after the arrest procedure. The film shows an institution ministered by well-intentioned judges, lawyers, parole officers, and social workers (two children of a woman discussing her case sit on the lap of Judge Turner, another seemingly benevolent patriarchal authority), but, like *Hospital* and *Welfare,* the juvenile courts of Memphis are besieged by a constant flow of clients, many of whom have problems beyond the ability of the institution to handle. *Juvenile Court* suggests the continuous flow of cases by concluding almost every major sequence in the courtroom with the bailiff announcing the next case. The film is also punctuated several times by a courthouse receptionist answering a barrage of phone calls and by shots of people waiting around on benches, as in *Welfare.* Judge Turner himself remarks on the large number of child abuse cases he has seen. The film's very length (144 minutes, Wiseman's longest to this point) speaks of how much work the courts must handle.

Given the heavy volume of cases, those who minister the institution try their best to move people through the system as swiftly as possible—sometimes at the expense of the clients themselves. This view of the juvenile court system becomes chillingly clear in the final, lengthy sequence concerning the case of Robert Singleton. The sequence acts like a summary of the entire film and is chilling in large part because it presents the gap between the institution's goals and its practice in such an understated way (although one suspects that the filmmaker, himself a lawyer, could not but have responded with outrage to the situation). Singleton, charged with armed robbery although he only drove the getaway car, had no weapon himself and did not enter either of the places that were robbed. He claims that his life was threatened by the man who actually committed the two robberies and that he was forced to act as the man's accomplice. His claim is apparently supported by the unsubmitted testimony of the other man involved. Singleton's defense lawyer, who can hardly be adequately prepared since he had taken on the case just that morning, claims to believe that the boy had no intention of going along with armed robbery and that a trial might exonerate him. Judge Turner decides, however, that in the boy's best interests Singleton should plead guilty in juvenile court and serve several months at a youth training school rather than face trial, which might result in a penitentiary term of twenty years. In a private discussion in chambers, Singleton's lawyer explains that in his view neither society's nor the boy's best interests would be served by having him tried as an adult; the lawyer is willing to enter a plea of guilty if the court decides in favor of retaining jurisdiction. But Singleton wants to "fight it out in court and prove that I'm innocent." The lawyer's view, as he reports to the judge, is that "the boy has lost all control over himself," and that he is "not in condition to make a decision." The judge agrees, even though he took the opposite position in an earlier molestation case.

The film, though, shows no evidence of irrationality in Singleton, only his different view, his wish to have his day in court, and his sobbing when he is refused and sentenced. During the time in chambers and for most of the time in the courtroom, the camera omits Singleton from its view, just as he seems to be excluded from the undue process that is deciding his fate. In one brief shot we see him sitting alone on a bench against a wall, isolated both visually and aurally from the proceedings. In the plea bargaining process, the question of guilt is pushed aside, displaced by the question of jurisdiction (just as Michael's principles become less important than the fact that he take some form of detention in *High School*).

Singleton's lawyer attempts to console him by encouraging him, again reminiscent of *High School*, to "handle this like a man," and by telling him that in time his record can be erased because "this

(*Juvenile Court*) The doors of justice close on the youthful offender in the final sequence.

is America." Wiseman establishes this larger connection early in the film through several different short but nevertheless significant shots that suggest an analogy between the institutions he examined previously and juvenile court. In one of these, for example, a detention center guard searches a boy, an image that refers back to the strip searches in *Titicut Follies*. There follows a shot of three boys getting haircuts, an image that also appears in *Basic Training* and that echoes the shaving in *Titicut Follies*. Shortly after this we see boys doing calisthenics, followed by a shot of the court files; the uniform exercises are reminiscent of similar shots in *High School* ("Simon Says") and, again, *Basic Training*, while the files remind us of the impersonal treatment of clients that culminates in the paperwork and bureaucracy of Wiseman next film, *Welfare*. Singleton is led out of the courtroom ("An injustice has been done," he cries), the shot holds on the courtroom door as everyone files out, and then the door closes, an image of the boy's now-sealed fate. Wiseman follows this with two concluding shots of the exterior of the courthouse building and the street, exactly reversing the fim's two opening shots. Unlike *Law and Order*, the "fearful symmetry" of this structure here expresses less a sense of futile continuation—although this is suggested elsewhere, in the cutaways of the receptionist, the bailiff, and the people on the benches—than a closed system that "traps" people, as Singleton says, as often as it provides justice.

The ironically titled *Welfare* is the closed system *par excellence,* a nightmare vision of institutional bureaucracy out of control. In this film, Wiseman sums up all the institutional and social problems explored in the earlier documentaries. It is no accident that, chronologically, *Welfare* comes between *Primate* and *Meat;* the titles of these films express how far, for Wiseman, living has become objectified, commodified, a matter of mere existence. Phrases like "nothing we can do about it" and "it isn't our responsibility," heard in the earlier films, insistently return in *Welfare.* Here, social and economic relations are reduced to verbal exchanges between welfare workers and clients, the clients seeking the money that the workers have the power to dispense. *Welfare* foregrounds the economic disparity shown in some of the earlier films, since everyone seeking help from the welfare system is penniless, many seeming on the verge of starvation. As Mr. Hirsch, the final client shown in the film, says: "There's no middle class anymore. There's just the rich and the poor."

John J. O'Connor is, of course, correct when he says that *Welfare* is the most pointless of Wiseman's films, for we are all aware of the entangled mess that this system has become.[36] But such a criticism misses the essential point of Wiseman's cinema. It is also the case that most everyone who views *High School* has suffered through that experience. It is, as Pauline Kael notes, "an obvious kind of film to make," but for her the film's power derives in good measure precisely from this fact.[37] Wiseman's documentaries heighten our awareness of routine life in America or, perhaps more accurately, present us with aspects of this life that we assume we know. It is no coincidence that Wiseman would go on to make films entitled *Deaf* and *Blind,* films that urge us to regard our world more closely than we normally do. Wiseman's camera looks intently at aspects of daily life that, exactly because they are so common, we in fact often overlook. We are all aware of, although we may prefer not to think about, the horrors of mental institutions, what Marion Crane in *Psycho* euphemistically refers to as "someplace." Just as *Titicut Follies* depicts life in Bridgewater with such power that it cannot be ignored, *Welfare* is at once obvious and revelatory—in a sense, anticipating the transcendental style of *Essene* and *Deaf and Blind.*

In *Welfare* the camera leaves the building just once, at the beginning. After this we remain confined within, unlike most of Wiseman's films which at the very least offer periodic exterior shots as rhythmic pause or release (even the enclosed world of *Missile* is relieved by the occasional outside shot of Vandenberg Air Force Base). Here, though, our physical point of view remains claustrophobically confined within the harsh walls of this one New York City welfare office. When a white racist is tossed out of the building by uniformed guards, the camera moves into a close-up of one of their nightsticks wedged between two door handles to prevent the man from reentering—and us from leaving. This place is an absurd *huis clos,* and we must wait it out along with the system's needy clients.

The first words we hear in the film, the receptionist's "please have a seat," is thus not only a self-reflexive acknowledgment to the viewer that the film is now beginning but also an ironic invitation to sit through a long ordeal as the applicants themselves must. *Welfare* is one of Wiseman's longest films to date (exceeded in length only by *Canal Zone* and *Near Death*), its running time an expression of the labyrinthine, self-contained system of procedures and paperwork through which welfare applicants must navigate. Even at the end of the film, the ambient sounds of the welfare office carry over into the final credits, as if interminable. This film is Wiseman's *Bleak House,* but instead of the pervasive symbolic fog with which Dickens's novel opens, *Welfare* is ironically bathed throughout by the artificial harshness of what James Wolcott aptly calls a "firmament" of fluorescent lights.[38]

Entrapping the viewer within the building, Wiseman refrains from making its physical layout clear. The geography of the place is confusing to the viewer, just as the procedures are to many of the clients. Physical space is subordinated to cinematic space. Within the welfare center Wiseman suggests, again, a circular structure similar to that of *Law and Order* and *Juvenile Court.* The first couple interviewed in the film are shown again at the end, waiting. Clients are frequently trapped in a variety of Catch-22 situations, the circular logic consistent with the film's structure. One client, for example, wants to move but cannot because there is no record of housing violations, but she is unable to get a buildings inspector to come and record the necessary violations. Another client becomes ineligible for benefits because he missed his appointment at the welfare office while attending his fair hearing required by welfare procedures. Toward the beginning of the film, a man seeking immediate help says that he is getting a "run around." The phrase is echoed periodically by several other clients. Toward the end of the film a woman who, speaking for her mother, angrily complains that she is caught in a never-ending "vicious cycle." Even Miss Hightower, who had put off the psychiatrist on the telephone and finally hung up on him in *Hospital*, claims she is getting a "fast shuffle" by the institution. Thus things have comes "full circle," as Hightower has changed roles from that of victimizer to victim.

During the first interview with the couple seeking emergency benefits, they are instructed to proceed first to the housing office on the fifth floor and then to return to the employment office on the fourth floor. Thus we learn that the welfare office occupies several floors in the building. But most of the interviews seem to hover in an indeterminate space, a Kafkaesque world in which people never seem to get their cases heard. Like Mr. Hirsch in the film's final sequence, everyone appears doomed to wait for Godot. Tangible assistance from welfare, even though many people's needs are immediate, seems unattainable, like Kafka's castle. The best one can hope for, apparently, is an appointment to return tomorrow. While Dan Armstrong makes a convincing case for the film's similarities to *Waiting for Godot*,[39] perhaps *Act without Words I* is the Beckett play closer in vision to *Welfare*.

As in both Beckett and Kafka, reality in *Welfare* seems unsettlingly indeterminate. Some applicants have multiple names and so even their identities are unclear. *Welfare*, in fact, depicts a world where meaning has crumbled. All of Wiseman's films reveal people speaking naturally and spontaneously, so that their discourse is frequently confused, hesitant, inaudible, vague. This is, of course, the difference between *lange* and *parole*, a difference that observational cinema, because of its unscripted quality, captures so well. *Welfare* contains more than its share of incorrect usage. One client,

for example, complains that he is being required to "relocate in-
stamatically," while the white racist speaks of how quickly blacks
"progenerate" and how they are inferior to whites "biologically
and nomalogically and pharmanoloty." But here, to a greater extent than in any of the other films, language is often drained of
meaning. The welfare workers speak of "reentertaining applica-
tions" and "financial servicing" for the clients. (Their language anticipates the euphemistic discourse of military indoctrination in
Basic Training and the "linguistic detoxification" of nuclear weapons explored in *Missile*.) "Whey I say 'you,' I don't mean you," explains one client to a worker. One woman, according to a case
worker, is "using a loose term, but broadly," with the result that
she is accusing herself of child abuse. Sometimes language is used
without faith, merely as signifier; one man uses strong language to
present himself assertively, then switches immediately to a sweet,
endearing tone and expression when he learns that he will be
given an interview tomorrow.

Welfare is the culmination of the institutional tendency to, as
Eliot puts it, fix people in a formulated phrase (as in the dismissive
diagnosis of Vladimir in *Titicut Follies*). *Welfare* emphasizes the
wielding of language for institutional control as explored in *High
School* and *Basic Training* ("it depends on the language," as one
teacher declares to Rona's father). Because of the importance of
language in *Welfare*, the soundtrack dominates the film to a
greater degree than in any of Wiseman's other documentaries. For
the most part, the camera remains content to film people talking.
And they do indeed talk, voluminously, more often at cross purposes than not. The interview with Valerie Johnson, the woman
whose name seems to have disappeared from the welfare rolls,
alone lasts a full twenty-two minutes. Consistently dense, the
soundtrack is filled not only with dialogue but with the constant
chatter of typewriter keys, background noise, and voices.

The film, like the welfare center itself, is swamped with various
kinds of forms. We see or hear about application forms; referral
slips; notarized, registered, and certified letters; verifications of
pregnancy; marriage licenses and driver's licenses; bills and re-
ceipts; change of address forms and prenatal forms; written bud-
gets and pay stubs; food stamps; medicaid cards and social security
cards; housing deeds, disability checks and pro-ration checks; car-

bon copies and photocopies. One client complains that she has to "get a notarized letter for this, a notarized letter for that." Another client, standing aimlessly against a post, launches into a monologue about the "rigamorole of forms" he must fill out. "Papers, papers, papers," he says, finally dropping them on the floor and leaving in frustration. Even the woman on the telephone, who has provided "every goddamn thing they've asked for," still cannot get "serviced." The film is punctuated with shots of files and records, timeclock cards, computers, and printouts. Valerie Johnson has become, in effect, a nonperson in the Orwellian sense. Her situation makes the incarceration of the unfortunate Mr. Buttle in *Brazil* (Terry Gilliam, 1986), whisked from his apartment because of a computer misprint, seem not so far-fetched. Johnson's friend remarks with resignation that "if they don't have your record, they don't know nothing about you. You could be Jane Doe."

This enclosed world of *Welfare* ("we go to court, from the court to the hospital, from the hospital to Social Security, to Welfare, back to Social Security, to the court," states an angry client) is like a pressure cooker that inevitably reaches the boiling point. After over two hours of seeing clients frustrated in every possible way, we are not surprised when two of them, Mr. Rivera and Mrs. Gaskin's daughter, can contain themselves no longer. They move around the desk, traversing the boundary that separates workers and clients, just as their emotions have spilled over, to confront the welfare worker Elaine, who also loses her temper ("Get a job," she snaps at Rivera). The anger and frustration of both worker and clients in this climatic scene are the understandable result of everything that has come before. After the climax comes the denouement, the calm after the storm. Mr. Hirsch, made to sit and wait alone on a bench, looks up and addresses the neon firmament and an absent God, saying he will wait as long as deemed necessary.

As in *Hospital*, the workers have become inured to the pain and misfortune of the clients, and, perhaps to maintain their own sanity, many have adopted a "strategy of withdrawal."[40] Just as the nurse in *Hospital* who is thinking of taking a neglected child home with her is warned not to get too involved, so the welfare workers constantly dismiss clients by sending them to "39 Broadway." In one problematic case, a supervisor instructs a worker to reject or accept the client, "either one," not wanting to become involved any further. Wiseman discovers a found equivalent of Sirkian irony (which he uses again in *The Store*): Christmas decorations bedeck the welfare center, a counterpoint to actual social relations. The regulations and procedures have overwhelmed all that is human (hence the spiritual quest of *Essene* and the *Deaf and Blind* films). "Void this 913," says one worker, using a kind of newspeak to avoid the reality of the client's fate. Like the split between morality and technology in *High School* ("Scientifically and technologically, Northeast is an advanced school. . . . morally, socially, this school is a garbage can," says one insightful student), in the welfare center, one client complains, "You give me technicality. I'm telling you about a condition."

Welfare also brings to a head the racial tensions in American society touched upon in several of the earlier films, especially *Law and Order*. At one point in the film, the black guard who is taunted by the white supremacist responds to the claim that black people are out to "get whitey" by saying "what goes 'round comes 'round." This is the ultimate expression of the film's circular motif, for it returns us to the prejudice and social inequities documented in the earlier films. For Wiseman it is significant that the alienated, disillusioned singer of "The Dock of the Bay" in *High School* is a black man, for he sees the song as expressing nothing less than the black experience in America. The black guard says he trusts no one, and from his point of view we all act like savages; "That's the way this country was founded," he observes. He has fought in a war and killed for a country from which he feels alienated, like the persona of the Redding song. He is, he says, just surviving (a phrase echoed in *Basic Training*). How ironic it is, then, that at a time when the welfare center is particularly understaffed, one worker is obliged to take the afternoon off for her biannual "disaster training." They prepare for fire, flood, even the atomic bomb, according to Elaine—but the disaster is clearly right here, right now. "Man, it's getting late," is the dire prophecy of the white racist; "The streets are gonna run with blood." In the final scene Mr. Hirsch predicts that if things don't change fast, in fifteen years there will be no more United States of America.

The Native American at the beginning of the film likens the reservation to a concentration camp. Wiseman's early documentaries show that we have created our own penal colony, for just as the inmates of Bridgewater in *Titicut Follies* are literally incarcerated, so the people in *High School, Law and Order, Hospital, Juvenile Court,* and *Welfare* are, in a variety of ways, imprisoned. America, these films suggest, is in some ways a social bedlam. In a letter submitted as testimony in the *Titicut Follies* litigation, Wiseman said the film is "about various forms of madness"[41]—a claim that, in a sense, can be made about all of these films. They show us how, in the words of William Carlos Williams, "the pure products of America go crazy."[42] People in these six films have become disillusioned, broken, made hopeless by the failure of the American dream. Democratic ideals have crumbled in a world where the American promise of equality has become, in Mr. Hirsch's words, "when somebody has and somebody hasn't and the one who hasn't tries to rip off the one that has and the one that has tries to keep what he's got." To return once again to the end of *Hospital,* Wiseman's camera on the highway recalls the famous ending of *Invasion of the Body Snatchers* (Don Siegel, 1956). Like Kevin McCarthy, it shouts a warning about contemporary life that begs to be heeded.

NOTES

1. Alexis de Tocqueville, *Democracy in America,* ed. J. P. Mayer and Max Lerner, trans. George Lawrence (New York: Harper and Row, 1966), II: 478ff.

2. Alan Westin, " 'You Start Off with a Bromide': Conversation with Film Maker Frederick Wiseman," *Civil Liberties Review* 1, no. 2 (Winter/Spring 1974): 52.

3. Wilfred Sheed, "Films," *Esquire,* March 1968, p. 55.

4. Dan Armstrong also discusses this aspect of the film in his essay, "Wiseman's Realm of Transgression: *Titicut Follies,* the Symbolic Father, and the Spectacle of Confinement," *Cinema Journal* 29, no. 1 (Fall 1989): 20–35.

5. Richard Meran Barsam, *Nonfiction Film: A Critical History* (New York: Dutton, 1973), p. 274.

6. Quoted in Christina Robb, "Focus on Life," *Boston Globe Magazine,* January 23, 1983, p. 29.

7. Michel Foucault, *Madness and Civilization: A History of Insanity in the Age of Reason,* trans. Richard Howard (New York: Pantheon Books, 1965), p. 265.

8. See, for example, Richard Dyer, "Entertainment and Utopia," *Movie* 24 (Spring 1977): 2–13; rptd. in Rick Altman, ed., *Genre: The Musical* (London and Boston: British Film Institute/Routledge & Kegan Paul, 1981), pp. 175–89. This idea is also explored by Armstrong in his "Wiseman's Realm of Transgression."

9. Robert Hatch, "Films," *The Nation*, October 30, 1967, p. 446.

10. See Barsam, *Nonfiction Film*, p. 274; Beatrice Berg, " 'I Was Fed Up with Hollywood Fantasies,' " *New York Times*, February 1, 1970, sec. 2, p. 25; Brendan Gill, "The Current Cinema," *New Yorker*, October 28, 1967, pp. 167–68. The connection between the two works has been made most recently by Dan Armstrong in "Wiseman's Realm of Transgression," pp. 29–30.

11. Thomas W. Benson and Carolyn Anderson, *Reality Fictions: The Films of Frederick Wiseman* (Carbondale and Edwardsville: Southern Illinois University Press, 1989), p. 331.

12. Arthur Knight, "Cinéma Vérité and Film Truth," *Saturday Review*, September 9, 1967, p. 44; Amos Vogel, *Film as a Subversive Art* (New York: Random House, 1974), p. 187.

13. Foucault, *Madness and Civilization*, p. 250.

14. Stephen Mamber, "The New Documentaries of Frederick Wiseman," *Cinema* 6, no. 1 (n.d.): 34; and Mamber, *Cinema Verite in America: Studies in Uncontrolled Documentary* (Cambridge: MIT Press, 1974), p. 219.

15. The presiding judge in the case, Harry Kalus, called the film "a nightmare of ghoulish obscenities." Litigation focused on the question of whether proper consent had been obtained from the Bridgewater patients shown in the film and whether they had been competent to give such consent, although Wiseman sees this as a false issue raised to deflect attention away from the conditions at Bridgewater itself. The result was that the film was banned from public screening in Massachusetts. According to the ruling, only "legislators, judges, lawyers, sociologists, social workers, doctors, psychiatrists, students in these or related fields, and organizations dealing with the social problems of custodial care and mental infirmity" were able to screen it, and a signed statement, filed with Wiseman's Zipporah Films, was required by law from anyone wishing to view it. According to Wiseman, the decision marked the first time in U.S. legal history that a work of art had been restricted for a reason other than obscenity or national security—although Brian Winston reports that it was, more accurately, "the first time that an injunction was obtained on the grounds of failure to obtain consent *outside of advertising*." "The Tradition of the Victim in Griersonian Documentary," in Alan Rosenthal, ed., *New Challenges for Documentary* (Berkeley: University of California Press, 1988), p. 281.

16. Robert Coles, "Stripped Bare at the Follies," *New Republic,* January 20, 1968, pp. 18, 28–30; Richard Schickel, "The Sorriest Spectacle: *The Titicut Follies,*" *Life,* December 1, 1967, p. 12; Wilfred Sheed, "Films," p. 52, 55; Knight, "Cinéma Vérité and Film Truth," p. 44; Gill, "The Current Cinema," pp. 166–67; and Vincent Canby, "The Screen: *Titicut Follies* Observes Life in a Modern Bedlam," *New York Times,* October 4, 1967, p. 38.

17. Charles Taylor, *"Titicut Follies,"* Sight and Sound 57, no. 2 (Spring 1988): 99.

18. Alan Rosenthal, *The New Documentary in Action* (Berkeley: University of California Press, 1971), p. 70.

19. Levin, *Documentary Explorations,* p. 322.

20. Donald E. McWilliams, "Frederick Wiseman," *Film Quarterly* 24, no. 1 (Fall 1970): 24–25; Rosenthal, *The New Documentary in Action,* p. 72; and Berg, " 'I Was Fed Up with Hollywood Fantasies,' " pp. 25–26.

21. Thomas Benson, "The Rhetorical Structure of Frederick Wiseman's *High School,*" *Communication Monographs* 47 (November 1980); 238. See also Benson and Anderson, *Reality Fictions,* chap. 3.

22. Westin, " 'You Start Off with a Bromide,' " p. 56. See also Rosenthal, *The New Documentary in Action,* p. 73.

23. Levin, *Documentary Explorations,* pp. 317–18.

24. Benson, "The Rhetorical Structure of Frederick Wiseman's *High School,*" p. 236.

25. Stephen Mamber, "Cinéma Vérité and Social Concerns," *Film Comment* 9, no. 6 (November/December 1973): 12–13; Mamber, *Cinema Verite in America,* pp. 234–40; Harry M. Geduld, "Garbage Cans and Institutions: The Films of Frederick Wiseman," *The Humanist* 31, no. 5 (September/October 1971): 36–37; Edgar Z. Friedenberg, "Ship of Fools: The Films of Frederick Wiseman," *New York Review of Books,* October 21, 1971, pp. 19–22; Richard Fuller, " 'Survive, Survive, Survive': Frederick Wiseman's New Documentary: *Basic Training,*" *The Film Journal* 1, nos. 3–4 (Fall/Winter 1972): 75; and Thomas R. Atkins, "Wiseman's America: *Titicut Follies* to *Primate,*" in Thomas Atkins, ed., *Frederick Wiseman* (New York: Monarch Press, 1976), p. 12. See also my chap. 3.

26. Rosenthal, *The New Documentary in Action,* p. 73.

27. Bill Nichols, *Ideology and the Image* (Bloomington: Indiana University Press, 1981), pp. 209, 235.

28. Brian Winston, "Documentary: I Think We Are in Trouble," *Sight and Sound* 48, no. 1 (Winter 1978/79): 4.

29. Victor W. Sidel, *"Hospital* on View," *New England Journal of Medicine* 282, no. 5 (January 29, 1970): 279.

30. Geduld, "Garbage Cans and Institutions," p. 37.

31. G. Roy Levin, *Documentary Explorations: 15 Interviews with Film-makers* (Garden City, N.Y.: Anchor/Doubleday, 1971), p. 316.

32. Armstrong, "Wiseman's Realm of Transgression," p. 27.

33. Stephen Mamber, "The New Documentaries of Frederick Wiseman," pp. 35–36; and Mamber, *Cinema Verite in America,* p. 224.

34. McWilliams, "Frederick Wiseman," p. 23.

35. Janet Handleman, "An Interview with Frederick Wiseman," *Film Library Quarterly* 3, no. 3 (1970): 7.

36. John J. O'Connor, "TV Review: Wiseman's *Welfare* Is on Channel 13 Tonight," *New York Times,* September 24, 1975, p. 91.

37. Pauline Kael, "The Current Cinema," *New Yorker,* October 18, 1969, p. 202.

38. James Wolcott, *"Welfare* Must Be Seen," *Village Voice,* September 29, 1975, p. 126.

39. Dan Armstrong, "Wiseman's Cinema of the Absurd: *Welfare,* or 'Waiting for the Dole,' " *Film Criticism* 12, no. 3 (Spring 1988): 2–19.

40. J. Louis Campbell III and Richard Buttny, "Rhetorical Coherence: An Exploration into Thomas Farrell's Theory of the Synchrony of Rhetoric and Conversation," *Communication Quarterly* 36, no. 4 (Fall 1988): 269.

41. Carolyn Anderson, "The Conundrum of Competing Rights in *Titicut Follies," Journal of the University Film Association* 33, no. 1 (Winter 1981): 18.

42. William Carlos Williams, "XVII: To Eloise," *Spring and All,* in eds. A. Walton Litz and Christopher Mac Goulan, *The Collected Poems of William Carlos Williams,* (New York: New Directions, 1986), vol. 1, p. 217.

CHAPTER 3

The Big Parade

Basic Training (1971) • *Manoeuvre* (1979) • *Missile* (1988)

Wiseman has made three films focusing on various aspects of the United States armed forces, each several years apart and spanning his career. *Basic Training* deals with the standard eight-week training course for new army recruits at Fort Polk, Kentucky. *Manoeuvre* examines the annual rehearsal of the rapid deployment of American troops from Ft. Polk, Kentucky, to join NATO forces in Europe. *Missile* documents the fourteen-week training program for air force officers at Vandenberg Air Force Base to man the launch control centers of land-based Minuteman ballistic missiles. (*Sinai Field Mission,* made just prior to *Manoeuvre,* might be included in this group as well, but as it is closer conceptually to *Canal Zone,* it will be discussed with the other films about cultural institutions.) Wiseman himself had been in the army from 1955–56, but his personal experience is less the reason for his interest in the military than the fact that it affords an extremely concentrated view of the institutional life that so concerns him.

In these three films, the maintenance of power and the processes of ideological indoctrination, primary aspects of institutional functioning explored in Wiseman's other films, are revealed with special clarity. Lt. Hoffman puts it bluntly in his welcoming speech to the men in *Basic Training:* "The best way to go through basic training is to do what you're told, as you're told, and there'll be no problems." Also, the repetitiveness of institutional processes explored in, say, *Welfare, Meat,* and *Model,* are reminiscent of military procedure. Officers in both *Basic Training* and *Missile* stress

(*Basic Training*) Silhouetted compositions of marching soldiers ironically invoke the nostalgic vision of John Ford's cavalry films.

the continuity between military and civilian life by emphasizing the former's participation in various civic functions. If there is a difference between military and civilian institutions in Wiseman's films, it is a matter of degree, not of kind. According to the company commander in *Manoeuvre*, the army is "a good cross section of American society," and for the commanding general in *Missile*, the Minuteman crews are "a microcosm of our great society."

These films may not represent Wiseman's greatest work, but, importantly, they show a greater interest in formal matters than the earlier documentaries. For example, *Basic Training* periodically features shots of marching soldiers silhouetted against the rising or setting sun that possess the compositional beauty and iconographic resonance of some of John Ford's cavalry shots (the kind of image that Wiseman employs with greater thematic weight in *Meat* and *Sinai Field Mission*). Similarly, *Manoeuvre* contains images of tanks moving into the frame that establish bold lines of compositional direction in the manner of what Eisenstein calls graphic conflict that perfectly express the aggressive penetration of Germany by the American forces. In one particularly striking shot in *Basic Training,* soldiers march in the foreground as if "beneath" a large American flag waving in the background. Here, Wiseman finds a visual equivalent to the military's reliance on iconographic language that expresses the extent to which the individual is subject to the state—a point reiterated by the image of the soldiers entering a transport plane shot from a position within or under it, its dark, jagged edges seeming like a giant maw about to consume the men. Also, whereas previously Wiseman's camera has almost always been, as one might expect of observational cinema, at eye level, in *Basic Training* there are for the first time several striking shots from both high and low angles for thematic purposes.

Basic Training—logically and chronologically the first film of the group—introduces the viewer to military life along with the inductees. Immediately, the men lose their individuality, are made anonymous, as demonstrated in the brief montage sequence with which the film opens. The men leave their civilian identities behind, becoming anonymous parts of the military machine. In the first shot the trainees arrive on a bus, from which they walk unhurriedly to the barracks dressed in a variety of civilian clothes. Their difference at this point is emphasized by the soldier giving the speech in the final graduation scene, who notes that they "arrived in blue jeans, sandals, tennis shoes, and T-shirts." In the second shot, they are assigned bunks by number. In the third shot, they are measured for uniforms, the tailor calling out measurements. Next come three shots of men having their hair cut short, a recurrent Wiseman image signifying loss of individuality and absorption into the institutional system. In one of these shots, a man is in the process of losing his distinctively long sideburns. Then there are quick shots of fingerprinting, ID photos being taken, and a trainee, in answer to an interview question, giving his social security number. Numbers are repeated later, in scenes showing physical exercise, the demonstration of the M-16 A-1 weapon ("not to be confused with the M-16"), and in the many marching scenes. At the end of the "overture" sequence, the men run in their new uniforms, a marked contrast to their leisurely gait in the first shot. A sergeant then informs them of the proper way to address someone of higher rank. In short order, the men have become unindividuated in both appearance and behavior. They are then arranged for a group photo, carefully posed just as they have been (re)composed for military life. This brief, rapidly edited sequence unambiguously sets the tone for the entire film.

The pomp and circumstance of music in the films further emphasize the loss of individuality within the larger group. The function of music is established immediately in *Basic Training*, when the commanding officer and his entourage smartly march into a room to welcome the trainees accompanied by the musical fanfare of "The Caissons Go Rolling Along." The military exercises in *Manoeuvre* also begin with marching band music and accompanying ceremony. Proper toothbrushing techniques are presented to the men in *Basic Training* in an instructional film with innocuous rhythmic accompaniment on the soundtrack. Wiseman's camera tilts from all the men brushing their teeth, imitating the demonstration on the screen, to a close-up of one trainee's foot, tapping in time to the music.

Basic Training is punctuated with shots—"like a musical refrain"[1]—of the men drilling, keeping time with marching tunes. In these (and in similar shots in *Sinai Field Mission* and *Canal Zone*), the camera frequently tilts down to isolate in close-up the legs and feet of the men, emphasizing the influence of what Marechal in *La Grande Illusion* (Jean Renoir, 1936) calls "the thud of marching feet" and the importance of keeping in step. As in *High School,* no one is allowed to march to the beat of a different drum, but all follow what Vonnegut describes in *The Sirens of Titan* (1959) as the "rented a tent, a tent, a tent" of the snare drum. And if, like the hapless recruit Hickman, they have trouble keeping in step, they are drilled over and over again until they get it right. In *Missile* the pervasive subliminal hallway "muzak" at the Vandenberg Minuteman training center adds significantly to the conditioned detachment of the trainees from everyday life. In the war movies of Samuel Fuller, there is a similar emphasis on feet, but while for Fuller the effort of moving forward is an expression of human will, in Wiseman's military films the imagery implies the opposite, the immersion of individual consciousness in the movement of the mass.

Because the two-month basic training period may be seen as a condensed version of institutional functioning generally, critics have been quick to notice many connections between *Basic Train-*

ing and some of Wiseman's other films—especially *High School* which, as suggested in the previous chapter, establishes connections with the military. As Mamber notes, "In *High School,* Wiseman repeatedly points up militaristic aspects of the high-school experience; in *Basic Training,* he emphasizes the high-school-like aspects of the training process."[2]

Both films feature marching bands, and both feature scenes focusing on the bandleader's hands keeping time. Also, both films show the goals of their respective institutions to be the stifling of individuality and the maintenance of the institutional system. The girls gym class, showing the performance of calisthenics by faceless girls, seems like the fitness part of basic training. The boys gym class features a ball game that encourages aggressive competition, another aspect of military indoctrination emphasized in *Basic Training.* The vice-principal, with his disciplinary approach and military brush cut, treats the students like soldiers, saying: "We're out to establish that you're a man and can take orders." Parents endorse institutional attitudes in both films. In *Basic Training* one couple visiting their trainee son sounds very much like the vice-principal, repeating several times the common view that the basic training process will make him a "true man."

Inversely, *Basic Training* often seems like high school. Training consists of classroom-like lectures as much as it does the acquisition of physical skills. Both films show instructors lecturing (in *Basic Training,* they are, appropriately, often shot from an extreme low angle). Their auditors, whether students or soldiers, are shown in individual close-ups as they listen. Indeed, some of the lecture subjects, like dental hygiene, seem more appropriate in a school context than in the army. In both films, classes make use of instructional movies. The trainees pose for a class photo, and the film concludes with its own graduation ceremony, complete with "valedictorian" address. The attempt of the chaplain (described by one reviewer as "a Baptist Barry Sullivan in burnt cork"[3]) to instill motivation in Hickman is quite similar to the counselor's advice to the girl in *High School* who "messes around." The disciplining of Pvt. Booker, the soldier caught fighting, is remarkably similar to the office scene in *High School.* And, finally, just as the girl who wanted to wear a short dress to the prom is told that it is nice to be individualistic, but only when deemed appropriate, so in *Basic*

Training Pvt. Johnson is told by Lt. Hoffman that "every person is an individual, but there are things that are regulated, that you have to do."

Wiseman's editing emphasizes that in boot camp, as in high school, people are given contradictory messages. The chaplain's words of encouragement to Hickman, that "if you fall down in the mud, you have to be willing to get up," are obviously contradicted by the crawling scenes, in which the instructors prevent the men from rising. Hickman is also told by his drill sergeant, "you're gonna have to think about what you're doing, Hickman, or you'll never make it," even though the men are explicitly instructed at the outset that they should simply follow orders ("to do what you're told, as you're told"). Although the trainees are encouraged to become fighting machines, they are also sent to corrective custody (CC) for punishment if they fight with each other. To make the similarities between school and the military perfectly clear, Wiseman edits *Manoeuvre* such that when the brigade commander asks, "are there any questions?" there is a cut to the next scene before anybody can respond; he did the same with the fashion and typing class scenes in *High School*.

In fact, the men in *Basic Training* often seem more like schoolboys than adults. As one mother explains to her son, the army is the transition stage between being a teenager and an adult. So, as if a child, Hickman is shown by his sergeant how to lace his boots; the sergeant, like a parent concerned about whether his son is properly dressed and fed, asks him where his hat is and whether he had his breakfast that morning. Elsewhere a drill sergeant chews out a soldier for bringing a can of pop onto the firing range, the kind of prankish flouting of authority ("messing around") typical of youth. In the final training exercise of the film, on the infiltration course, the men prowl about with rifles, giggling as they go, as if playing a game like Capture the Flag.

Just as the men are conditioned in military discipline, so Wiseman plays with the viewer's generic expectations of Hollywood war movies. But unlike the men, Wiseman's position is a resistant one. He plays off the genre in several ways for the purpose of dispelling its glorification of combat. In her study of Hollywood war movies, Jeanine Basinger offers a list of the genre's elements that includes a hero; the faceless enemy; an objective; a harmoniously functioning, ethnically diverse fighting unit that she calls a "democratic ethnic mix"; and sometimes, a "last stand" fight.[4] All of these can be found in some form in these three documentaries—except for the hero, who, significantly, is notable only in his absence.

Traditionally, the thrust of the genre is the elimination of unmanageable individualism and the welding together of a fighting unit (infantry platoon, bomber, or submarine crew) of mixed ethnic background, representing a microcosm of the American melting pot ("a good cross section of American society"). Hence the genre's treatment of stars (James Cagney, John Wayne) who iconographically embodied the essence of stalwart American individualism. Resistant at first, they become model servicemen. If they stubbornly remain uncompromising individuals, they suffer a rare death, as happens to Wayne in *Sands of Iwo Jima* (Allan Dwan, 1949). Even the existentialist Bogart persona ultimately commits himself to the Allied cause in, for example, *Casablanca* (Michael Curtiz, 1942) and *The African Queen* (John Huston, 1951), movies Dana Polan calls "conversion" narratives.[5] When Lt. Hoffman tells a black private who cares about no one but himself in *Basic Training* that "the army's not just one man, it's millions of people," and that he must work with the group, he echoes the message of virtually every classic instance of the genre. Hence one reviewer observed that the depiction of basic training in Wiseman's film seems rather close "to the old Warner Brothers Gung-Ho Fighting Flicks of the feckless forties. The sergeants, and even more, the lieutenants and captains are saying the same things."[6] Yet there is a crucial difference. While the classic war films depict the compromise of individualism as a noble sacrifice necessary for the war effort, the Wiseman trilogy views the military as unacceptably dehumanizing.

One might expect the "democratic ethnic mix" to be the most important generic element in these films, since Wiseman typically approaches the military, like other institutions, as a cultural "spoor." But the ethnic mix here is neither democratic nor harmonious. The absence of racial issues, which served obvious propaganda purposes in the genre classics of the World War II era, is as clearly present in Wiseman's military films as in his earlier films. Early on in *Manoeuvre*, the white company commander says in an

interview with an American television news crew that he has noticed no "new racial problems" in the army, but this claim is denied
by the evidence already shown in the earlier *Basic Training*. His response is somewhat disingenuous, for does he mean that there are
no racial problems, or no *new* ones? That is, are the problems the
same old ones?

In *Basic Training* awareness of racial difference is present from
the beginning. In the initial montage sequence, a black soldier
posing for his photograph is coaxed into smiling by being asked to
say something nice about George Wallace. As well, there are two
alienated black soldiers in the film, both reminiscent of the guard
in *Welfare*. One is "tired of people" and would rather spend his
time in jail than participate in the unit's activities. The other wants
out of the army, claiming to be "a man without a country." Both
black soldiers are like the persona of the Otis Redding song in
High School, whose alienation for Wiseman symbolizes the fate of
blacks in America. Wiseman underscores the racial significance of
the second soldier's attitude by juxtaposing it with a scene of the
promotion of the white Lt. Hoffman to captain in which the presiding officer tells Hoffman that he has "equal opportunity now."[7]
Also, in the combat practice sequence, Wiseman presents first
a white and then a black soldier in separate close-ups, facing in
opposite screen directions, shouting violent encouragement to
the opponents.

In *Basic Training* Basinger's "faceless enemy" is the Vietcong,
who are talked about but never shown and whose status as enemy,
unlike the Nazis or Japanese in World War II, as at least one of the
instructors acknowledges, is not completely accepted by Americans. The irony of *Manoeuvre* in this context is that the "enemy" is
another NATO detachment. In essence, they are their own enemy.
This becomes frighteningly clear in *Missile*, where the entire institutional structure is designed as a safeguard against American
military personnel using their own weapons, and in the general's
concluding speech, wherein he imagines a Soviet *doppelganger*.
And since the "enemy" moves from a qualified Other to ourselves,
the "objective" in the films becomes less clear, from winning a
war (*Basic Training*) to playing at war (*Manoeuvre*) to maintaining
a system in the event of a war that could not in any case be
won (*Missile*).

Just as Wiseman plays with genre in these films, so he maintains a ludic spirit by employing in all three (and in *Sinai Field Mission* and *Racetrack* as well) an elaborate game motif, most prominently in *Manoeuvre*. As Marshall McLuhan has noted, "games, like institutions, are extensions of social man and of the body politic."[8] In *Basic Training*, the theme is initiated by the sergeant who introduces the "movie matinee." Like George C. Scott's opening speech as the eponymous general in *Patton* (Franklin J. Schaffner, 1969), itself based on several of his actual speeches prior to the invasion of Normandy, the sergeant emphasizes the winning tradition of the American military by making an analogy to great teams in the history of sport, none of which, he says, can boast the same record ("all the great champions that you've never thought of never went undefeated the whole time"). In *Missile*, the two-person crews are referred to as teams, and, according to one instructor, "just like a football team, or a basketball team, you know, it takes teamwork to win in the game." In a sense, the entire training program in *Missile* is a glorified game, a more elaborate version of *High School*'s Project SPARC, for the trainees must pretend that they are in real missile silos controlling real missiles, but a dummy missile planted on the grounds of Vandenberg Air Force Base serves as an ironic emblem of the entire enterprise.

Manoeuvre makes the most elaborate use of this motif, since the NATO exercise it chronicles is, of course, a war game. As the tanks pull out from Ramstein Air Force Base in West Germany, they pass a sign that says "Reforger is fun." ("Reforger" and "Crested Cap" are the official names for the exercise.) Battalions are referred to as teams; the controllers (designated to assess "kills"— that is, to keep score) are called umpires and referees. The commander makes an analogy between the manoeuvre and the seventh game of the World Series. Later, he says that the day the enemy attacks will be "the fun day," and that "we're gonna bring home the marbles." A department of defense observer interviews a soldier in a scene that seems very much like a pregame interview with an athlete about the lack of home field advantage.

According to General Steele, the aim of the manoeuvre is "to reproduce the fog of battle that is such a real factor on any battlefield" and to simulate the pressure and stress of combat that cannot be provided by textbooks or in the classroom.

(Unsettlingly, this comment throws the entire training program in
Missile into doubt.) The sergeant's advice to the men at the com-
mencement of the exercise to "be safe," reiterated later in the field
by the company commander, thus seems, in context, rather silly.
Indeed, the film's presentation of the exercise reveals that the attempt to duplicate actual battle conditions is ludicrous and impossible. On their way to their chosen defensive positions, the men
are cautioned to watch out for civilians in BMWs, and the tank
convoy is temporarily stopped by nothing more than an elderly
German forest warden with a shovel (a "population problem"). As
the troops await assault by the enemy, civilians curiously skirt the
area with binoculars and cameras, children ride by on bikes, a
farmer plows his field, and controllers leisurely chat with German
women. Some of the soldiers play a game of touch football—appropriate, given the terminology of the sport (enemy territory,
penetration, blitz, long bomb).

The film's treatment of these manoeuvres as a game is very
much in keeping with the view of warfare advanced by such writers as Johan Huizinga. His analysis of warfare demonstrates that
historically combat has been approached in the spirit of "play,"
which he defines as a temporary order set apart from the flux of
life by a clearly defined structure (a set of rules). Play, games, and
sport are "pretend," although this does not mean that such activities lack seriousness. Warfare, in fact, is "the most intense, the
most energetic form of play and at the same time the most palpa-
ble and primitive."[9] According to Huizinga, warfare expresses the
values of justice, fate, and honour necessary for civilization. (Huizinga traces a direct line of descent from the medieval knight to the
modern gentleman, the latter term used consistently in the films
by officers and NCOs to address their men.) However, if one participant in war refuses to play by the rules, then these civilized values disappear and are replaced by barbarism and unredeemed
violence. From the American point of view, this was the case in
Vietnam, as we learn from instructors in both *Basic Training* and
Missile, since the Vietcong engaged in guerilla warfare and en-
listed the services of women, children, and men out of uniform. In
Missile, the commander acknowledges that warfare today is more
complex than in the past, when combatants were clearly identified
and when after the battle the rules of the game clearly allowed for

"rape and pillage and whatnot." *Missile* also shows that the ever-present threat of nuclear destruction and the consequent strategy of limited military engagement has undermined any possibility of war as noble play.

Now the rules of warfare are negotiable rather than noble, as we see in the lengthy argument between a missile lieutenant and a controller in *Manoeuvre* over "kill credit," and in the bargaining over "kill ratios" between German and American officers. The American officer explains to his men that, despite having performed well, they lost in the exercise as a result of "the play of the game." The negotiations, he explains, were discussed "over the hood of the jeep because we couldn't go in the woods anywhere because of the rain last night"—hardly the fog of battle. The controller sums up the film's view of the entire endeavor: "This is not a real war, man. Why you think you in a real war? If this was a real war, half of this shit that's going on wouldn't even happen. When you was on the road coming here you'd be dead now."

Wiseman allows his ludic spirit free reign in *Manoeuvre*, sparing us little of the absurd he manages to find in the situation. A German controller, unhappy with a developing situation, says he will temporarily stop the war. Like Tweedledum and Tweedledee, the two sides agree on a time to resume battle. The German tells his American counterpart that the experience has been "enjoyable," and cheerfully departs calling, " 'bye, and happy war." An officer laughs when his situation is defined by a controller as a "last stand" (undercutting yet another element of the classic war film identified by Basinger). Another chuckles when the battalion commander says they'll all go down together. Images of George Romero zombie movies are conjured up by one officer's report that the enemy are "all dead and sitting in a holding area," and by the commander's request for "all your dead crews out there waving hand and arm signals."

Gen. Alexander Haig's speech about preparedness and equivalence ("a crucible of collective security") is followed by a reception for the soldiers in which an army band performs the song "We've Only Just Begun." The song's lyrics ("Talking it over / Just the two of us . . . / So much of life ahead") ironically contrasts with Haig's hawkish position. The film also features several hilarious conversations, including the argument over kill ratios ("You think you know this shit, now. You don't know shit. Not this shit. I know this shit"). This strong comic tone infuses all three films, suggesting, as in Joseph Heller's *Catch-22* (1961), that war is an absurdity requiring a sense of humor.

Missile humorously comments on the military bureaucracy by emphasizing its acronyms, reminiscent of several jokes in Howard Hawks's postwar service comedy, *I Was a Male War Bride* (1949). The film's dialogue and images are filled with acronyms. Such jargon leads to discourse like this, by one of the program's instructors: "So PRP, the same type thing applies to pilots. We have what's called duty not involving alert, DNIA. You get sick, they gotta give you medication that may make you drowsy, you go DNIA and you can't go on alert, because that would violate PRP. Pilots DNIF, duty not involving flying. Same exact concept."

Basic Training is the most consistently funny of the three films. It has a strong undercurrent of black humor, yet another quality it shares with *High School*. Several writers have commented on the irony of the scene in which Pvt. Booker is given correctional custody for fighting by alluding to what is probably the best remembered line from Stanley Kubrick's *Dr. Strangelove* (1963), that there is no fighting allowed in the war room.[10] (In fact, the subtitle of Kubrick's dark military comedy—*How I Learned to Stop Worrying and Love the Bomb*—could well serve as an alternate title for *Missile*.) There is a bizarre discussion about karma and reincarnation, ironically counterpointed by continuous gunfire from the firing range; it concludes with one sergeant's apparently serious assertion that the descendants of Atlantis have infiltrated NASA. As in *High School*, Wiseman occasionally plays with his editing in *Basic Training*. Perhaps the funniest instance of this is when the scene where a trainee is instructed in how to clean the latrine cuts to the class practicing proper toothbrushing techniques. It is at once a joke about "a war on tooth decay," as David Slavitt suggests;[11] a pun on the cleaning of enamel; and a wry comment on the foul language frequently associated with the military (although this is much more in evidence in *Manoeuvre*).

Wiseman concentrates his comedy in the figure of the hapless Hickman, the trainee who has trouble with everything from marching to making his bed. As the other trainees learn to march in unison, Hickman's incompetence stands out more and more.

While attempting something as simple as reversing direction while marching, behind Hickman we see the other men marching with increasing uniformity and skill. And just as they tend to march in the opposite direction from Hickman within the frame, so the lack of ability by this one individual in the foreground sets him up as a foil to the many in the background, all of whom are quickly becoming professional soldiers. (Their growing proficiency also provides Wiseman with a visual way of "marking time" in the film.) Hickman, at least initially, seems a real-life Sad Sack, in the tradition of Charlie in *Shoulder Arms* (Chaplin, 1918) and Lou Costello in *Buck Privates* (Arthur Lubin, 1940). Periodically we see the platoon in close order drill, with Hickman hopelessly attempting to keep in step with the rest of the men. How can he possibly pick himself up by the bootstraps when he cannot even lace them properly? He is, in short, a marvelous found example of the comic misfit literally out of step with society.

While *Basic Training* may invoke in its depiction of Hickman the lowbrow humor of the service comedy, it does so only to underscore its seriousness by, once again, making viewers examine their own responses. These men, after all, are training for combat in Vietnam—a fact introduced with jarring suddenness when, during the first class about weapons, we see one trainee ask somewhat innocently whether these guns they are now handling for the first time have ever been used to kill people. After hesitating for a moment, the instructor responds to this "pretty heavy" question by admitting that in Vietnam it is kill or be killed. There are in fact some rather chilling moments in the film, and it is Wiseman's ability here at balancing the comic and the serious (in David Denby's words, "comic military disciplines alternate with intimations of mutilation and death")[12] that in large part gives the film its distinctive power. So Hickman, as funny as he may seem, has at the same time his tragic potential, not unlike the unfortunate draftee Pyle in Kubrick's *Full Metal Jacket* (1987) who eventually snaps, killing his sergeant and then himself. Perceived as inept by the other men as well as by the viewer, Hickman is threatened with a "blanket party," the same ritual hazing to which Kubrick's Pyle was subjected. Hickman's response, we discover, was to attempt to overdose on drugs. The first sergeant diagnoses him as having suicidal tendencies ("In other words, it seems like he wants to knock

hisself off"). Thus we can never be entirely "at ease" laughing at
Hickman, and inevitably we feel somewhat guilty about respond-
ing this way initially.

There is yet a further complication to our response. We also appreciate Hickman's ineptitude because, just as the film's humor
serves as a corrective to the military's deadly seriousness, so Hickman represents a quality of human imperfection that is all but
eliminated as the men become trained soldiers. Indeed, *Basic
Training* suggests that as men become good soldiers, so they lose
their humanity. In one training sequence, the men cheer, encouraging each other to "get him from behind" and "hit him in the
head," as they fight two at a time. Even after the whistle blows,
signaling the combatants to stop, we see one pair continue on,
their potential for violence now fully aroused. In several of the
fight training sequences, Wiseman shoots the men from a high angle, the camera meditating on "what fools these mortals be." In
one instance, the camera pans a field filled with pairs of soldiers
boxing, a shot of metaphysical import, before singling out individual pairs in close-up. Ultimately, *Basic Training* offers a vision of
masculinity not unlike that of William Goldman's *Lord of the Flies*
(1954); the innate violence beneath the civilized exterior of boys
emerges as the veneer of civilization is stripped away. In Wiseman's film, this stripping is symbolized by the quick loss of civilian
clothes and identities, as shown at the beginning. This vision of
masculine violence is also suggested in the toothbrushing scene,
where several of the men are shown, in effect, foaming at the
mouth. In one scene the men fight dummies, the objects serving
as metaphors for the extent to which the men have been aggressively indoctrinated with a military view.

Significantly, most of the actual training in the film is bracketed
by crawling scenes. During two scenes toward the beginning, the
men look like mad bugs, their limbs flailing in the dirt. Just before
the two crawl scenes near the end of the film—one in daylight,
the other at night—the men silently apply makeup to themselves,
the only noise the loud buzzing of insects. During the first period
of bayonet practice, the men shout "yaaah" as they whirl, lunge,
and thrust in unison to the instructor's commands, and similar
sounds are repeated by the men in several other scenes. In short,
these "grunts" are abandoning language for screams of violence.

The men are reduced merely to animal instinct: "You probably won't have anything in your mind except survive, survive, survive," as one instructor tells them.

This capacity for violence is associated with sexual aggression and disfunction in all three films, and would seem to demonstrate the opinion of several commentators that warfare is at least in part a substitute for sexual experience.[13] On the firing range in *Basic Training,* a demonstrator fires his weapon extending it from his crotch, accompanied by a crude joke from the instructing sergeant. In the earlier latrine-cleaning sequence, urination is described in terms of weaponry: "That's where people try to shoot from way back over there." One soldier's description of the impersonal, pneumatic bliss to be obtained from a Louisville prostitute is paralleled by the introduction of the M-16 A-1 rifle: "Nut for nut, screw for screw, rivet for rivet," boasts the instructor, "it is exactly—exactly, my friends, the same as the one I have in my hand."

Most important is the scene where one trainee is visited by his family, who concentrate their attention and conversation on his rifle, fetishistically investing it with unmistakable phallic implications. In this scene the relation between sexuality and aggression is given a particularly American emphasis. The mother's view of the experience as a rite of passage for her son and her repeated assertion that it will make him "a true American soldier, a true man" evokes D. H. Lawrence's famous description of Cooper's Natty Bumppo as representative of the American psyche: "hard, isolate, stoic, and a killer."[14] In retrospect, Kaminsky's mad monologue in *Titicut Follies* about the connection between American military aggression and sexual pathology would seem to possess an unsettling quality of prophecy.

Manoeuvre contains much footage of tanks, cleverly presenting them as the phallic embodiment of cultural penetration. This suggests a view of American imperialism, as in *Canal Zone,* as a form of rape. The film begins with shots of the troops' considerable gear being loaded onto military planes for transport to Germany. But the Americans bring their cultural baggage with them as well. As the convoy moves through the rural German landscape, we hear conversations on the radio between tank crews. The young men assess the German women they pass ("All of them are nice looking. Even the thirteen year olds"), as if they were back home cruising the local strip for some "action" on Saturday night. Some of the men pick apples from atop the tank turrets, others stop to pick corn ("nice lookin', too"), apparently without permission of the landowner, suggesting in context defloration.

In another scene, the briefing in the tent, the field commander explains the battle plan, speaking several times about "penetration," while one of the officers in the group smokes a big cigar, a visual rhyme with the tank cannons. Indeed, rumbling through sleepy German towns, their ominous metallic clank permeating the soundtrack, the tanks suggest phallic aggression, as in Bergman's *The Silence* (1963). Cars pull up on sidewalks to avoid the oncoming tanks, damaging them. Trees are uprooted in the forest as tanks move through it, despite the commander's explicit instructions not to destroy any foliage since this is a watershed area. There are many brief shots in the film of tanks moving laterally, entering the frame from one side and exiting from the other. Wiseman consistently holds these shots just long enough for the tanks to disappear across the opposite side of the frame from which they entered. Their sweeping movement across the frame underscores their potency.

The cannons are emphasized in these shots, since they are the first part of the tanks to be seen. Sometimes they protrude from the foliage, where the tanks are entrenched, as if a profanation of nature. In one shot, taken from atop the turret, cows scatter as a tank passes by, its cannon leading the way. (Near the end of the film a couple of soldiers, looking at a nudie magazine, laughingly refer to a woman with large breasts in one of the photographs as "a guernsey.") Occasional low angle shots from close to ground level, as tanks move toward the camera, emphasize their power even further. Also, some of the shots begin by showing objects, such as houses, at a great distance, and so the viewer scans these shots "in depth." This "space" is then violated by the sudden appearance of a tank entering the foreground from either side of the frame, "violating" the viewer's perception of depth. In short, Wiseman uses a wide range of cinematic devices to depict the tanks in this manner.

In *Missile*, sexuality is entirely sublimated by the overwhelming presence of the giant missiles in their silos "down deep in the bowels of the earth." (One thinks of Slim Pickens straddling a nuclear

(*Manoeuvre*) Tanks are consistently framed so as to suggest penetration and violation.

bomb like a bull out of a chute, or a giant phallus, at the end of *Dr. Strangelove.*) Indeed, there seems to be an emotional malaise hanging over everyone in the film, making the warning to the instructors to avoid "fraternization" superfluous. As Col. Ryan, the commander of the program, talks about how this is the most difficult and intensive of all military training programs, one of the trainees yawns widely. Later, an instructor boasts that he has been practicing a blank look for years. Even though these people are learning to tend the weapons that have the potential to destroy life on the planet, Col. Ryan is puzzled by the attitude of one of the trainees, guessing that for some reason he must be feeling "a little bit of apprehension."

Indeed, the military state of mind in *Missile* seems a clear example of what Robert Jay Lifton and Richard Falk have defined as "numbing," the psychic defense of excluding or minimizing feeling because the realities of nuclear war are too horrifying for the mind to bear.[15] This numbing enables people in the contemporary world of nuclear proliferation, in the words of the sergeant in *Basic Training*, to "survive, survive, survive." The people in *Missile*

joke about the weapons to avoid confronting their devastating reality, an illustration of what Lifton and Falk call our inability in the
nuclear age to "imagine the real." For example, the Titan system
is laughingly said to be so volatile that missiles could be launched
at the drop of a wrench; yet they fail to perceive the irony in the
colonel's concern about "the nuts . . . who seek to come in and kill
people and destroy property and that sort of thing." Like plain
folks, they go about their normal routines, barbecuing hamburg-
ers, playing softball, and drinking Coke, seemingly insensitive to
the deadly realities of their work, which they refer to simply as "a
profession" and "a business."

According to Lifton and Falk, one of the primary manifestations of numbing is a "linguistic detoxification," an attempt to "*do-
mesticate* these weapons in our language and attitudes."[16] This is
clearly shown in the film, most obviously, in the use of acronyms.
Their language also employs many euphemisms. To tame the possibility of the unthinkable, the accidental launching of a missile is
referred to merely as a "big error," and the violation of Weapons
Systems Safety Rules (that is, a release of radioactivity or a nuclear
detonation) is described as "a biggie . . . one of those times when
the old career dissipation light comes on." Similarly, the trainees
are told that if complications arise during a launch process, they
should "get a successful launch and take care of any other problems that happen afterwards." (The implication is, of course, that
there will be an "afterwards.") The detached discourse of *Welfare*
has here become, in Lifton and Falk's phrase, "nukespeak," what
Allen Ginsberg calls "black magic language."[17] Such language is already detectable in *Basic Training*, where, for example, the men
are told to call their M-16s a "weapon, rifle, piece, or what have
you," but never to refer to them as guns. In *Manoeuvre*, terms like
"survivability" and "more survivability" mask the deadly reality of
armed conflict.

Similar is the army's consistent invocation of tradition and history through the use of words charged with iconographic power.
Yet the words are used emptily—a perfect example of what Roland Barthes calls the "depoliticized speech" of cultural myth.[18]
Frequently the men are asked to live up to the traditions of "their
forefathers, and theirs before them." "It all started back, way back

there about the Boston Tea Party, and it kept workin' up," one instructor tells the men in *Basic Training*. The speech at the end of the film by the soldier winning the American Spirit of Honor Award, described by Slavitt as "not only a Hallmark card, but echt-American,"[19] invokes such predictable mythic moments of American history as Valley Forge, Gettysburg, and San Juan Hill. His discourse is a string of clichés: "When Fascism reared its ugly head, the American Spirit came forth and slew the dragon." (The name of the presiding general, we note with amusement, is B. G. Cantley.) In short, such language, like the "nukespeak" in *Missile*, attempts simultaneously to minimize the reality of warfare and to bolster ideology by invoking cultural iconography and mythology.

In *Missile,* emotional numbing is expressed not only by the discourse on the soundtrack but also visually and structurally by the film's emphasis on enclosure. At the beginning of the film, a building is shown displaying a sign that reads "Welcome to space and missile country," as if this were a land apart. In the training program's opening seminar, Col. Ryan acknowledges that in their underground capsules missile crews will not have full access to information about a situation (although he reassuringly adds that "you're not going to be working completely in a vacuum"). Wiseman's characteristic transition shots are, in this film, especially thematically resonant. The hallways he shows have no discernible entrances or exits and are filled with vapid Muzak and blinking red lights—a totally artificial environment. The film's structure reinforces this sense of isolation and apartness in two ways. First, Wiseman methodically alternates interior shots of classes and training sessions with outdoor shots of the buildings as an introduction to each sequence. Through contrast, the outdoor shots show how enclosed the interior spaces are, like the "world" of *Welfare*. As well, the specific views given in these shots are significant. In one of the typical traffic shots, for example, a warhead is transported. In two others, construction pylons on the road visually rhyme with the shape of the warhead. In yet another, a military building is consumed by fire, foreshadowing the kind of devastation a nuclear strike would bring. If that final shot of traffic in *Hospital* suggests that "the world is too much with us," the traffic shots in *Missile* adumbrate our potential to "lay waste our powers."

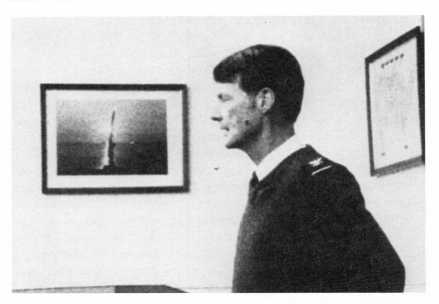

(*Missile*) The photograph of the missile in flight belies the colonel's words about deterrence.

Second, Wiseman brackets (encloses) the film with two different speeches about the necessity of strong deterrence, the same philosophy espoused by Gen. Haig but undercut by editing in *Manoeuvre*. For Lifton and Falk, this view of stockpiling and preparedness as an effective deterrent to nuclear war is in large part self-justification—what they call "nuclearism." The self-justification is obvious. "Our country needs us to do just what we are doing," the general says. "Frankly, if we don't need that kind of a deterrent force, they don't need us." Stylistically, this bracketing provides a closed structure and suggests entrapment, as do the frames of *Titicut Follies, Law and Order,* and *Juvenile Court*. By bracketing the film with this argument, Wiseman suggests the entrenchment of the system; counterarguments are "closed out" of the text. But the irony of the general's last words that abruptly conclude the film—"we're a people who are concerned about God"—hauntingly remain to be pondered as the credits appear.

In an early scene, Col. Ryan articulates the philosophy of deterrence to the trainees. Behind his head on the wall is a photograph of a missile launching, the image directly contradicting his

(*Missile*) The scale of the model pistol suggests the human potential for violence.

words. This happens yet a second time, later in the film. As he explains that the missile crews have at their fingertips the awesome power "to launch the world into nuclear darkness," his hands work, as if on their own accord, already in flight. When he speaks of "measured response," one of his hands ironically forms the shape of a pistol. In the class on firearms, we see a giant mock-up of the M-15 Smith & Wesson Combat Masterpeice handgun; the size of the weapon (emphasized by Wiseman's framing it in close-up) underscores its potential for use ("Mr. Nixon, drop the bomb/ 'cause I don't wanta go to Nam," sing the men as they march in *Basic Training*). A soldier who has done fieldwork in Europe unearthing artifacts from World War II shows a photo of himself posing by gravestones, providing a pointed editorial comment.

Missile, finally, reveals how, according to Lifton and Falk, in the nuclear era the mind comes to be determined by technology "rather than the mind-set controlling and restraining the technology."[20] The film shows the military system for authenticating and executing launch orders, an elaborate technological structure that supposedly precludes the possibility of a fail-safe scenario.

This is a system designed, ironically, to prevent itself from being employed in every case except one. The system, elaborately detailed in the film, constitutes what Lifton and Falk cite as a dominant "nuclear illusion": "the illusion of a 'systems rationality'—of a whole structure of elements, each in 'logical' relation to the other components and to the whole."[21] Thus the launch control panel without the MCU's, says one instructor, is just "a hunk of iron." The system seems perfect, a pure form removed from reality and history (analogous to the film's treatment of physical space). Accordingly, in the hermetic world of *Missile* (amazingly, the switch on the launch control panel indicating war plans A and B is unconnected), history begins to fade. Already the trainees respond to the one soldier's research about World War II as little more than an archeological curiosity from the barbaric past.

If "the flow of history," as Gen. Haig calls it in *Manoeuvre*, has begun to fade in *Missile*, then Wiseman's aim in these films is to prevent history from repeating itself. The project of these films is to counter such illusions, both nuclear and conventional, and the numbing that they result in. They proceed toward this end not only by playing with generic conventions and by examining the institution's ideological discourse but also, particularly in *Manoeuvre*, by adopting a self-reflexive strategy that makes us view combat itself, like narrative cinema, as a construction—a "theater of war," so to speak. Just as the generic conventions of war movies are thwarted in these three films, forcing us to adopt a new position toward the cinematic depiction of the military, so we are encouraged to look at military operations themselves as elaborate fictions, like the film on military history with its cast of "historical characters" shown to the men in *Basic Training*.

Manoeuvre begins with the process of transporting men and equipment from the United States to Germany for the "reforger" exercise, consistently presented by Wiseman so as to allude to the event as a fictional construction. Several times cameras are shown. In the film's third shot, ID photos of the men are taken; later, one soldier takes a snapshot of some friends. There are also two scenes showing a television news crew shooting a story. As in the production of movies, the physical apparatus (military equipment), costumes (uniforms), musical accompaniment (military band at the reception), and even advance publicity (the officer's orientation speech in which he valorizes the exercise's "special effects") are all arranged before "shooting" begins. The men constitute a cast of thousands. Deplaning in Germany, they even enter from the wings, as it were. The battalion is turned over to the general in charge of the exercise, who becomes, in effect, the "director."

Significantly, this is Wiseman's only film wherein the opening title credit is not shown immediately but is delayed until the transport planes (and the "plot") take off. The delayed title, like a Brechtian placard, serves as a further reminder that Wiseman's film, like the NATO exercise itself, is an elaborate fiction. During the argument over assessing kills—in other words, a script conference—the controller makes an explicit distinction between the exercise and "real life." Wiseman foregrounds this distinction, asserting, moreover, that to do so is a more truthful (less fictional) account than either Hollywood war movies or even television news "stories." Thus Wiseman films the news crew from behind, showing the act of production and presenting a wider view than what their camera shows (the same strategy that he later exploits for similar reasons, although more fully, in *Model*). We see not only the physical apparatus of the camera but the discussion about the background and a retake when the reporter flubs his lines.

Manoeuvre is, finally, a war movie without action, where fighting is discussed rather than shown. The action, explicitly acknowledged within the text as "simulated," undercuts the typical Hollywood approach to combat as glorifying spectacle, not unlike Jean-Luc Godard's *Les Carabiniers* (1963). Denied this visual pleasure, and constantly reminded that what we are watching is a text, we are forced to think about warfare rather than passively view it as spectacle. At one point the men are warned about any "unduly curious" civilians with cameras, for they may be guerillas. Wiseman is, in effect, such a guerilla, for in these films he snipes at the institution of the military, deconstructing both its fiction and our suspension of disbelief, uncloaking the cover of night by which ignorant armies clash.

NOTES

1. Richard Fuller, " 'Survive, Survive, Survive': Frederick Wiseman's New Documentary: *Basic Training,*" *The Film Journal* 1, nos. 3–4 (Fall/ Winter 1972): 75.

2. Stephen Mamber, "Cinéma Vérité and Social Concerns," *Film Comment* 9, no. 6 (November/December 1973): 12–13. See also Mamber, *Cinema Verite in America: Studies in Uncontrolled Documentary* (Cambridge: MIT Press, 1974), pp. 234–40; Harry M. Geduld, "Garbage Cans and Institutions: The Films of Fredrick Wiseman," *The Humanist* 31, no. 5 (September/October 1971): 36; and Fuller, " 'Survive, Survive, Survive,' " p 75.

3. David R. Slavitt, *"Basic Training,"* *Contempora* 2, no. 1 (September/ February 1972): 11.

4. Jeanine Basinger, *The World War II Combat Film: Anatomy of a Genre* (New York: Columbia University Press, 1986), pp. 61–62, 73–76.

5. Dana Polan, *Power and Paranoia: History, Narrative, and the American Cinema, 1940–1950* (New York: Columbia University Press, 1986), pp. 75–76.

6. Slavitt, *"Basic Training,"* p. 11.

7. See also Benson and Anderson's comments about Hoffman's racist remark to Booker that he is not "back on the block. You do not go around just beating people up," in *Reality Fictions: The Films of Frederick Wiseman* (Cabondale and Edwardsville: Southern Illinois University Press, 1989), p. 172.

8. Marshall McLuhan, *Understanding Media: The Extensions of Man* (New York: Signet, 1964), p. 208.

9. Johan Huizinga, *Homo Ludens: A Study of the Play-Element in Culture* (Boston: Beacon Press, 1955), p. 89.

10. Edgar Z. Friedenberg, "Ship of Fools: The Films of Frederick Wiseman," *New York Review of Books,* October 21, 1971, p. 92; and Chandra Hecht, "Total Institutions on Celluloid," *Society* 9 (April 1972): 46.

11. Slavitt, *"Basic Training,"* p. 10.

12. David Denby, "Television: Taps," *New York,* October 4, 1971, p. 69.

13. According to Lawrence H. Suid, *Guts & Glory: Great American War Movies* (Reading, Mass.: Addison-Wesley, 1978), p. 9, this is the view of Joseph Heller, David Halberstam, and Pete Hammill. Suid quotes Halberstam's observation that many soldiers, "while they are heterosexual . . . really don't like women; they replace sex with war."

14. D. H. Lawrence, *Studies in Classic American Literature* (London: Heinemann, 1964), p. 59.

15. Robert Jay Lifton and Richard Falk, *Indefensible Weapons: The Political and Psychological Case Against Nuclearism* (New York: Basic Books, 1982).

16. Ibid., pp. 106–7.

17. Ibid.; Allen Ginsberg, "Wichita Vortex Sutra, Part II," in Stephen Berg and Robert Mezey, eds., *Naked Poetry* (Indianapolis and New York: Bobbs-Merrill, 1969), pp. 207–20.

18. Roland Barthes, *Mythologies*, ed. and trans. Annette Lavers (New York: Hill and Wang, 1977), p. 143.

19. Slavitt, *"Basic Training,"* p. 11.

20. Lifton and Falk, *Indefensible Weapons*, p. 9.

21. Ibid., pp. 22.

CHAPTER 4

Blood of the Beasts

Primate (1974) • *Meat* (1976) • *Racetrack* (1984)

Racetrack, focusing on the sport of horseracing and the running of the Belmont Stakes, shows how presumptuously proprietary people are about animals. Yet the film establishes clear parallels between humans and animals in, for example, feeding (horses in the stalls; workers in the cafeteria), grooming (horses being curried; jockeys in the barbershop), competition (horses in the winners' circle; John Morris in the spotlight at the evening reception singing "New York, New York," a song about surviving the urban "rat race").

Racetrack reveals no stylistic discoveries on Wiseman's part, and its handling of cinematic devices is not nearly as provocative as in the two earlier films, *Primate* and *Meat*. Indeed, these two films build on the promise of the military films by demonstrating both a deeper understanding of what institutional life has done to human consciousness and a developing ability to express these themes in cinematic terms. Among Wiseman's most complex films, they convey the filmmaker's "theory" of the events by masterfully positioning the spectator so as to implicate him or her in the institutional processes shown.

James Wolcott observed in his review of *Welfare,* which was made between *Primate* and *Meat,* that Wiseman seemed poised to break through the barriers of the documentary approach."[1] Wiseman himself has remarked that with *Primate,* he was attempting to make a film where the visuals tell the story, which is to say that he approached his material more than ever as cinema.[2] Individual

(*Meat*) The geometric quality of shots such as this one of feed on conveyor belts reinforces the film's determinist view.

shots are often composed with the kind of deliberate mise-en-scène shown to be at work in the military films. For example, in *Primate* a close-up of an ailing, screeching chimp is suddenly obscured by a closing door and fastening lock, which come to block our view of the animal—a wonderfully precise visualization of how, according to the film, the researchers have "blocked out" nature in their scientific pursuits. In *Meat,* some shots of the cattle feed being steamed and processed on conveyor belts and sides of beef hanging in cold storage have a symmetrical austerity and consequent thematic weight worthy of Fritz Lang's distinctive mise-en-scène.

Beyond the similarity of the well-composed shot, though, *Primate* and *Meat* manifest different but equally ingenious structures. Significantly, *Primate* took all of fourteen months to edit, the longest period spent by Wiseman editing any of his films. Both films feature a greater reliance on editing within the sequence. Entire, sometimes considerably lengthy, sequences are frequenty composed of many shots. According to Liz Ellsworth,[3] *Primate* contains 569 shots which, given the film's 105-minute length, works out to an average of about eleven seconds per shot, approximately one-third the average shot length of *Titicut Follies* and one-half that of *High School* or *Hospital*. My own count of the shots in *Meat* totals 552 (a 12.28-second average), which is remarkably close to that of *Primate*. The films tend primarily to carry the viewer along through compositional patterns and the rhythm and logic of the editing. Often there are sequences in both films with little or no dialogue. Significantly, the only sound in many is ambient noise, for the most part the sounds of various machines at work. Dialogue, of course, is still important, but it is less crucial in these two films than in any of the others. In *Meat,* for example, the "beefkill" sequence, depicting the cattle being unloaded, killed, disemboweled, inspected, and placed in cold storage, contains no dialogue at all (the workers shout and make noise, but use no words). It is comprised of ninety-two shots taking twenty minutes of screen time. In *Primate,* the sequence showing the removal and sectioning of a monkey's brain (including a clean-up break and cutaways of animals) is comprised of over one hundred shots, lasting for over twenty-three minutes—almost one fourth of the film—yet it contains very little dialogue.

However, this is not to say that these two films are without long takes or camera movement. During the electro-ejaculation procedure in *Primate,* for instance, the camera bounces back and forth between close-ups of the two researchers conducting the experiment, who face the center of the frame from either side. Like the animal, the viewer is, as it were, caught in the middle, their pawn or plaything. In the union negotiations with the company personnel director in *Meat,* Wiseman pans between the parties, seated on opposite sides of the room, the camera's movement here expressing the gap between their negotiating positions. It is clear, though, that in these two films (unlike *Racetrack,* which seems stylistically closer to some of the earlier documentaries) Wiseman uses camera movement and the long take, both essential elements of the observational style, more sparingly and more purposefully than previously, and that he does not hesitate to employ whatever stylistic devices are suited to his overall purpose.

Both films also demonstrate Wiseman's growing sophistication in positioning viewers in challenging ways and closely linking them to thematic concerns. Most obviously, the films' very subjects—primate research and meat packing—are topics that are likely to make viewers somewhat uncomfortable. The earlier films perhaps allow the viewer the consolation of liberal guilt, but *Primate* and *Meat* make such a response more difficult. The mounds of ground beef Wiseman shows, just after Ken Monfort's discussion of morality in meat packing, inevitably speak to the ethics of our national lifestyle and implicates all of us. *Primate* is Wiseman's most openly acerbic film since *Titicut Follies* and possibly his most extended experiment in the manipulation of viewer response. As one might expect, it generated more controversy than any Wiseman film since his first. *Meat,* surprisingly, is quite the opposite, so understated and apparently detached that for many viewers it is, if anything, merely puzzling or perhaps mildly annoying. Hence the general response to it was relatively mild. In fact, it may be seen as the first in a long string of Wiseman films that have generated only lukewarm response because they lack the "hard-hitting" qualities of the early documentaries. Wolcott, for example, while admiring *Meat,* found its style too austere, while John J. O'Connor thought it unclear in focus, "unsure of itself."[4] However, the divergent reactions to these two films are actually the result of Wiseman's different approach in his effort to intimately bind the spectator through the viewing experience to the implications he perceives in the institution under scrutiny.

The titles of both films are pointedly ambiguous, suggesting in some measure the reduction of human as well as animal life. Indeed, *Primate* and *Meat* are perhaps this filmmaker's bleakest, most pessimistic views of American institutional life. Life is alienated, deterministic, and, as in the famous opening passage describing the Central London Hatchery in Huxley's *Brave New World,* wholly technological and commodified. "The overalls of the workers were white," Huxley writes, "their hands gloved with a pale corpse-coloured rubber"[5]—a detail that applies to the Yerkes researchers, the Monfort workers, and even the medical team during the operation in *Racetrack.* Both films feature many close-ups of machinery and technology in action, displacing the human element. In *Primate* the animals are continually under the silent surveillance of the researchers who, like Big Brother, observe their every action.

(*Primate*) An animal's hand struggles to grasp food dangling just out of reach, an absurdist image of the primates' helplessness before greater forces.

"We don't want them doing things sexually when we're not in a position to see it," explains one scientist. In *Meat* the computerized feed building looms on the horizon like an Orwellian ministry.

Existence in *Primate* and *Meat* seems to be determined by forces beyond individual control, as indifferent to our fate as flies to wanton boys. After the lengthy but compelling sequence in *Primate* where the squirrel monkey's brain is removed, one of the researchers merely concludes, rather anticlimactically: "That's sort of interesting." In the muscle experiment, as in *Welfare*, existence becomes an absurd struggle to reach unobtainable goals. A monkey's hand is shown in close-up reaching for the bits of food that dangle just short of its grasp. The animals become puppets, their behavior, movement, and sexuality controlled by various wires and electrical impulses (one scientist boasts that they are now getting readings from "in the brain itself").

Just as in *Racetrack* movement is consistently regulated for people as well as animals by fences, gates, aisles, highway lanes, and entranceways (blinders prevent the horses from seeing anything off the beaten path—a metaphor of ideology at work), so in *Pri-*

mate and *Meat* life is constrained by a variety of pens, corrals, cages, and boxes ("a five foot monkey in a three foot space" is how one box in *Primate* is described). Ultimately the animals themselves are transformed into objects in boxes, cartons of steak at the end of *Meat*. In this film, at the end of the path (the entrance to the plant) the inevitable man waits with cattle prod and stun gun. The film builds on Dean Jagger's metaphor in *The Dark City* (William Dieterle, 1950) that "people are like sheep frightened by the smell of death in a slaughterhouse. They run down the passageway with the other sheep, thinking there's freedom, but there's always a man with a sledgehammer waiting."

All of this, however, is not to say that these films are defeatist or nihilistic, for it is precisely in their ability to elicit vivid response from the viewer that they suggest, for want of a better word, redemption. The strong presence in both films of Wiseman's characteristic black humor works, in part, as the acting coach says in *Model*, to relieve the tension of horror. In the face of emotional numbing—the result, as we have seen, of bureaucracy and technology—comedy is a sign of our ability to feel deeply. Neither the experimentation upon nor the butchering of animals would seem subjects appropriate for a humorous treatment, especially in the age of militant animal liberation. Nevertheless, the humor is strongly present in both films, and given their subjects, makes for many viewers a most uneasy blend of tones that serves to amplify an already uncomfortable viewing experience.

In *Meat*, there is the sight gag of a football (pigskin) game on television in the plant, and the song "What Kind of Fool Am I?" ("What kind of man am I? / An empty shell") plays from a portable radio as workers butcher sides of beef. In the spirit in which Hitchcock views *Psycho* as a comedy, Wiseman himself claims that *Primate* "is actually a rather bizarre comedy—I think it's a riot."[6] Two scientists talk about the copulating positions of gorillas as a photo of two animals in the act hangs on a wall between them, functioning like a cartoon thought balloon ("I've some pictures inside," one says tantalizingly). Later comes the ludicrous discussion about the variables of the electro-ejaculation experiment ("Do we use fresh semen on Tuesday or Wednesday?"). The film also invites us to view the hirsute scientists as "primates" themselves (Wiseman claims that he chose the opening close-ups of behavioral scientists more for the way they look than for their scientific achievements). This running joke culminates in the scene where one scientist has to show an ape how to swing on a trapeze.

Primate was shot at the Yerkes Primate Research Center at Emory University in Atlanta, Georgia. The film's ostensible subject is the scientific experimentation and research conducted there using various species of monkeys and apes as subjects. It is on this level that the film's material generates controversy, for the topic, like abortion, is one that inevitably elicits strong feelings. The emotional response such material is likely to elicit is, if anything, exacerbated by what Patrick J. Sullivan describes as Wiseman's strategy of giving us "bewilderingly little information about the nature of the experiments, the goals of the research group, the rationale for individuals' behavior."[7] Indeed, with the exception of one sequence where the scientist lucidly explains the purpose of his experiments in measuring primate muscular activity, the viewer remains in the dark about the nature of and justification for most of the experiments shown in the film. This, of course, only serves to heighten one's sympathy for the animals and anger toward the scientists, since the experiments are made to seem pointless—eliciting reactions such as Sullivan's, that the Yerkes Center appears to be "a concentration camp of behavioral research."[8]

Dr. Geoffrey Bourne, director of the Yerkes Center, responded publicly to the film by calling it "grossly misleading," claiming that much of the material shown was taken out of context. In an irate letter published in the *New York Times,* Dr. Bourne insisted that "in fact, the film shows no vivisection, no cruelty, no pain caused to any of the animals and no callousness—except the effects deliberately created by the camera tricks used by Mr. Wiseman."[9] Bourne's letter goes on to describe the film as a "mishmash of synthetic sadism, confusion, misunderstanding, misrepresentation and obsession with sex." The one specific example he cites is the scene concerning the critically ill epileptic chimpanzee (the film transcript indicates that the chimp is suffering from heat stroke) who is hosed down to reduce a high fever that, according to Dr. Bourne, was in no way the result of experimentation. From his point of view, the chimp's life was saved by the institution's dedicated staff, but, unfortunately, the viewer has no way of knowing this because of the material and information omitted by Wiseman. Indeed, when the scientists express concern that the fever may have damaged the animal's brain, we are likely to snicker at their apparent solicitude, given that the sequence immediately preceding this is the removal and sectioning of the squirrel monkey's brain.

According to the *New York Times,* for the film's scheduled broadcast in December 1974 on New York's WNET (the station that produced it), Bourne submitted a three-minute videotaped disclaimer that he requested be shown before the film. WNET rejected the request (in the end, the videotape was shown only on WETV in Atlanta), and proposed instead to televise a discussion between Bourne and Wiseman. But Dr. Bourne declined, arguing that that would be nothing more than a publicity stunt for the film. He lodged a formal complaint with the FCC, charging the film with "gross distortion," and even threatened legal action. When the film was shown on December 5, WNET reported receiving over 150 complaints from viewers, including a bomb scare and a threat on Wiseman's life. In the end, only 81 of the 222 PBS stations showed the film that night, and many refused to show it at all. The *Nova* staff of WGBH in Boston produced a follow-up show, a half-hour discussion entitled *The Price of Knowledge?,* which was distributed to the PBS network. The show featured Wiseman, biologists Richard Lewontin and David Baltimore, Harvard philosopher Robert Nozick, and Yerkes researcher Adrian Perachio (the primatologist in the film conducting the telestimulation experiment). According to Wiseman, none of the participants accused the film of being inaccurate.

Wiseman did not feel obligated to provide full exposition about the experiments in *Primate,* since the research activity at Yerkes is not the film's primary concern. Even as a graduate student in the film remarks to one of the researchers when hypothesizing about the sexual behavior of gorillas, no account, not even a scientific one, ever provides the whole story. Moreover, as one of the scientists notes later in the discussion about pure research, pieces of information take on different meanings depending upon their context—a point particularly appropriate to Wiseman's mosaic structures. Wiseman himself concedes that he does not have strong opinions about animal research and that he is not an animal liberationist or even a vegetarian. He cheerfully admits that while shooting *Meat,* "I ate steak every night I was up there, usually something I met earlier in the day." Elsewhere, he states that he saw no animal cruelty at the Yerkes Center, and even accepts the argument that such experiments are "vital to research."[10] For him, the importance of the work at the Yerkes Center is to "question the implication of this kind of research for human behavior."[11] One of his interests in showing the gap between institutional ideology and practice has always been to show how the ideology "is used for the purposes of social control within the group."[12] This is made explicit during the birth of the foal at the beginning of *Racetrack.* When it is suggested that the pregnant horse be given a tranquilizer, a woman remembers that when she gave birth she had to have an epidural because her husband "couldn't stand it anymore." The Yerkes Center and the Monfort Plant are, then, two more cultural "spoors" that for Wiseman embody contemporary American society.

Unfortunately, because *Primate* deals with such an emotionally charged issue, the publicity it generated, as with *Titicut Follies,* concentrated more on the sensationalism of its ostensible subject than on the thematic or aesthetic issues it raises. Writers were quick either to take an antivivisectionist position or to defend the Yerkes researchers against unfair treatment by Wiseman. In a review that vents its spleen more on the activities of the Yerkes Center than on the film, for example, Chuck Kraemer said *Primate* is "grisly, with enough vivisection, exotic behavior modification, implantations, vomiting and probing to turn the strongest stomach."[13] Even the relatively lengthy article in *Bioscience* magazine, despite its generally calm and detached recounting of "The *Primate* Controversy," echoed Sullivan's complaint that the film fails to address the political and ethical issues of primate research in any clear way, that the information necessary for viewers to make an informed judgment is lacking, and that it "simply divided its audience on the basis of already formed prejudices."[14]

However, Wiseman's humanist concerns in *Primate* are successfully translated into a cinematic treatment that is, in fact, precisely controlled. Most obviously, the film encourages the viewer's inherent inclination to anthropomorphize the apes and monkeys, and to identify with the animals as if they were feeling human emotions. Some reviewers did note that the viewer's identification tends to be located with the monkeys and apes. For example, the squirrel monkey becomes for one writer the film's "star,"[15] while another critic unproblematically claims that the close-ups of the animals' faces reveal "their feelings of panic, suspicion and open hatred of their keepers."[16] Gary Arnold clearly acknowledged his identification with the animals, noting how their faces "register responses of pain, resistance and frustration" but then checked himself because "such responses are . . . thoroughly unprofessional," in other words, excessively subjective.[17] Having failed to perceive how and to what purpose the film deliberately encourages such "unprofessional"—that is, unscientific or uncritical—reactions, no one has seriously reflected on the implications of this spectator position. In context, it is less an instance of the pathetic fallacy on the part of the viewer than it is a central aspect of the film's strategy and meaning.

Wiseman encourages us to endow the animals with human qualities and feelings through, for example, the film's extensive use of facial close-ups. Just as these close-ups magnify the faces of the animals on the screen for our visual scrutiny ("bigger than life," says one scientist about the image of a monkey's face captured on video in the zero gravity experiment), so they amplify our tendency to project human qualities onto animals in the first place. There are approximately as many close-ups of animal faces as there are of human faces in the film. Moreover, the animals' faces are often shot in the same manner as typical human reaction shots that amplify drama, further inviting us to see them as human-like. For example, a doomed squirrel monkey is followed to a table where a blood sample is taken. Wiseman cuts to a close-up of its clearly grimacing face, presumaby a pained protest. The cut is obviously motivated by the wish to increase viewer identification with the animal at this dramatic point. Much the same can be said of those typically expressive close-ups of hands, so frequent in Wiseman's work. There are many shots of animal hands in *Primate* as poignant as the close-up of the monkey tossing the bone in the famous opening of Kubrick's *2001: A Space Odyssey* (1968). As when a chimp feels a seashell in the language experiment or when a monkey reaches out from within its cage to defend itself from being injected with an anaesthetic, animals' hands seem as gesturally

eloquent as some of the human body movements captured elsewhere by Wiseman's camera. Because they are almost always either in cages (they are frequently shown standing by the cage
doors or hanging from the ceiling, positions that emphasize their
entrapment) or subjected to experimentation, our tendency to
sympathize makes us even more responsive to them and their
situation.

Several specific shots of animals in the film encourage us to respond to them as if they were human because the images suggest
similarities to shots involving people from previous Wiseman
films. The shaving of the squirrel monkey's head (in addition to
anticipating the sheep shearing in *Meat*) reminds us of similar
shots in *Titicut Follies, Basic Training,* and *Juvenile Court.* A rhesus
monkey has a tube forcibly inserted through its nose (the same
thing happens to a horse during the operation in *Racetrack*), like
Malinowsky in *Titicut Follies* and an elderly patient in *Hospital.* Surgery is performed on an anesthetised monkey, its arms spread out
like those of the patient in the opening shot of *Hospital* (see p. 00).
A newborn chimp's ability to hang from a bar is timed by a lab
technician, reminding us of the girls gym class in *High School* and
the trainees in *Basic Training.*

Another shot of an orangutan (although not a reference to a
specific image from a different Wiseman film) works similarly.
The orangutan, shaved so that its muscular activity can be electri-
cally monitored, is photographed with its back to the camera, making it look surprisingly human in physique. The species name,
from the Malay for "man of the woods," is itself a linguistic anthro-
pomorphism, like the Judas goat in *Meat.* This visually undercuts
the scientist's theory of divergent primate evolution, for such shots
enhance our thinking of the animals as being "like" people.

Within the film, the staff of the Yerkes Center themselves anthropomorphize the animals. Baby chimps are brought into "newborn reception," like human babies in any North American
hospital. They are dressed in diapers, soothingly rocked, and fed
with bottles. When they are a little older, they drink from cups. A
nurse prattles at them as at human babies, calling them "boys" and
"girls" and referring to herself as "mommy." Some, like the chimp
Lana who can sign for candy and juice, have begun to master the
rudiments of symbolic language and so are engaged in conversation by researchers.

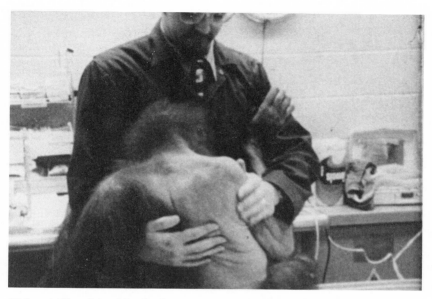

(*Primate*) The shaved back of an orangutan looks surprisingly human.

It could be argued, in fact, that the animals seem more expressive, more alive, than the Yerkes researchers. At the very beginning of the film, Wiseman presents a series of eight shots of scientists (identified in the transcript simply as "various famous behaviorists") followed by another series of shots of primates in their cages. The scientists, as we see them, are images of images, still photographs hanging on a wall at the center. They are motionless, like the image of Dr. Yerkes himself, ossified in this opening sequence in the form of a bust. By contrast, the animals move about, obviously alive. They touch and hug each other, unlike the humans who maintain a public, professional distance from one another. The energy of the animals seems even to spill out of the frame. With charming impulsiveness, Lana, apparently having had enough conversation, jumps from the table in the direction of the camera, causing it to shake before the shot abruptly ends.

The scientists, seeming insensitive and manipulative, compare unfavorably to the animals. One researcher remarks, as if surprised, that a monkey seems "very sensitive" as an electrode is being fitted into his brain. Later, a woman observing the electrode procedure[18] genuinely wonders if the animal "resents" being

(Primate) Camera placement in the film, as in the beginning and end of this shot, frequently positions the spectator within the space of the research facility.

restrained. The chimp John is literally "jerked around" as a lab assistant coaxes him over to the bars of the cage with grape juice so that he can masturbate him with a lubricated plastic tube. The duplicitous actions of the people in the film are expressed visually by the fact that in most shots, humans are shown either in profile or wearing surgical masks, in both cases their faces partially hidden.

Primate, then, clearly provides the spectator with an emotional point of view that is more closely aligned with the animals than the humans. This viewpoint is organized physically and perceptually as well as emotionally in terms of what the animals see and feel, and, to some extent, what they might think (in Bruce Kawin's terms, as both subjective camera and "mindscreen").[19] We are placed in a position similar to that of the animals, for we know so little about the experiments that the objectives and methods are often obscure. Like the animals, we lack comprehension of what is going on around us. Just as the orangutan is lured with juice and the monkey is enticed into its constraining device with a banana,

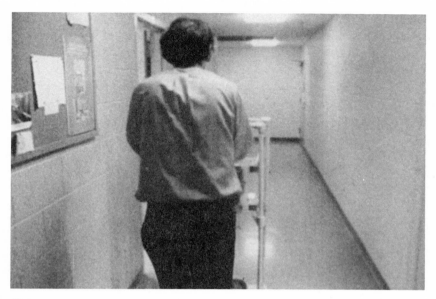

(*Primate*)

so the viewer is offered at the beginning of the film the carrot of witnessing benevolent research where animals learn sign recognition and language skills, raising a false sense of security which is then increasingly undermined. Like domesticated animals, we place our blind trust in the good will of experts, but the film pulls the rug out from under us.

In *Primate* Wiseman alters his more common practice of following people down hallways in two ways. Compare, for example, how the camera follows the inmate Jim back to his cell in *Titicut Follies* or the stunning sequence shots in hallways in *Blind*. In *Primate*, instead, Wiseman most often places the camera in the middle of corridors in an immobile fixed position—that is to say, he films these shots as if from a cage. He only pans left or right to follow the researchers as they walk down the halls toward the camera and then past it. Consequently, if they are carrying equipment, as they usually are, in the first part of these shots it is being wheeled toward or pointed at us. Alternately, several times when researchers walk past the camera, Wiseman cuts to another position in advance of the person (normally a difficult point of view to construct in observational cinema). It is as if we, like the animals, were already there, trapped, and can only wait for their unwelcome arrival.

In both cases we are placed, in Nick Browne's terms, as a "spectator-within-the-text,"[20] which aligns us with the position of the research animals. Thus, even though the close-ups of the animals' faces may not be more numerous, they carry a greater emotional weight, for the techniques of spectator identification are consistently mobilized on their behalf. Moments of animal identification in cinema are rare, as Edward Branigan acknowledges.[21] Films almost never ask the viewer to identify to any significant extent with an animal unless it is presented as a dramatic "character" with recognizable human qualities. Hence what is noteworthy about *Primate* is its attempt to construct a sustained emotional identification with animals without presenting them as rounded individuals.

It could be argued that the close-ups of animals' faces in *Primate* and the numerous shots of them in seemingly helpless subjection (reinforced by the selective presentation of information about the experiments), constitutes another instance, like the uncomplimentary close-ups of teachers in *High School,* of Wiseman's unfortunate reliance on "cheap shots" for easy emotional effect. *Primate*'s style, it is true, forces the viewer to identify with the animals, but this effect is central to the film's theme. Primate research exists on the horns of a dilemma. On the one hand, it is supported (as the film's final sequence aboard the air force jet makes perfectly clear) by government funding, obtained by emphasizing the biological similarities between humans and other primates. On the other hand, the argument against the moral objections to such research is that these creatures are, after all, just animals. Therefore, by encouraging us to sympathize with the animals, and to think of them as being "like" people, the film encourages us to experience directly this dilemma. Rational argument is necessarily informed by emotional response, for after seeing *Primate,* a viewer, whether previously sympathetic or hostile to primate research, can no longer think about the issue in quite the same way. In the end, while of course we do not really come to know the animals' point of view, we have felt it to the extent that we have become somewhat estranged from the locus of human values embodied by the researchers. Indeed, to some extent the scientists come to seem

(*Meat*) The reduced scale of the animals in extreme long shot graphically foreshadows their treatment as raw material for "animal fabrication."

peculiar, themselves subjects for observation, one among several species of primates. In Sklovskij's sense, they have been made strange. Like the stereotypical mad scientists of countless science fiction and horror films, their quests come to seem "unnatural." Interestingly, Wiseman has described the film as a "science fiction documentary."[22]

Meat places the viewer in an entirely different relationship to its profilmic events. Where *Primate* systematically employs subjective camera techniques, *Meat* is resolutely third person. Where the tone of the former film is emotional and angry, that of the latter seems cool and dispassionate. As Wolcott so aptly describes the film: "Instead of ham-fisted proles driving screaming blades into Goya carcasses, two young women calmly monitor the grain feeding of cattle from their *Space: 1999* control center."[23] Near the beginning of *Meat* we see several extreme long shots of cattle in the feedlot from a very high angle. Visually, this reduces the animals to such an extent that they look like the specks in a Larry Poons painting or similar to the microscopic slides of blood, brain, and sperm cells we see in *Primate*. This great physical distance from the animals establishes the film's overall perspective, as do the connotations of omniscience indicated by the angles of the shots. If *Primate* encourages the viewer to anthropomorphize the animals, *Meat*, even while it shows us the seeming terror in the eyes of the cattle as they are being herded, scrupulously avoids subjective camera techniques. Here, as in Alfred Hayes's poem "The Slaughterhouse": "Whatever terror their dull intelligences feel / or what agony distorts their most protruding eyes / the incommunicable narrow skulls conceal."[24] Only once in the film—as the cattle are being funneled up a long ramp in the depth of the shot—is the camera placed in the pen, along with the animals.

The film shows the entire process of meat packing—what Ken Monfort, the owner of Monfort Meat Packing in Greeley, Colorado, where the film was shot, calls "animal fabrication"—from the animals grazing in apparent freedom to the shipping to market of identical small cuts of meat. Wrapped in plastic, stamped by government inspection, and sealed in boxes, the final product bears little resemblance to the animals at the beginning of the process. Even the language used to classify the animals as products— "light heiferettes," "ungraded goosenecks in combos," "tri-tips"— strips ("flays") them of life. Every part of the animal is accounted for in the process, from hide to intestines. It is nothing if not efficient, seemingly honed to perfection. The work, like the animals themselves, has been sliced into little pieces, each worker repeatedly performing a single task on the disassembly line. There is no room here for what the narrator of Georges Franju's *Le Sang des Betes* (1948) calls "the *art* of flaying," where everything is done with hand-tools, or for a master butcher like Henri Furmel to demonstrate his impressive manual skill. Instead, power saws slice easily through the carcasses in seconds, flaying is done by giant machines that effortlessly peel away skin, and hooves are clipped off by powerful, ominous-looking scissor machines.

Meat, like all of Wiseman's films, is concerned with process, although the process examined here is nothing less than processing itself. Animals, workers, and viewers are all processed in the course of the film. Because the work has become so repetitive, so mechanical, workers no longer take pride in their labor as they do in Franju's film. *Meat*, unsurprisingly, is the Wiseman film that lends itself most readily to a Marxist analysis of labor within advanced capitalism.[25]

In the cafeteria the workers, bored and alienated, eat in rows, arranged on either side of the long tables like the sides of beef in cold storage. Their faces, as they stare into the distance, doze and glance at their watches, seem as expressionless as those of the dead animals moved through the "beefkill" procedure on hooks. While Wiseman was filming at Monfort, the fortuitously named Governor John Vanderhoof came to campaign for reelection, and Wiseman brilliantly incorporated his visit into the film. He photographs the governor as he proceeds down the rows of workers, automatically asking each how he is today, shaking hands mechanically as he goes (like General Haig in the mess hall in *Manoeuvre*). The camera isolates the governor's hand in close-up repeating the handshake gesture as he moves down a table, emphasizing its similarity to the repetitive work in the plant, in particular to the movement of the cutting machines. That this sequence is placed immediately after the one with the cylindrical egg salesman emphasizes the extent to which politics has become a matter of salesmanship.

The connections between the animals and the workers are established in an understated manner that befits the numbed alienation of the workers. The lengthy "beefkill" section of the film concludes with a clean-up sequence that begins with the workers punching out their time cards. Their time is slotted and calculated by company management, analogous to the treatment of the animals by the workers. They then hose themselves and their equipment clean, just as they had done previously with the various cuts of meat. The later "lambkill" section of the film, which concludes with the lamb carcasses being washed, weighed, tagged, and put into cold storage, ends with a sound bridge from the coming sequence, the negotiations between the union and company representatives. While we see the lamb carcasses in cold storage, we hear the personnel director say, "I reviewed the area that we've talked about" before the scene cuts to the director's office where this conversation is taking place. This creates an ambiguity about whether "the area" is one for the workers or the meat. This ambiguity is strengthened by the unintentionally ironic fear of the worker Bill that the company is "gonna start chopping our heads."

The film's style matches perfectly the alienated, desensitized world shown inside the Monfort Plant. In addition to constructing

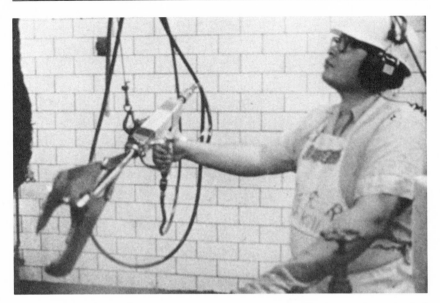

(*Meat*) The framing of plant machinery and the campaigning governor's glad hand suggests the extent to which the idea of "processing" informs the film.

the point of view of an "ideal" (detached) observer, an "absent one" who in this case is positioned so as to see each step of the process clearly, the camera, in comparison to Wiseman's other films, tends to move very little. The minimal movement the film does exhibit is primarily functional, serving to contain the flow of animals through pens and on ramps or to keep within frame the various tasks performed by workers. Long takes generally are reserved for dialogue sequences. Still, on the few occasions when camera movement is employed to any significant degree, as in the previously mentioned union bargaining sequence, it tends to further express this pervading sense of alienation and confinement. But mostly the shots are stationary, and they accumulate with a rhythmic regularity that reflects the stultifying, repetitious tasks of the workers. The one notable exception is the cattle auction at the beginning of the film, where the speed of the transactions is mirrored by the rapid pace of the editing. This sequence is comprised of thirty-eight shots and takes less than a minute and a half of screen time. After this initial excitement, though, the film settles into its steady rhythm.

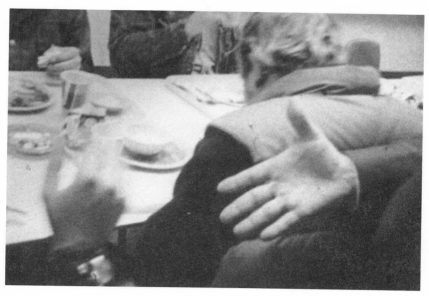

(*Meat*)

The shots are embedded in a structure that brilliantly conveys in the viewing experience this sense of alienated labor. The film is divided into two parts, each showing the slaughtering and packing process from beginning to end. The first part, which lasts about an hour (roughly half of the film), shows the process applied to cattle. As it nears completion, one cannot help but wonder what else the film can show. The answer, as many viewers are probably dismayed to discover, is that it chronicles the process once again, from the beginning. The second time around, the process, this time involving the smaller sheep, is not only repetitious but decidedly anticlimactic. While the cowhides must be removed by big machines, the sheepskins are peeled away merely by a firm tug of the hand. Similarly, the jaws of the cattle must be pried open by placing them in special metal receptacles, whereas the sheep skulls are unceremoniously squashed, like nutshells, by giant stamping machines, reminiscent of what happens to the diminutive squirrel monkey's head in *Primate*. With the cattle, at least there is drama. In one scene, a stubborn cow refuses to be prodded into one end of a holding pen along with the others; several times the animal

must be prodded before it agrees to go along with the rest. The
sheep, by contrast, need no such prompting; they move along as a
crowd, unquestioningly following the Judas goat without protest
toward their inexorable fate.

If *Primate* is structured by a sense of mounting horror, as experiments seem to become increasingly grotesque and violent, *Meat*,
then, works oppositely, draining what it shows of drama, as the animals themselves are drained of blood. In short, Wiseman has stra-
tegically placed the slaughter of the smaller animal second, to
make it seem even less "interesting." It may be true, as John
O'Connor asserts, that the repetition of the process "adds nothing
to our comprehension of the system,"[26] but it does not follow that
this repetition is without meaning. For the film quickly induces
disinterest, even boredom in the viewer who, given the film's subject, might be disappointed by the absence of those "ham-fisted
proles driving screaming blades into Goya carcasses." Indeed, how
very quickly the film moves from the potential frisson of the ab-
attoir to the dull banality of routine. In the space of two hours, the
viewer comes around to the detached consciousness of the workers
themselves. The film "prods" us to realize how quickly and easily
we too may be processed.

At the same time, similar to the military documentaries, the
film plays with the viewer's generic expectations by encouraging
our awareness of how we have been "processed" by popular cinema. Just as the meaning of *Basic Training* is in part determined by
its inflections of the conventions of the war film, so *Meat* engages
our experience of westerns. The film immediately evokes the
genre in its opening shots of bison grazing and cowboys on horse-
back, and early on the dialogue mentions a "stagecoach from
Denver."

The first shot of the film is a long shot of a small buffalo herd;
then come two shots, taken at a closer range, of two or three of the
animals. A second or closer look, in other words, reveals a decrease
in their number. This is no thundering herd of the Wild West. At
once we are reminded of how the mighty herds of buffalo that
once roamed the plains, as "numerous as fishes of the sea," were
brought near extinction by the westward course of empire—that
is, by capitalism and industrialism, those forces embodied in *Meat*
by Monfort. Thus the images of these mighty creatures, that "typ-

(*Meat*) The Western myth is deconstructed in iconographical images that acknowledge their own artifice.

ical American symbol of rugged strength and independence,"[27]
isolated at the beginning of *Meat* in little groups, serve as an iconographic reminder of the passing of the West and an index of the
contemporary working conditions the film proceeds to show. (In
its depiction of horses as commodities, as "tools" according to one
of the owners, *Racetrack* works similarly. As Edward Buscombe
notes, "a horse in a western is not just an animal but a symbol of
dignity, grace, and power.")[28]
   Similarly, the shots of the cowboys evoke a mythic past that is
contrasted by the contemporary working conditions inside the
plant. Wiseman consistently shoots the cowboys in the film's opening sequence so that, as in the shots of soldiers drilling in *Basic
Training*, they are silhouetted against the rising or setting sun.
These shots are reminiscent of many of the justly celebrated images in Ford's classic westerns, and evoke a similar nostalgic quality, for in *Meat* the days of the cowboy as the rugged individual
of American western myth are over. In *Stagecoach* (Ford, 1939),
John Wayne's Ringo Kid may have been "saved from the blessings
of civilization," but *Meat* shows that now, in the blunt words of

e.e. cummings, "Buffalo Bill's defunct." The trucks on which the animals are loaded are also photographed in silhouette against the sun, suggesting how these machines have replaced the horse. Indeed,the only broncos in the world of the film are the professional football players, referred to by a pennant above the feedlot computer.

These iconographically loaded shots at the beginning of *Meat* immediately establish the film's discourse as self-conscious. The silhouette shots of both horses and trucks call attention to themselves as images, since in many of them the sun is refracted in William Brayne's camera, and dust and dried drops of water are visible on the lens. The film forces us, then, to acknowledge the constructed status of such imagery in an industrial world where the values the imagery celebrates can operate only on the level of myth. The low angle shots of the cowboys do not function as images of mythic celebration, as in Colin Low's *Corral* (1954), but rather as ironic deflation.

In these films, the entire life cycle has been commodified, made unnatural, from birth (the caring of the baby chimps in the hospital at the beginning of *Primate;* the carefully supervised studding in *Racetrack*) to death (experimentation in *Primate;* animal fabrication in *Meat*). In the first dialogue sequence of *Primate,* a scientist tellingly confuses what types of animal behavior are observable in the wild and in captivity. One Yerkes researcher remarks in the planning meeting for the artificial insemination experiment that after artificially impregnating the female they will "let nature take its course," providing a howlingly funny punch line. Wiseman follows this sadly short-sighted comment with his own visual joke: he cuts to a shot of the monkey slated for the zero gravity experiment being wheeled down a corridor in a restraining device, a sort of technological tumbrel (see p. 00), hardly nature taking its course. Incredibly, the line is repeated almost verbatim in *Racetrack* when, after sequences showing the studding procedure and the birth of a foal, someone remarks, "ain't nature wonderful?" In the eerie final sequence of *Primate,* the zero gravity experiment aboard a climbing and diving air force C-130 jet, no one—neither the scientists nor Wiseman's cameraman—can keep his feet on the ground, and everyone begins to float in the air. Like the giddy finale of *Model,* a fashion show where models seem to twirl about endlessly, nature has been violated to the extent that we have lost our footing.

The cylindrical egg product in *Meat* is the perfect found metaphor for the technologization of nature examined in the film. The salesman says: "We just put a dozen eggs back together again into one convenient form." (The company, he adds, has "developed" some salads.) Thus technology has managed to blur the distinction between the raw and the cooked. The egg product's cylindrical container looks similar to the tubes of ground beef we see being prepared in the film's final sequence, the similarity of shape reinforcing the thematic connection. It is significant that technology has refashioned even eggs, for it "brings us at last," to quote *Brave New World* once again, "out of the realm of mere slavish imitation of nature into the much more interesting world of human invention."[29] Just as the horses in *Racetrack* are pampered because they are "worth millions," so in *Meat*, as in the early cattle auction sequence, life is quantified, a matter of weight and dollars ("We're going to weigh 'em in two, sell 'em in one"). Numbers and dollars, in fact, make up the content of virtually every dialogue in *Meat*: the auctioneer's patter, the exchange between the feed truck drivers and the computer operators, the tour of the plant given to the Japanese businessmen, Monfort's conversation with the cattle buyer, the salesmen's telephone chatter, the union negotiations with the company's personnel director, the employee benefits meeting, the newspaper reporter's interview with Monfort. Prices can be cut and scaled, just like animals. Even the weather is quantified (like the "weather inhibiting factor" in *Missile*), as the feedlot supervisor reports to Monfort the relevant data on the climate at the two feedlots.

The world of *Primate* and *Meat* is, in short, one where reason has triumphed over passion, the mind over the body. In our reification of scientific knowledge and technology, we have cut ourselves off from our own physical and emotional nature, just as the squirrel monkey's head is separated from its body. The extent to which we have become alienated from nature is visualized in *Primate* in the prophylactic barrier established by the incubator, the surgical masks and gloves, and padded gloves the scientists wear when handling the animals. Significantly, the image we see of Dr. Yerkes himself at the beginning of the film is a sculptured bust at the center—a head without a body. Bodies are continually violated and deadened in these films—in *Primate* by the penetration of a variety of devices, drugs, tools and artificial stimulation and in *Meat*

and *Racetrack* by the routinization of activity. In all three films animals themselves become tools to be utilized. The bodies of animals in *Primate* are anaesthetized despite their protest; in *Racetrack*
a man threatens a spirited horse with castration. But *Primate,* in
fact, suggests that we have in a sense castrated ourselves. Hence
that close-up of a researcher's hand, with long knife and banana,
seems extremely ominous. Similarly, the workers in *Meat* have
grown anaesthetized, stunned in a different but analogous way to
the animals they slaughter. As in *Welfare* and *Missile,* we have been
shackled by what William Blake calls "mind-forg'd manacles."

Wiseman's film practice is, in a sense, analogous to the work of
the scientists. As Calvin Pryluck has noted in his discussion of ethics in documentary, "scientific experiments and direct cinema depend for their success on subjects who have little or nothing to
gain from participation."[30] Just as the researchers watch their subjects, so Wiseman observes his; they dissect the animals, like Wiseman "cuts up" what he films through framing and montage. The
squirrel monkey's brain in *Primate* is removed and sliced into sections like meat, but also like the process of montage. And as in the
scene in *Hospital* where the human brain is examined, the monkey's brain is assessed in aesthetic terms ("one of the best we've
seen in a few weeks"). The scientists' response to the microscopic
slides ("shots") made from the brain samples—we see several fill
the entire frame—appears more aesthetic than scientific ("That is
beautiful," they enthuse). Wiseman similarly explores the compositional potential of observational cinema. In different ways, then,
both scientist and observational filmmaker murder to dissect.

Clearly, though, Wiseman's camera is superior as a method of
obtaining empirical knowledge. The scientists employ people to
observe the animals and at one-minute intervals to fill in checklists
containing "fifteen or twenty categories of behavior." At one point
a scientist asks a checker if she recorded her "impressions" in "a
short sentence." Another observational method involves tape recording verbal descriptions of animal behavior and taking periodic
still photos to document actions. But such procedures are inadequate to gauge the complexities of behavior. Thus Wiseman films
the checkers through links in a chain fence, the framing suggesting their narrower vision. Inevitably, we wonder why they don't
use videotape, or film, like Wiseman—like, in fact, the very film

(*Primate*) The observers observed; the framing suggests a more comprehensive view than that offered by scientific knowledge.

we are watching (video cameras are employed in some of the experiments; why not here?). *Primate* shows an orangutan giving birth, accompanied by the researcher's tape recorded narrative, which clearly provides less information than what we see. Certainly neither still photos nor words alone can duplicate the power of observational cinema.[31] Toward the end of the film the scientists discuss the relative value of pure and applied research. They profess the superiority of the former, although their claim is suspect since their work (like that of many "independent" filmmakers including Wiseman himself) is dependent upon government grants and private endowments. Wiseman acknowledges this economic reality and emphatically undercuts the idea of pure research in the final sequence of the film, the zero gravity experiment, by focusing on the air force logo on the plane as a van carrying the scientists, monkey, and camera draws near it on the runway.

Typical of Wiseman's approach and in contrast to the behavior modification of the scientists, both *Primate* and *Meat* allow viewers to come to their own conclusions. *Primate* ends abruptly, with the plane in mid-flight, leaving us, as so many of his films do, "up in

the air" with questions. How far will we go in our quest for knowledge? Is our path upward or down? At the end of *Meat,* only after
being stultified along with the workers is the viewer rudely awak-
ened; the institution is suddenly thrust into a moral perspective
when Monfort is asked by a local news reporter about his and the
consumer's (viewer's) moral responsibility. In Wiseman's cinema,
then, it is not only the filmmaker but the viewer as well who is cast
into the role of researcher. The last image in *Primate* is of the plane
in flight shot through cross hairs. In these films Wiseman has focused on his target, the increasing alienation of people from
the world and themselves. Yet, as suggested earlier, these films,
while depicting a bleak and seemingly deterministic world, is not
one without hope. For it is precisely our sympathetic, "unprofessional" responses to the animals in these films that at once allows
us to perceive them as more than mere tools for knowledge (*Primate*) or amusement (*Racetrack*) and to redeem us from our
contemporary malaise. If we ourselves are to avoid becoming
alienated, processed bodies, urge the films, we must feel deeply. It
is this emotional openness, and the difficulty achieving it, that informs the group of films discussed in the next chapter.

NOTES

1. James Wolcott, "*Welfare* Must be Seen," *Village Voice,* September 29,
1975, p. 126.
2. Interview with Wiseman in Eugenia Parry Janis and Wendy Mac-
Neil, eds., *Photography within the Humanities* (Danbury, N.H.: Addison
House, 1977), p. 71.
3. Liz Ellsworth, *Frederick Wiseman: A Guide to References and Resources*
(Boston: G. K. Hall, 1979), pp. 102–58.
4. James Wolcott, "Blood on the Racks: Wiseman's *Meat,*" *Village
Voice,* Novemember 15, 1976, p. 95; John J. O'Connor, "Wiseman's Latest
Film Is Another 'Reality Fiction,'" *New York Times,* November 7, 1976,
p. 27.
5. Aldous Huxley, *Brave New World* (New York: Harper and Row,
1969), p. 1.
6. Chuck Kraemer, "Fred Wiseman's *Primate* Makes Monkeys of Scientists," *New York Times,* December 1, 1974, sec. 2, p. 31. See also Thomas
R. Atkins, "'Reality Fictions': Wiseman on *Primate,*" in Thomas R. Atkins,
ed., *Frederick Wiseman* (New York: Monarch Press, 1976), p. 75.

7. Patrick J. Sullivan, "Frederick Wiseman's *Primate*," *New Republic*, January 25, 1975, p. 31.

8. Ibid, p. 32.

9. Dr. Geoffrey H. Bourne, "Yerkes Director Calls Foul," *New York Times*, December 15, 1974, p. 33.

10. Kraemer, "Fred Wiseman's *Primate*," p. 31; Wolcott, "Blood on the Racks," p. 95.

11. Cristine Russell, "Science on Film: The *Primate* Controversy," *Bioscience* 25, no. 3 (March 1976): 153, 218.

12. Quoted in Hillary DeVries, "Fred Wiseman's Unblinking Camera Watches How Society Works," *Christian Science Monitor*, May 1, 1984, p. 27.

13. Kraemer, "Fred Wiseman's *Primate* Makes Monkeys of Scientists," p. 1.

14. Russell, "Science on Film," pp. 151–54, 218. See also Ken Gay, "*Primate*," *Films and Filming* 21, no. 6 (March 1975): 37–38.

15. Timothy Jon Curry, "Frederick Wiseman: Sociological Filmmaker?," *Contemporary Sociology* 14, no. 1 (January 1985): 37.

16. Sylvia Feldman, "The Wiseman Documentary," *Human Behavior* 5 (February 1976): 69.

17. Gary Arnold, "Frederick Wiseman's 'Primates,' " *Washington Post*, December 5, 1974, p. B15.

18. The woman is identified in one interview (Atkins, "Reality Fictions," in *Frederick Wiseman*, p. 86) by Wiseman as the sister of the scientist conducting the zero gravity experiment. Dramatically, she functions as a surrogate for most viewers, unaware of the facts about primate research.

19. Bruce Kawin, *Mindscreen: Bergman, Godard, and First-Person Film* (Princeton, N.J.: Princeton University Press, 1978), esp. chap. 1.

20. Nick Browne, "The Spectator-in-the-Text: The Rhetoric of *Stagecoach*," *Film Quarterly* 29, no. 2 (Winter 1975–76): 26–38.

21. Edward Branigan, *Point of View in the Cinema: A Theory of Narration and Subjectivity in Classical Cinema* (New York and Berlin: Mouton, 1984), p. 104.

22. Thomas Atkins, "Wiseman's America: *Titicut Follies* to *Primate*," in Atkins, ed., *Frederick Wiseman*, p. 25.

23. Wolcott, "Blood on the Racks," p. 95.

24. Alfred Hayes, "The Slaughterhouse," in C. F. Main and Peter J. Seng, eds., *Poems*, 2d ed. (Belmont, Calif.: Wadsworth, 1965), pp. 33–34.

25. See, for example, Roland Tuch, "Frederick Wiseman's Cinema of Alienation," *Film Library Quarterly* 11, no. 3 (1978): 9–15, 49.

26. O'Connor, "Wiseman's Latest Film Is Another 'Reality Fiction,' " p. 27.

27. Norman B. Wiltsey, "The Great Buffalo Slaughter," in Raymond Friday Locke, ed., *The American West* (Los Angeles: Mankind Publishing, 1971), pp. 109–40; the quotations are from pp. 110 and 133, respectively.

28. Edward Buscombe, "The Idea of Genre in the American Cinema," Barry Keith Grant, ed. *Film Genre Reader* (Austin: University of Texas Press, 1986), p. 22.

29. Huxley, *Brave New World,* p. 8.

30. Calvin Pryluck, "Ultimately We Are All Outsiders: The Ethics of Documentary Filming," *Journal of the University Film Association* 28 no. 1 (Winter 1976): 24.

31. Hence *Primate* works to encourage rather than to "revoke" the viewer's look, as Stuart Cunningham argues in "The Look and its Revocation: Wiseman's *Primate,*" *Australian Journal of Screen Theory,* nos. 11–12 (1982): 86–95.

CHAPTER 5

You and Me

Essene (1972) • *Blind* (1987) • *Deaf* (1987) • *Adjustment and Work* (1987) *Multi-Handicapped* (1987)

In the appendix to his novel *The Devils of Loudun,* a short discussion of the varieties of transcendence, Aldous Huxley writes that "the worship of truth apart from charity—self-identification with science unaccompanied by self-identification with the Ground of all being—results in the kind of situation which now confronts us. Every idol, however exalted, turns out, in the long run, to be a Moloch, hungry for human sacrifice."[1] In Wiseman's films, such unfortunate worship finds its strongest expression, clearly, in the detached quest for knowledge by the scientists in *Primate.* The justification of pure research would seem indeed to constitute "the worship of truth apart from charity," the sacrifice being our closeness to the natural world and to each other.

This condition frequently manifests itself elsewhere in Wiseman's cinema, although perhaps not as dramatically, from the labeling of patients in *Titicut Follies* to the nightmarish adherence to procedure in the world of *Welfare*—instances of what Wiseman refers to as "the demeaning way in which words, which are essentially clichés, are used to categorize a person, so that as a result he will be treated as a member of a category, not a person."[2] Chuck Kraemer notes in his review of *Primate* that the film inevitably raises questions not only about science, but also about "the eternal tension between the rational and spiritual sides of man's nature."[3] This tension is articulated in the conflict the film raises in the viewer between a detached, scientific viewpoint and an emotionally charged identification. The group of Wiseman's films examined in this chapter—*Essene* and the four films that constitute the *Deaf and Blind* series—also explore this tension. But they examine institutions that offer the promise of an antidote to a world desperately in need of charity, understood in the spiritual sense of deep feeling and compassion for one's fellow men and women. They do so by employing a style that encourages empathetic response.

This tension is central to *Essene*. It is made explicit at the end of the film, when the abbott invokes the biblical story of Martha and Mary (*Luke* 10:38–42) to represent the "dichotomous relationship" of being in the world that exists in us all. On the one hand, says the abbott, there is "the Martha quality of egoism," which seeks to grasp the world through rationality: "It takes it apart, or it leaves it apparently fragmented." On the other hand, there is Mary, characterized by a "wisdom" that does not depend on the material world: "You don't possess things, and they do have a unity, they have an ecology." In *Essene* and the *Deaf and Blind* films, one finds a struggle to realize this "Mary" quality in an urge toward self-transcendence, an attempt to escape from what Huxley calls "the shell of the ego" and "the horrors of insulated selfhood"[4] through charity, in the Christian sense of a selfless love of others ("Charity envieth not; charity vaunteth not itself" [1 *Cor.* 13:4]).

Huxley identifies three kinds of transcendence—upward, downward, and sideways. The last of these is "horizontal self-transcendence," where the ego is subsumed by a larger idea or cause. In both subject and style, the five films examined in this chapter explore this spiritual aspect of community by emphasizing the importance, as well as the difficulty, of minimizing one's ego within a larger social context. To some degree, of course, all of Wiseman's films are concerned with the difficulties of establishing or maintaining a genuine sense of community,[5] but these five films stand apart in their embrace of that charitable selflessness Huxley terms "theophany." In so doing, they express—in a more general, secular sense—an optimistic humanism that counters the bleakness and pessimism that otherwise pervades Wiseman's cinema. Like Hawks's action films when considered in relation to his comedies, Wiseman's other work gains considerable depth from the different emphasis of these five films.

The central informing conceit of this charity is heightened awareness through the senses: vision, hearing, and touch (signaled explicitly by the titles *Deaf* and *Blind*). In these films Wiseman's purpose is, like D. W. Griffith's, to make us see with a sharpened spiritual as well as physical eye. By detailing the daily life at these institutions and giving us a personal understanding of the handicapped through his film style, Wiseman allows us to transcend the shell of the self and to experience the world as other people very differently do.

Essene seems to stand apart from Wiseman's other early documentaries not only because of its transcendent vision but because, unlike the others, it does not take as its subject a public, tax-supported, urban institution. Instead, as Wiseman himself notes,[6] the film looks at a private, voluntary community, an Anglican monastery associated with the Episcopalian church in southwestern Michigan. (The film's title comes from the name of an ascetic brotherhood founded in the second century B.C.)

However, the film remains similar to Wiseman's other documentaries in its examination of institutional organization and so, like those others, may be understood as yet another cultural "spoor." According to Wiseman, "the bureaucracy in a monastery, I've found, is quite similar to that in a high school or a hospital."[7] *Essene* is not primarily animated by a Christian worldview or in fact by an orthodox religious vision of any kind. On the contrary, as Wiseman himself acknowledges, *Essene* is very much concerned with the secular—although it would be flippant to describe the conflicts and tensions upon which it focuses, as one reviewer has, as "an ecclesiastical *Who's Afraid of Virginia Woolf?*"[8] The film is not melodrama but rather a philosophical investigation of a pragmatic struggle to erect a true community, with all the potential and difficulties that such a goal inevitably entails. Thus, as Mamber so aptly puts it, *Essene* is both Wiseman's "most specific and most universal work."[9]

This is not to deny the importance of religion as a theme in Wiseman's cinema, however. Wiseman says that he "is interested in the role religion plays in everyday life," a claim borne out by the fact that this is a subject to which he returns regularly. In fact, Christian ritual appears in some form in almost all of his films, most simply because it constitutes such a significant part of "the way we live." The films view orthodox Christianity as, at best, an apparently necessary palliative for some people in the face of hardship and, at worst, a self-serving institution for preserving the ideological status quo. Religion as the opiate of the people in Wiseman's cinema frequently takes the mild form of preaching a vague sense of "acceptance," as in the church service in *Sinai Field Mission,* but just as often it is overtly political, as in the hysterically antifeminist sermon in *Canal Zone,* where women's liberation is described as "Satan's way of breaking up homes, destroying what God has set up and his plan." *Canal Zone,* in fact, emphasizes the extent to which church and state are intimately connected (the film's penultimate sequence, for example, features a band playing both "Onward, Christian Soldiers" and "The Star-Spangled Banner"), even while the Christian preaching of brotherly love is expressed, ironically, in the socially polarized context of colonialism. People in Wiseman's films frequently use religion in bad faith, for their own purposes, like the boy in *Juvenile Court* who embraces the Christian Teen Challenge program for the second time, apparently as a convenient way of finding favor with Judge Turner. But Wiseman would agree with Huxley, for whom "herd-intoxication—even if it is done in the name of religion . . . cannot be morally justified."[10]

It is indeed interesting that Wiseman has cited Herman Melville's *The Confidence Man* (1857) as his favorite novel. Apart from its similarity to Wiseman's work in presenting a broad panoply of American morals and manners (a "congress of all kinds of that multiform pilgrim species, man")[11] and its microcosmic ship of fools (analogous to the director's approach to institutions), the book's black humor, particularly its treatment of religion, undoubtedly appeals to him. The narrative situation of the devil disguised as a good Christian testing the morals of men by spouting orthodox moral precepts, pointing out the hypocrisy of seemingly devout Christians in the process, is the kind of dark joke consistent with the humor and the uncomfortable challenges to the viewer found throughout Wiseman's films. The tone is established in *Titicut Follies,* which associates Christianity more with death than life. The film's two scenes of Christian ritual are of last rites and a funeral service, presumably for Malinowsky (although this ambiguity is also to the point). Wiseman introduces Christian elements rather sardonically, cutting from a physically dysfunctional inmate picking his nose to the hand gesture of the priest, Father Mulligan, performing the last rite. One inmate stands on his head, singing of sacred glory; the upside-down close-up of the man's face suggests Christianity is an inversion of values, specifically in that it asks us to endure the miseries of this life for the promise of a better one in the hereafter.

Wiseman's critique of the function of Christianity in American society is particularly trenchant in the military films. At one point in *Manoeuvre*, several of the men pause to pray with the chaplain before entering into "battle." The sequence comes as a surprise since nothing before it is concerned with religion but only with war preparation and strategy. The startling suddenness of this scene encourages us to consider the ritual in context, bringing to mind Melville again, this time in the form of his narrator's musings in *Billy Budd:*

> Bluntly put, a chaplain is the minister of the Prince of Peace serving in the host of the God of War—Mars. As such, he is as incongruous as a musket would be on the alter at Christmas. Why, then, is he here? Because he indirectly serves the purpose attested by the cannon; because too he lends the sanction of the religion of the meek to that which practically is the abrogation of everything but brute Force.[12]

The chaplain in *Basic Training* (whose impatient glance at his watch while counseling the hapless Hickman is a gesture of the hereafter compromised by the here and now) explicitly acknowledges the co-optation of Christian thought in his comment that "the Church has represented a crutch to us. A way of soothing our feelings of guilt." Unfortunately, even as he tells the men that he is going "to kick the crutch from under you," he actually reinforces it by declaring that God can give them the inner strength necessary to survive in the army. Hence the sharp irony of the ending of *Missile:* in the context of a training program where people learn the procedures for destroying the planet with nuclear weapons, the last words in the film, uttered by the commanding general in his speech to the trainees, is that "we're a people who are concerned about God."

Still, Wiseman's critique of Christianity is perhaps nowhere more powerfully expressed than at the end of *Hospital*. After all the human suffering we see in this film, a priest exhorts his congregation in the hospital chapel to forget about themselves and their fleeting physical existence because God is all. But again, in emphasizing the hereafter over the here and now ("We personally must resist the secularization of our time. We must be wary of placing God second," says the priest in *Racetrack*), orthodox faith hardly motivates us to do anything to improve our earthly existence—not just our physical suffering, but the socio-economic inequities that have created an institution like Metropolitan Hospital in the first place. All we can do, the priest suggests, is carry on stoically through this vale of tears, like the people in the film's last shot racing by the hospital in their cars. Enduring social conditions as God's will obviously goes against the reformist impulse of the documentary tradition generally and Wiseman's interests specifically, at least at this early point in his career. Because institutions are human and not divine creations ("God is not a man like, uh, social service," says one client in *Welfare*), they are what we make them.

In the material, alienated world presented in most of Wiseman's films, what real significance can God, understood in the general sense of spiritual value, have for us? It is this question that *Essene* seeks to explore in its quiet, intimate style, so distinctly different from the typical Hollywood "religious" film, with its emphasis on burning bushes, casts of thousands, and visual spectacle. The film is more philosophical, closer in spirit to the venerable tradition of American utopianism. With its vision of harmony between society, technology, and nature, *Essene* belongs to the utopian tradition in American art, but as in this tradition's best works, community and harmony are not achieved so easily as in *Star Wars* (George Lucas, 1977) by simply "letting the Force be with you." Nathaniel Hawthorne succinctly summed up the difficulties facing such attempts when he observed in *The Blithedale Romance* (1852), the novel about his experience at the experimental Fourierite community Brook Farm, that "Persons of marked individuality—crooked sticks, as some of us might be called—are not exactly the easiest to bind up into a fagot."[13]

Appropriately, the very first image in *Essene* is of a monk raking the grounds. We see another monk raking later, and in his final sermon the abbot makes reference to tension in the community with the specific example of someone having left the rake out overnight. The brethren are a group of distinct individuals, like Hawthorne's "crooked sticks." Everyone there, as Sister Alice points out, comes with a different background and influences, making communal harmony difficult. Yet this religious order, like so many earlier groups from the Fourierites to the Woodstock "nation," is a community of Americans optimistically seeking to improve a more perfect union. What they have in common, and what keeps them together, is that they have renounced material values and are genuinely seeking to discover selfless love.

At several points in the film there are short montages of vocationers or monks alone—one stands in a field, another walks in the woods, a third rakes leaves, and so on. The connection between these shots, established by the editing as well as by their similar temporal duration, suggests that even as they are at times apart physically, they are nevertheless connected by a common endeavor—partaking in the community even in their moments alone. This idea is reinforced by the sequences of ritual, such as the vigil and compline, where brethren gather to sing and pray together. In these sequences closeness is shown by common activities being performed, by the physical proximity of the participants, and by Wiseman's long takes and moving camera. Some shots are composed in depth, like the one that shows a group of monks praying simultaneously and receding into the background of the image. In the short haying sequence, three of the brethren are seen at work, but only in silhouette, so that we cannot identify them as individuals. Difference is thus subsumed in harmonious collective activity.

Early in the film Brother David identifies the problem when he says that people are both Christians and individuals, and that the latter "is the one we have difficulty with." The conflict is embodied by a tension between the young reformers and the old guard. On the one hand, there is the postulant Richard, who in his zeal to lead a spiritual and moral life vigorously seeks to escape the bounds of the "insulated self." Richard cries and is deeply troubled by the absence of true connection among the brethren. He and others pressure the community toward reform, which they see as a new, "God-given direction," in the words of Father Anthony. Already the mass is conducted in English, and the daily prayer meetings are more like group therapy or sensitivity sessions than

(*Essene*) Composition in depth suggests the intimate community of the brethren.

traditional prayer. The similarity is explicitly acknowledged by the vocationer Robert when he compares their prayer to the individual and group therapy sessions he participated in while living in New York.

On the other hand, there is tradition and egotism, as represented by Brother Wilfred. He is suspicious of change and reactionary in attitude ("There is so much a tendency today for something to be taken up at once," he complains to the abbot). Driving back to the monastery from town, he is framed with the rear-view mirror distinctly visible by his face, the image expressing the orientation of his vision in the past, in tradition. In his discussion with the abbot, Wilfred rails against people calling him by his first name, considering it an act of disrespect ("except among my very close chums, of which there were five"). He is defensive and hostile, literally seated up against a wall, feeling trapped and cornered by the abbot's gentle argument that the mutual experience of Christ is analogous to childhood friendship. Wiseman's camera moves into a close-up of Wilfred during the discussion, articulating his feeling of being entrapped by the abbot's Socratic rhetoric.

His hands are tightly folded across his chest for most of their conversation, and he frequently bites his lip—body language distinctly opposite to the open, expansive gestures characteristic of
the other brethren throughout the film. Wilfred rationalizes his
position by claiming that confusions would arise in using first
names since, for example, there are now two Davids at the monastery. For him, the homily "familiarity breeds contempt," which
he cites, is the gospel truth. Tellingly, he takes out his frustrations
by swatting at flies in the room before folding his arms across his
chest once again. Clipboards hang to one side on the wall behind
him during this discussion, suggesting his emphasis on the letter
rather than the spirit, while the telephone hanging at his other
side ironically counterpoints his stated refusal of intimate contact.

While the rest of the brethren seek spiritual community,
Brother Wilfred, "the implacable loner,"[14] sets off by himself on a
trip to town, the only brother to do so in the film. In both the supermarket and the hardware store, Wilfred is flanked by aisles of
consumer goods, emblems of the daily world's emphasis on the
material over the spiritual. The contrast between the two worlds is
emphasized by the juxtaposition on the soundtrack of gentle harmony in vigil and blaring pop music on the radio as Wilfred walks
down the street toward the supermarket. This lack of spirituality
in the material world is also suggested rather humorously by the
background music heard while Brother Wilfred is inside the market—a Muzak version of "On the Street Where You Live," a pop
debasement of spiritual epiphany in terms of romance ("Oh, the
towering feeling").

Comically, the friendly hardware store salesman addresses the
monk by his first name as he delivers his sales pitch, and the joke
is compounded by the fact that he uses the wrong name, calling
him Herb instead of Ed. Curiously, though, Brother Wilfred
seems perfectly at ease, amicably chatting with the salesman despite his jocular barbs. The salesman worries that Brother Wilfred
might purchase an inferior potato peeler: "Anything I hate to see
is one of the brothers prostrate on the floor bleeding from their
fingers." When the salesman kids him about their ascetic lifestyle—"All on tap? All answer the roll call? All come forth?"—Wilfred shoots back, "Damned if I know, by gosh." The only evidence
here of his cantankerous personality is his finding fault with every

model of peeler proffered by the salesman, and he remarks that, despite his choosiness over the utensil, "I'm not going to peel them so I couldn't care less." Ironically, in a later brief shot we see Wilfred cleaning vegetables—a shot that is funny but also suggests the greater strength of community. This sequence at once reveals that Brother Wilfred, the only one in the film shown outside the monastery grounds, is more comfortable in the material world, and that our daily social interaction is pleasant but superficial, lacking the substance of true contact the younger brethren so devoutly desire.

Between the viewpoints of Richard and Brother Wilfred is that of the abbot. It is he who maintains the apparently tenuous hold of the community, who prevents it from splintering, by seeking to steer a middle course between the letter and the spirit, between Martha and Mary, Wilfred and Richard. Some of the monks, meeting with the abbot, complain that Wilfred is "a very divisive element," even a misanthrope, since he seems to like no one. Father Anthony worries that their efforts to achieve community "are hopeless," since Wilfred fights everyone. Father Leo adds that this opposition has been the case with "our dear brother" from the beginning, the slight irony in his choice of words revealing the seriousness of the rift. Patience seems to be wearing thin, the community reaching a point of crisis. The abbot is keenly aware of both these tensions and his crucial position in relation to them, several times referring to himself as mediator. The inevitable clash of egos is nothing less than a battle. At one point he uses military metaphors ("shifting the troops," "blow the bugle") to describe it. In the chapter meeting that opens the film, the abbot describes his ultimate authority as "a shared responsibility," "more and more a community awareness of what we are doing," and "a corporate approval of our life." Thus he sees his role as seeking to discover "the unity behind what is being said" by the brethren. His sense of a corporate consciousness invokes an ideal socialist democracy, in opposition to the materialistic corporate existence of consumer capitalism (the town supermarket and hardware store).

Richard tells a lengthy and extraordinary parable of a man who wants everyone to dance the same dance, because he finds different dances chaotic and confusing. The elders, in response, simply nod and do nothing, but the man finds the dancing—"all these legs and arms and all this trouble and chaos, and all this noise and confusion"—so intolerable, that he ends up crippling his beloved and destroying himself. In the parable, as in the various institutions depicted in so many of Wiseman's other films, the individual is made to march in step ("If you don't have discipline you've got chaos," according to Father Leo). The abbot, however, acknowledges the unique spirit, what he calls "the divine mystery," of each individual and seeks to establish community without imposing the crippling "Pharisaical answer" wherein "you don't really deal with man, you simply impose a Sabbath or system or letter upon him." But, he admits, the problem remains for "family charity"; the brethren have no clear blueprint for achieving it.

Richard, tears rolling down his cheeks, talks in the garden with Sister Alice about the difficulty of transcendence, of truly opening oneself up to others. At their meetings, he says, one is "laid wide open," all one's foibles and faults revealed in the process. "It's like taking all the hard skin that was on the outside and ripping it all off and you have all that nice fresh skin underneath." (The school principal in *Blind*, worrying about a boy named Dallas whom he has tried hard to reach, similarly describes his frustration by saying "it tears your insides out.") These metaphors of flaying, of being opened, seem particularly resonant, referring as they do to images in *Hospital*, *Primate*, and *Meat*. The emphasis in *Essene*, though, is on healing. Richard's prayer for Father Anthony, to "make him whole," invokes a completeness that is in opposition to the atomizing, the dismantling, of the self and the body in *Primate* and *Meat*. But the self is only whole in contact with others: "No man is an island, entire of itself," a speaker says in a eulogy in *Canal Zone*, quoting John Donne. In the scene in the garden, Sister Alice responds to Richard with a simile of her own, telling him that to be open, to truly love, is "like being an open channel." Richard picks up on the image, saying that despite the difficulties involved, "there is always the 'river of joy' underneath." Significantly, this sequence is followed by probably the most genuinely moving scene in the film, when Richard sings the hymn "Deep River" at the piano.

During a meeting with the senior monks, the abbot remarks that the achievement of community, the corporate consciousness that is their goal, is obtained "by *listening* to one another and then *looking* for the unity behind what is being said." This, he adds, is an art that must be learned. In his discussion with the entrenched Brother Wilfred he emphasizes that what he is trying to do is simply to "illuminate" what others mean to say. The film ends with the abbot asking the brotherhood, but also the viewer, "Will you listen, really deeply? . . . Will you listen?" The abbot's question is fundamental, for to do so is to directly counter the "strategy of withdrawal" that characterizes human affairs in, say, *Welfare* or *Hospital*.

Wiseman picks up the challenge of the abbot's question and passes it on it to the viewer in the *Deaf and Blind* films. The crippled state of the man in Richard's parable becomes in these four films a variety of literal, physical conditions. Listening and looking are crucial to these films, both as subject—the films were shot at the Alabama Institute for the Deaf and Blind (AIDB) in Talladega—and theme. Just as in many ways the handicapped people in the films triumph over their physical limitations, so analogous spiritual success may be achieved by the viewer through attention and empathy. The *Deaf and Blind* films seek, in Kracauer's terms, to redeem physical reality, but only as a step in attaining a forgotten spirituality. Toward the end of the last of the four films, *Multi-Handicapped*, a black house parent sings a spiritual about "One More River to Cross"—another reference to the channel that must be traversed for community to be achieved. The experience of viewing the *Deaf and Blind* films becomes, as it were, the bridge.

On the simplest level, the *Deaf and Blind* series—in terms of conception, possibly Wiseman's most ambitious work to date—requires a greater commitment from viewers. The four films together possess a running time of almost nine hours. Wiseman views the four feature-length films (their proper sequence is *Blind, Deaf, Adjustment and Work*, and *Multi-Handicapped*) as independent works, "but also working as one nine-hour film." He says that he went to the institute initially intending to make one film, but soon realized that this would be insufficient because the different handicaps are so distinct. In one film, he would be able to devote only about twenty minutes to each, with the result that all would be "trivialized"; even at its present length, he adds, "it risks being trivial." But the combined length of the films and the complex structure of four separate yet connected works suggest that for the filmmaker the topic contains significance beyond the ostensible subjects.

The series chronicles the daily life of teachers, administrators, and students (both children and adults who seek to enter the work force) at AIDB, one of the nation's better institutions of its kind. With only a few notable exceptions, the films eschew the extraordinary to concentrate on the normal, the daily. When, for instance, a deaf and blind girl, a student in the Helen Keller school, is strapped into her seat for lunch in *Multi-Handicapped*, there are no hysterics and flying silverware, as in *The Miracle Worker* (Arthur Penn, 1962), only an orderly, uneventful repast.

The pace of the films is extremely leisurely. The establishing montage at the beginning of *Deaf*, for example, is composed of thirty-two shots—the last a slow pan to the AIDB campus—taking almost three minutes of screen time. Such undramatic sequences, their unhurried pace exacerbated by the very length of the series, have caused some to perceive the films as boring and aimless. Perhaps somewhat extreme but not atypical is the ungenerous preview by Jeff Jarvis that appeared in *People* magazine prior to the PBS screenings. He says that in *Blind* (apparently the only film of the series he managed to sit through) "we can see uninterrupted, unending scenes of cars going by and then of a train going by. I wanted to go bye too but had to keep watching, becoming more irritated with every long minute." He concludes that the film is indistinguishable from what millions of Americans are now doing themselves with their home video cameras.[15] But along with the more astute Robert Coles, the attentive viewer must seriously wonder, "Exactly who is 'bored' by these films?"[16] The answer, it seems, is those who have been conditioned by Hollywood cinema to expect more "drama" in movies. Like *Essene*, though, *Deaf and Blind* minimizes the easy pleasure of spectacle. Significantly, the first montage of Talledega shots in the first of the four films, *Blind,* includes a shot of the marquee of a defunct movie house, the sign of an exhausted conventional cinema to which the *Deaf and Blind* series announces its opposition.

What the films in fact do when they decline overt drama is to renew for our eyes and ears the simple sights and sounds of the world that most of us, unlike the students at AIDB, have the luxury to take for granted. In doing so, they restore a sense of connection and proportion that all but gets lost in the rush of contemporary existence. In several ways, the *Deaf and Blind* series gives us the time, the opportunity, to rediscover such simple joys. In short, *Deaf and Blind* encourages us look and listen with an intensity that takes us out of ourselves and connects us both to the natural world and, through admiration for their stoic bravery and strong will, to those deprived of the senses to do so. Perceiving in this manner, the viewer moves and is moved beyond the boundaries of the insulated self, becoming what Emerson called "a transparent eye-ball," where "all mean egoism vanishes."[17]

In this important sense the *Deaf and Blind* series is strikingly different from Wiseman's earlier school documentary, *High School*, although much invites comparison. They both show dance and cooking classes, discipline scenes with teachers and principals, and numerous hallway shots as transitional devices. However, the scenes in the *Deaf and Blind* films consistently seem both less dramatic and more caring than those in *High School*. If the hallways in *High School* are filled with peripatetic movement and a constant din, in *Deaf* the hallway shots are quiet, orderly, uncrowded. Whereas *High School* features narrow-minded teachers who impose their values on their students, the pedagogical philosophy of AIDB is commendably flexible. It is "a program of instruction, not a set of guides and not a set of constraints," says one of the teachers at the beginning of *Multi-Handicapped*. Unlike the vice-principal in *High School*, who moves aggressively forward toward the student and toward the camera, the principal in the *Deaf and Blind* films invites problem children into his own space. And instead of the martial music that calls everyone to keep in step in *High School*, in these films students in one class are told "to let the music go inside you," while another student during a piano lesson is advised to take his time practicing, even if he has to forget the time signature to get the notes right.

The simple fact that the films are shot in color serves as a constant reminder of the world around us, offering a lovely palette that we often fail to appreciate. Beginning immediately with *Blind*, we are constantly aware that we can see things many of the people in the film cannot. The difference between the viewer's perceptual

ability and that of the people at AIDB is made immediately clear
in the film's first classroom sequence, where children must follow
the instructions on a recording: "This is a story about colors." The
children are assigned colors and must stand up and sit down when
their color is called. As we see, for them this is a difficult task, and
several are clearly at a loss.

At the beginning of *Deaf*, too, a student learns to sign the words
for different colors, and the first classroom sequence in *Multi-
Handicapped* involves color recognition. As well, several objects in
Blind serve as especially forceful reminders of the world of color to
which we are privileged, including the bright red Crimson Tide
jersey worn by the blind boy Jaimie during his long talk with the
principal, a child's sky blue Toronto Blue Jays shirt in the music
therapy class, and the prominent sign in the school gym that identifies it as the "Home of the Redskins." Continually the *Deaf and
Blind* series brings us back to the delight of color. When the house
parent turns out the light at day's end in *Blind,* for a moment we
are suddenly cast into the darkness that these blind people must
endure constantly. As night falls at the end of the film, we may be
disappointed that the world is temporarily without light, but we
take comfort in the knowledge that the light will return with the
morning sun. Moreover, our hearts may leap up to behold the lu-
minous silver of the moon shining overhead in the exterior shot
before the Halloween party—elsewhere another shot even presents a beautiful field of flowers, Wordsworth's "host of golden
daffodils"—but at the same time we are fully aware that the people in the film are deprived of this pleasure.

Both our reliance on light and the films' emphasis on dailiness
are forcefully established early in *Blind* in one of the film's most
stunning sequences, both technically and emotionally. Jason, a
young blind student proud of his schoolwork, wants to go to another classroom to show his paper to Mrs. Williams, another
teacher. But to do so, he must find his own way out of the room,
along the hall to the stairway, down the stairs, and along another
corridor to Mrs. Williams's classroom. Then, of course, he must reverse his path to return to where he began. Wiseman patiently follows Jason through the entire process, which lasts over five
minutes, the duration of the event emphasized by the lack of editing. There is only one cut, as the boy leaves the first classroom.

According to Wiseman, this cut was motivated purely by technical considerations, as John Davey had to juggle the camera to keep up with the boy as he went through the doorway, a jarring movement that he felt would have distracted the viewer. But Jason's pluck and resolve are so impressive that the cut is hardly noticeable, its effect negligible. The camera remains tightly framed on Jason, which not only underscores his achievement, but also duplicates somewhat for the viewer his sightlessness, as we are not allowed to see much of the physical space surrounding him, nor indeed, even the faces of the teachers.

Several other sequences in the films work in a similar manner, including an even lengthier sequence showing a girl named Charlotte being taught how to get around with the use of a cane. This sequence takes about fourteen minutes, almost three times as long as the one with Jason. It contains only four cuts, and two of the shots are approximately five minutes in duration. Charlotte first appears at the end of the sequence with Jason, saying she wants to go down to Mrs. Williams's class too, but when asked by the teacher, admits that she is not yet capable of doing so by herself. All of Charlotte's subsequent hard work involved in negotiating the school space with the cane reveals how much learning and effort it had taken Jason to be able to do what we have seen. Thus our admiration for the boy grows even greater.

In *Adjustment and Work,* a blind man gets a detailed lesson in the geography of a kitchen, learning where the different drawers and cabinets are, the utensils that are in them, and how to put them away. The sequence, composed of five shots, takes as many minutes. There is also a lengthy sequence that parallels the one with Jason, showing the subsequent difficulties the boy will inevitably face when he is older. A blind man attempts for the first time to negotiate some streets in downtown Talledega, as a teacher gives him periodic instructions. The man must make several turns and cross several streets, one a four-lane thoroughfare, finding curbs in the process, all the while careful to avoid the traffic—emblems of the workaday world speeding by. As in the sequences with Jason and Charlotte, the camera focuses on the man's feet and cane as he makes his way, emphasizing the difficulties of each step. For all of Jason's success, this sequence reminds us that his hard work is by no means over. Thus, whenever we see people feeling their way around a hallway in any of the four films, however briefly, we can appreciate the obstacles, if not the terror, they must occasionally experience at not being able to perceive their environment fully.

The films encourage us as well to listen deeply, in the words of the abbot. During Charlotte's cane lesson in *Blind*, she must concentrate on the sounds of things and learn to distinguish between similar sounds. She correctly identifies Miss Reed's classroom by the sound of the piano, but then wrongly deduces her location because she confuses the noise of the water fountain with that of the clothes dryer. The girl's honest joy at now being able to move about with a cane ("I deserved a drink of water for that, didn't I?" she asks, after finally finding the fountain) is infectious; we cheer her on and are disappointed at her mistakes. When Charlotte and her instructor briefly step outdoors, moving from one building to another, the rush of ambient street noise dominates the soundtrack, suddenly putting her achievement into perspective. One of the methods with which the blind man negotiates the busy Talledega streets is to listen for parallel traffic. With him, too, we listen attentively, hoping he makes it ("If you're lucky," says his instructor). So just as the blind people in the film must listen carefully to the world around them, the viewer, through the mobilization of identification, finds him or herself doing the same.

In *Deaf*, the emphasis on sign language requires the viewer to pay particularly close attention to gesture, an important part of signification in movies in general and in Wiseman's cinema especially. We learn that many signs (such as those for "tea bag" and "milk") are not arbitrary but precise gestures, like mime. Early in the film, along with some of the parents, we are given a lesson in signing where we discover that to some extent we all use sign language—a codified system of gestures—without understanding it as such. In another lesson we learn that different places have different signs for the same word or concept ("ugly," "coke"), which is to say that the language is rich enough to sustain a variety of "dialects." There are many shots of students conversing in sign language, but the film provides us with no "translation," and so the viewer must be extremely attentive in order to get a sense of what's being said. During a field trip to the local courthouse and jail, there is a particularly astonishing moment when a prisoner suddenly thrusts his hand between the bars of his cell, signing something to the children about why he is there. The viewer ignorant of sign language is especially frustrated at this moment; surely the man is saying something of significance. When the children are introduced to the judge in his chambers, his insistent nervous laughter betrays his discomfort—and likely our own—at being unable to converse with the deaf.

The importance of such communication, and the unfortunate result of its lack, is made devastatingly clear in the sequence with the fourteen-year-old Peter in *Deaf*. It is forty-five minutes long, or about one-third of the film. Its length and central placement attest to its significance. Because of his deafness, Peter has been rejected by his natural father, and he also feels rejected by and angry toward his mother. In his anger, he refuses to look at his mother, who continues talking to the principal and the teacher, Dr. Meecham. Only after several minutes does the viewer realize that the mother has no signing skills, a fact that she explains and justifies by saying that she has three other children and cannot find the time to learn. Whether this is true or not (according to Dr. Meecham in the lesson on friendship shortly after, if someone really wants to be the friend of a deaf person, it is a necessary part of that commitment to learn to sign), the mother and son have become locked in a self-defeating dynamic wherein they neither look at nor listen to one another.

The fundamental importance of communication is constantly reiterated in the films. Dr. Meecham tells Peter that what is important is "to communicate with each other and to communicate with people here at school." Elsewhere in the same film, she suggests to the students that if they see a lonely person they should approach him or her and offer their friendship. One of the coaches reminds his team before the football game in *Deaf* that "You gotta pay attention and remember to communicate with each other. . . . All of us here love each other." Even Washington Irving's classic story "Rip Van Winkle," discussed in a lesson in *Deaf*, endorses the point, for it offers the moral that one cannot escape the difficulties of a relationship with "a quieting draught out of Rip Van Winkle's flagon" (through a strategy of withdrawal, as in *Welfare*).[18] At the end of the lesson about the richness of sign

(*Multi-Handicapped*) The importance of sympathetic contact is shown throughout the *Deaf and Blind* films and *Essene* (next page).

language, Wiseman cuts to a close-up of an electronic learning tool as its prerecorded voice states "I have a limited vocabulary." That is to say, there is no adequate substitute for the depth and contact of human communication.

Touch, as the physical emblem of communication, is also emphasized in these four films. Its importance is established early in *Blind,* in the sequences where Jason and Charlotte feel their way around the school. Charlotte also learns about the different kinds of canes by feeling them. The blind man learning to cross the street is told to "feel" the traffic coming across his chest, and a teacher responds to the boy who wants to go play with the other children by telling him to follow the sound of their voices and to "get that feeler out." In the first scene in *Multi-Handicapped* the driver touch signs with a deaf and blind man as he gets off the schoolbus. In the wrestling lesson in *Blind,* the students learn by empathic touch ("I want you to feel the position he's in," the coach instructs them), and in the music therapy class body awareness is emphasized through touch. In *Deaf,* a teacher gives a speech lesson to a deaf boy by touching his throat box.

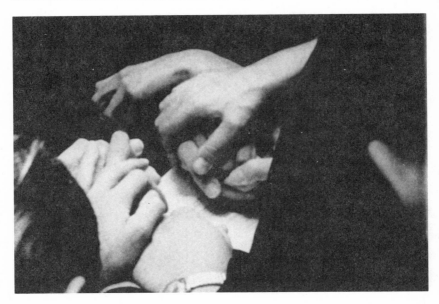

(*Essene*)

Often, students are rewarded with hugs or kisses instead of or
in addition to verbal encouragement, reminiscent (but without the
therapeutic ambiguity) of the holding therapy in Allan King's
Warrendale. For example, the principal explains that while the boy
Peter was depressed and suicidal, he "hugged him a lot," and the
meeting ends with Peter being encouraged to hug his mother. In
short, the four films are filled with gentle, exploring, and touching hands: the hands of workers in *Adjustment and Work* putting
dishes away or screwing nuts to bolts, the hands of students talking
to each other and combing each other's hair, the hands of pupils
feeling out solutions to puzzles in *Multi-Handicapped.*

Several of the children in the films cry out for the contact they
have been deprived of. One boy, Dennis, disrupts his class because
of his desperate need for attention. Another is afraid of his
mother, who drinks, and would rather stay at the school than go
home for visits. What he needs, says Dr. Meecham, is "people who
really care." Peter wants to see his father who, according to his
mother, has rejected him and does not love him. The "missing

children" sign, visible in the courthouse during the school trip in
Deaf, refers also to the many abused children, not only in *Deaf and
Blind*, but throughout Wiseman's cinema.

The subtle force with which the *Deaf and Blind* films prompt us
to look and listen more deeply than usual raises the rhetorical
question about who exactly is deaf and blind. As Dr. A. G. Gaston
explicitly acknowledges in his closing speech in *Deaf*, the idea of
"handicap" can be taken metaphorically, on many levels. Indeed,
his point is essential to these four films. Frequently the films play
on the idea by creating an ambiguity about whether people shown
in the films are in fact handicapped, and even question the term
itself. In the opening raceway sequence in *Blind*, for example, it is
not clear that the kids in the band are blind until the announcer
identifies them (although we might suspect it, given the film's title
and the AIDB sign briefly visible on the side of a schoolbus). Nor
is it clear that the announcer himself has a physical handicap until
after his introduction, when the camera pulls back slightly to reveal that he lacks an arm. Similarly, in the painful sequence in *Adjustment and Work* where the slow-learning Donna tries to
comprehend that fifty cents equals half of a dollar, it is only toward
the end that we realize her patient instructor, too, is blind. When
we see people signing in *Deaf*, often we do not know if they are
deaf or if they are hearing people who have made what Dr.
Meecham calls "the necessary commitment" and learned sign language. The blind Willy protests to his supervisor in *Adjustment and
Work*, "We're not sick; we're just people." So in sequences like
these, as in the interviews with Vietnam veterans in Peter Davis's
Hearts and Minds (1974), we are forced to attend to the people
first, before we categorize them and relegate them to the status
of "handicapped."

Significantly, staff and students in both *Blind* and *Adjustment and
Work* frequently speak of seeing, despite their physical limitations.
In *Blind*, one child wants to "watch" the other kids playing on a
fire engine. When Jason heads out of the classroom to find Mrs.
Williams, he calls back, "See you all later." A blind man learning
his way around the kitchen says, when coming across the potato
peelers, "I've seen them before." Teachers frequently tell students
when giving them instructions to "look" and "see," while the

students say "I see" when they understand instructions. Indeed, these handicapped people sometimes demonstrate a deeper perception than many persons of "normal" sensory ability. Several times in the films we are reminded of how people who can see often do so only superficially, relying on surface appearances. In *Blind*, for example, William, who wants to become an auto mechanic, is advised by his supervisor "to at least look busy" in order to satisfy his foreman. Similarly, while his goals are certainly laudable, the principal in *Deaf* dubiously attempts to reconcile Peter and his mother by forcing the boy to alter the unhappy expression on his face. "I don't see you smiling," the principal declares and, holding a mirror to Peter, he says, "I want to see your teeth," as if putting on a happy face will necessarily change the "very depressed" way the boy really feels.

The *Deaf and Blind* films, shot in the South, are (with the exceptions of *Essene* and, interestingly, *Model*) the only Wiseman documentaries in which racism does not appear as an important issue. In Wiseman's films racism is seen to pervade the way Americans interact, most obviously in *Basic Training* and *Welfare*. (For one writer, even *Primate* features a strong racial theme. In the film, he says, "there are four groups: white researchers, machines, apes and blacks, in roughly that order.")[19] However, if one believes the extreme utopianism of Dr. Gaston's speech in *Deaf*, racism is merely a curse of the unenlightened past. In a sense, this is true for the blind, for whom race is hardly an issue. Unlike many people with sight, they have the insight to disregard, to see through, the veneer of skin color. Indeed, in all four of the films handicapped of different races are shown to communicate, to touch, to live with each other seemingly as equals. As *Essene* reminds us, what the abbott calls "the divine mystery" in each person, his soul, and what Father Leo calls "the treasure," "the pearl," is hidden within the shell, beneath the surface.

Despite Wiseman's admitted cynicism about the effective capability of cinema, there is a sense in these documentaries that film in fact can be instrumental in effecting empathy and understanding. When in *Essene* the abbot asks Father Anthony for specifics about Brother Wilfred's intimidation of the younger men, the latter replies that he cannot offer direct proof because he was not there "with a little pad and a camera." Wiseman, however, is, and the specifics offered to viewers in these films provide ample evidence of the struggle to transcend ego and be truly charitable. The very style of the films encourages us to participate in the quest for community. In Richard's parable about dancing, what had looked like chaos to the man becomes beautiful patterns from a different vantage point; so Wiseman's mediating camera and his editing make profilmic reality more vivid and meaningful.

In the austerity of its construction, *Essene* seeks to capture the spiritual values that inform the order. As Sullivan notes, *Essene* contains fewer sequences than any of Wiseman's previous documentaries,[20] thus establishing a slow, deliberate pace ("like watching a flower blooming through a process of slow motion," as Brother David defines spiritual growth). As well, the film eschews montage within sequences for long takes, mirroring the quiet asceticism of the brotherhood. Generally, the camera moves slowly and gently, as if caressing the people it is filming, just as they embrace each other. In one prayer meeting, the camera in one lengthy, rapturously fluid shot slowly circles the group, as if a participant in their communal embrace. During mass the congregation embraces in the kiss of peace, and the camera slowly moves down the line as the embrace is passed to over a dozen people.

The film is intimate in style and more than Wiseman's other films dominated by close-ups of hands and faces radiating spirituality. The hands we see in this film are quite different from, for example, the aggressive, probing fingers of *Primate*, the mechanical, repetitive hand movements in *Meat*, or the frequently ironic hand gestures in *High School*. Instead, the hands here seem gentle and, in keeping with the emphasis on contact, eager to touch others. When the abbot talks about the importance of community, his fingers are knit together, expressing the values he invokes; when he speaks of intuition opening him up, making him sensitive to the needs of the brethren, they spread as if in supplication. Frequently hands are seen folded in prayer or touching others, as in the vigil for Father Anthony or after Richard's parable. Richard's embrace of Sister Alice after their talk about the pain of loving is a beautiful moment, shot in a bucolic, sunlit grove, as if a visualization of Hopkins's line, "Glory be to God for dappled things."[21]

The dominance of facial close-ups in *Essene* is, of course, typical of many documentaries, but also, given its subject, reminiscent of

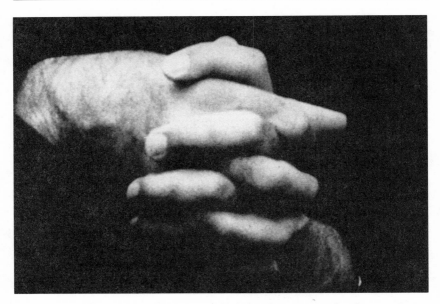

(*Essene*) A monk's knit hands express the hope for community that motivates the order.

Carl Dreyer's *La Passion de Jeanne d'Arc* (1928). The films share a common religious subject as well as what Paul Schrader has called "the transcendental style," a manner of expressing "the holy," a sense of unity beyond the individual in which the self participates. According to Schrader, "day-to-day reality" is first solidly established and then undermined, serving as "a prelude to the moment of redemption, when ordinary reality is transcended." Schrader argues that the films of Yasujiro Ozu, Robert Bresson, and Dreyer generally avoid techniques of expressive stylization in order to present everyday reality more straightforwardly. There is then introduced a "disparity," "a growing crack in the dull surface of everyday reality," so that the viewer begins to sense some greater force in life than daily existence. This crack in everyday reality becomes "an open rupture," leading to some sort of "decisive action" that, in turn, culminates in stasis, "a frozen view of life which does not resolve the disparity but transcends it." In Ozu's films, for example, there is frequently a coda, a final still life image, that expresses oneness.

Clearly, documentary possesses great potential for expressing the transcendent. Although Schrader discusses no documentary films specifically, he acknowledges their importance to his thesis. In his analysis of Bresson, Schrader remarks on the documentary film's ability to record reality's surface and quotes the director's intention in *Un Condamné à mort s'est échappé* (A man escaped, 1956) to create a documentary tone that is "a celebration of the trivial."[22] Bresson's minimization of dramatic plot, acting style, and avoidance of expressionist camerawork and montage, all of which act as "screens" to reality, seem remarkably close to Wiseman's observational style in these five films. Schrader also quotes Susan Sontag on Bresson, who argues that Bresson's style is a challenge for the viewer because it eschews the "easy pleasures" of conventional cinema[23]—again, very much like Wiseman. Yvette Biro expresses a view similar to Schrader's, although she uses the terms "profane" and "mythic" to refer to cinema's transcendent possibilities. More than Schrader, however, Biro emphasizes the role of the documentary in achieving cinema's mythic potential, man's urge to "go beyond himself" by mythicizing everyday life through the camera's observation, magnification, and celebration.[24]

If, as Schrader states, for Bresson "the raw material taken from real life is the raw material of the Transcendent," then Wiseman's cinema, at least in these five films, functions similarly. The disparity between documentary realism and spiritual passion that characterizes Bresson's work is true of *Essene* and of the *Deaf and Blind* series as well. Wiseman's editing in these films may not be quite "deadpan," as both Schrader and Sontag say of Bresson, but Wiseman always connects his shots with basic cuts (as opposed to process shots like fades, dissolves, or wipes); certainly he avoids almost completely the kind of shock editing he earlier employed in *Titicut Follies* or the heavily ironic montage of *High School*. Like the three directors Schrader discusses, Wiseman frequently presents static, well-composed images of the environment, particularly in the establishing exterior shots that have become a stylistic trademark. This creates a disparity between the implacable surfaces of physical reality and the spiritual depth of the people who dwell within these spaces[25]—a direction, it would seem, in which Wiseman was moving since that final shot of *Hospital*.

The attainment of stasis, suggestive of transcendent unity, may be seen in the Talledega shots at the beginning and end of the *Deaf and Blind* films. Ozu, says Schrader, often ends his films with an image of stasis that "is the same restrictive view which began the film: the mountain has become a mountain again, but in an entirely different way." Similarly, the shots of the people of Talledega going about their daily business on the street or in cars take on a profoundly different quality at different times, as in the final shots of *Blind*. These shots bring us back to the short montage that opens the film and frames the other three films. At the end of *Blind* the shots are at night, and what strikes us most is a new awareness of our dependence on light. We see a riot of lights— automobile headlamps, traffic lights, the garish neon of stores and restaurants on the town's main strip—lights that now possess the importance of beacons because we rely on them to guide us through the darkness. Here, the disparity between common activity and what we have come to know about blind people makes nature seem more impressive, our little goings to and fro more petty. Similarly, Richard's parable in *Essene* features one quite lengthy shot that begins with a harmoniously composed triangular composition of Richard flanked by two other monks and ends with an almost identical composition (the only change is that Richard is embraced by a fourth monk). The *tour de force* cinematography in this sequence wonderfully expresses the unity of which Richard speaks and the transcendental style's "return to the mountain."

Schrader further suggests that the three filmmakers he discusses in his book share the use of irony as "a temporary solution to living in a schizoid world," a world of disparity. Irony and a black sense of humor are, as we have seen, characteristic of Wiseman's work. But with the exception of the sequences concerning Brother Wilfred in *Essene*, these five films seem markedly less ironic in tone than Wiseman's other documentaries, focusing as they do on the gap ("disparity") in institutional theory and practice. Both Mamber and Armstrong view the monastery in *Essene* as another institution of social control,[26] seeking perhaps to fit this film into patterns that apply to the other early documentaries. But neither the film's style nor its unique emphasis on the abbot in fact support this view. Similarly, while it is true that we see the AIDB staff in *Multi-Handicapped* reach for and stumble over generalities

(*Essene*) Richard's parable is an expression of transcendental "stasis."

that hardly describe the impressive work with the handicapped they actually do—and the film moves back and forth between such sequences to heighten our perception of this disparity—this is hardly the central focus of the series. This unfortunate exercise in administrivia is more than balanced by the patient, caring work of the teachers and house parents chronicled throughout the four films. If anything, then, we smile rather than snicker at these scenes. "So it goes, the bemused filmmaker seems to be telling us," writes Coles in response to this aspect of the film,[27] echoing the tag phrase of Vonnegut's wry acceptance of the transcendent in *Slaughterhouse Five* (1969). Even here, Wiseman's irony is less pointed, more understated, than elsewhere.

Wiseman does unleash his irony upon one particular institutional disparity in the *Deaf and Blind* films, one which itself "transcends" this particular institution; it is nothing less than the distance between the function of AIDB and the ideology of the American dream itself. This emphasis on national values as an institution follows from those documentaries (*Model, The Store*) made prior to *Deaf and Blind* that, as discussed in the next chapter,

(*Essene*)

redefine the concept of "institution" from an ideological perspective. The *Deaf and Blind* films are filled with exhortations and reminders about the greatness of America ("The American Dream is Alive and Well in the School," says a sign on a classroom wall in *Deaf*), but Wiseman consistently juxtaposes them to the more somber realities confronting handicapped people. In a sense the difficulties of job training emphasized in *Adjustment and Work* and *Multi-Handicapped* work in counterpoint to *Blind* and *Deaf,* undercutting the Algeresque optimism of the first two films.

At the end of *Deaf,* Dr. Gaston delivers a speech about the greatness of America, a country where individuals can triumph over their "handicaps" (in his case, being black) and achieve success. Gaston himself was born in poverty, his grandparents slaves, yet now he owns several companies worth over fifty million dollars. According to Dr. Hawkins, the man who introduces Dr. Gaston, it "probably couldn't happen in any other country in the world, that a gentleman could accomplish so much, so much, from such a meager beginning." In the speech, the value of individual effort is stressed, yet all along these films insist on the importance of human interdependence for success. In *Blind,* students mouth the same conventional patriotic sentiments, speaking of limitless educational opportunity and potential in America. But the speeches ring somewhat hollow, for they are comprised largely of cliché (like the valedictorian's speech at the end of *Basic Training*). And, of course, the claim is undercut by what follows.

For example, Chris, a thirty-seven-year-old black man in *Adjustment and Work*, wants to withdraw from his job training program and seek immediate employment in order to earn some money. He has been a student most of his life, and, as he tells the interviewing staff, his friends are all working. Even though he is described as having "scores in the upper average range of intelligence," whenever he goes somewhere for a job interview, his application is rejected because he is blind. Chris is motivated less by fantasy or a dream than by hard reality, and he simply wants to get on with his life. Then, too, there is William, who wants to work in auto mechanics, although his supervisor reports that this does not seem a feasible vocation for him because of the obstacles involved. "Looking down the road ten years from now . . . he will probably still be a mechanic's helper," he predicts. Despite the anomalous success story of Gaston, the choices for most handicapped people are limited, and there is little hope that with the right combination of pluck and luck they will rise in their field of employment. Tellingly, during the class visit to the county judicial building in *Deaf,* Wiseman inserts a shot of the lobby newsstand vendor, a blind man, sitting motionless and alone.

Toward the end of *Adjustment and Work,* in the Industries for the Blind building we see the work so many blind people actually end up doing: bending file folders, making brooms, mops, and ties, or making first-aid and M-16 equipment pouches for the army. "They do that Monday, Tuesday, Wednesday, Thursday, Friday, sometimes on Saturday. And that's work," the guide explains. Wiseman emphasizes the point by having the droning, repetitive sound of the file folder machines carry over the film's final credits, similar to the sound bridge at the end of *Welfare.* The fact that the workers are making brooms and mops is especially significant in the context of Wiseman's cinema; in so many of his films we see the disparity between rich and poor concretized in the contrasting images of white and blue collar workers, of professionals and janitors. Indeed, the last image of *Adjustment and Work* is of some-one sweeping up. "Everyone makes at least minimum wage, and some of them with fringe benefits are making as much as $5.25 an hour," someone proudly explains to Dr. Gaston. While it is true that employment will give some of these handicapped people self-respect, many do not feel fulfilled, and absenteeism is identified in the preceding scene as a major problem.

The opening racetrack sequence of *Blind,* preceding even the typical expository montage that opens the other three films in the series, acts as a prologue or prelude, establishing immediately this crucial aspect of the series. At the Talledega Raceway, the school band of the Alabama School for the Blind prepares for a perfor-mance during a day of stock car racing. Impressive customized cars sponsored by large corporations (Busch, Winston, Coors, and Goody's headache tablets, "the official pain reliever of NasCar") parade by, with bathing beauties (including Miss Montgomery In-ternational Raceway) perched atop them. These beautiful cars and women serve as compelling icons of the wealth and beauty that characterize the American dream. (Even Gaston later depicts success in terms of cars: "The fellow who drives an automobile, he is somebody," he declares, adding, as proof of America's greatness, that his gardener drives to work in a Cadillac.) The camera is po-sitioned so that the women are waving at both the raceway audi-ence and the film audience, implicating the viewer in our culture's typical emphasis of material over spiritual values. By contrast, the marching bands in the same sequence are shown from a variety of perspectives.

The American dream as presented at the racetrack is a dream that the children in the band, because of their handicap, can never attain. They are situated in the center of the track, surrounded by—that is, inside, yet outside—the dream. The only race cars we see them drive are those in video machines, as shown at one point in *Adjustment and Work,* or by servicing the vending machines along life's highway, as one man with failing vision hopes to do. The band proceeds to play "America the Beautiful" and "Gonna Fly Now," the theme from *Rocky* (John Avildsen, 1976). But the tune teeters off-key, then finally collapses—a telling failure, for these young blind people can never charge up the steps of city hall like Rocky Balboa.

(*Blind*) **Miss Coors** seems to wave to the camera, implicating the viewer in the materialism of the American dream.

As "the cosmopolitan" so appropriately asks in *The Confidence-Man:* "What is an atheist, but one who does not, or will not, see in the universe a ruling principle of love?"[28] The *Deaf and Blind* films remind us that we need others to help us achieve selfhood just as Martin Buber (specifically referred to by Robert in *Essene*) claims that "The basic word I-You can be spoken only with one's whole being. . . . I require a You to become; becoming I, I say you."[29] Brother David expresses a similar view at the beginning of that film, when he says that you are "endeared" to someone you watch "becoming," because you are "becoming" at the same time. In these films Wiseman forces us to attend to, to endear ourselves to, people becoming. In *Essene,* the vocationer Bill draws attention to a poster on the wall in Father Anthony's office showing a naked man crouched in a corner with the caption, "Because you are afraid to love, I am alone." Without love, these films say, we are all isolated and vulnerable, handicapped.

One of the most moving sequences anywhere in these films occurs in *Blind,* when blind children pretend to walk on a tightrope, keeping their balance with heart-shaped objects the teacher calls their "magic heart." "Don't forget to hold your heart up," the teacher reminds the children as they pretend to walk the tightrope between dependency and self-sufficiency. If they succeed, they "walk way above the crowd"; with the encouragement and charity of others, they may attain the heights of personal achievement. If it is true that in our daily lives, as Emerson says, "we never touch but at points,"[30] Wiseman attempts in these films to engage these points by bringing us closer together through empathetic, transcendent experience. It is perhaps only through such experience that we become "balanced," restoring the footing lost at the end of *Primate*.

NOTES

1. Aldous Huxley, Appendix, *The Devils of Loudun* (London: Chatto & Windus, 1961), p. 375.

2. Quoted in Sylvia Feldman, "The Wiseman Documentary," *Human Behavior* 5 (February 1976): 69.

3. Chuck Kraemer, "Fred Wiseman's *Primate* Makes Monkeys of Scientists," *New York Times*, December 1, 1974, sec. 2, pp. 1, 31.

4. Huxley, *The Devils of Loudun*, pp. 371, 374.

5. Feldman, "The Wiseman Documentary," p. 69.

6. Alan Westin, " 'You Start Off With a Bromide': Conversation with Film Maker Frederick Wiseman," *Civil Liberties Review* 1, no. 2 (Winter/Spring 1974): 52.

7. Quoted in Thomas Meehan, "The Documentary Maker," *Saturday Review of the Arts* 55, no. 49 (December 1972): 14.

8. Malcolm Boyd, "To Worship and Glorify God," *New York Times*, November 12, 1972, p. 17.

9. Stephen Mamber, *Cinema Verite in America: Studies in Uncontrolled Documentary* (Cambridge: MIT Press, 1974), p. 240.

10. Huxley, *The Devils of Loudun*, p. 374.

11. Herman Melville, *The Confidence-Man: His Masquerade*, ed. Hershel Parker (New York: Norton, 1971), p. 6.

12. Herman Melville, *Billy Budd, Sailor (An Inside Narrative)*, ed. Harrison Hayford and Merton M. Sealts, Jr. (Chicago and London: University of Chicago Press, 1962), p. 122.

13. Nathaniel Hawthorne, *The Blithedale Romance* (New York: Norton, 1958), p. 85.

14. Patrick Sullivan, *"Essene," Film Quarterly* 27, no. 1. (Fall 1973): 56.

15. Jeff Jarvis, "Tube," *People*, March 13, 1988, p. 11.

16. Robert Coles, "Senses and Sensibility," *New Republic*, August 29, 1988, p. 60.

17. Ralph Waldo Emerson, *Emerson's Nature—Origin, Growth, Meaning*, ed. Merton M. Sealts, Jr., and Alfred R. Ferguson (New York and Toronto: Dodd, Mead & Co., 1969), p. 8.

18. Washington Irving, "Rip Van Winkle," in *Washington Irving: Selected Prose*, ed. Stanley T. Williams (New York: Holt, Rinehart and Winston, 1964), p. 106.

19. Peter Sourian, "Television," *The Nation*, October 15, 1977, p. 382.

20. Sullivan, *"Essene,"* p. 55.

21. Gerard Manley Hopkins, "Pied Beauty," in *The Poems of Gerard Manley Hopkins*, ed. W. H. Gardner and N. H. MacKenzie (New York: Oxford University Press, 1970), p. 69.

22. Paul Schrader, *Transcendental Style in Film: Ozu, Bresson, Dreyer* (New York: Da Capo, 1988). The quotations here are from pp. 39–49, 63.

23. Ibid., p. 64. The Sontag quotation is from "Spiritual Style in the Films of Robert Bresson," *Against Interpretation* (New York: Farrar Straus & Giroux, 1966), p. 191.

24. Yvette Biro, *Profane Mythology: The Savage Mind of the Cinema*, trans. Imre Goldstein (Bloomington: Indiana University Press, 1982), esp. chaps. 3 and 4.

25. For similar views on the sacred in film, see Michael Bird, "Film as Heirophany," in John R. May and Michael Bird, eds., *Religion in Film* (Knoxville: University of Tennessee Press, 1982), pp. 3–22; and Amédée Ayfre, *Conversion aux Images?* (Paris: Éditions du Cerf, 1964).

26. Mamber, *Cinema Verite in America*, p. 244; Dan Armstrong, "Wiseman's Realm of Transgression: *Titicut Follies*, the Symbolic Father, and the Spectacle of Confinement," *Cinema Journal* 29, no. 1 (Fall 1989): 21.

27. Coles, "Senses and Sensibility," p. 59.

28. Melville, *The Confidence-Man*, pp. 136–37.

29. Martin Buber, *I and Thou*, ed. and trans. Walter Kaufmann (New York: Charles Scribner's Sons, 1970), p. 62.

30. Ralph Waldo Emerson, *Journals of Ralph Waldo Emerson*, 8 vols., ed. Edward Waldo Emerson and Waldo Emerson Forbes (Boston and New York, 1910), IV: 238.

CHAPTER 6

When Worlds Collide

Canal Zone (1977) • *Sinai Field Mission* (1978) • *Model* (1980)
The Store (1983)

The four films discussed in this chapter clearly demonstrate how Wiseman's film practice has moved beyond the liberal humanism that informs most of his previous work and grown more sophisticated and increasingly politically conscious in recent years. The theme and method of these later films is similar to contemporary deconstructionist criticism in that they seek to identify cultural myths and ideological constraints at work in institutions, including the institution of cinema. The presence of several American flags during the shooting of the Toyota advertisement at the beginning of *Model* explicitly acknowledges that visual images are, in Roland Barthes' distinction, cultural rather than natural.[1] In these films, Wiseman examines cultural institutions while at the same time critiquing his own documentary practice as one of many signifying systems. In this sense, the films mark a clear progression from the self-reflexive strategy of *Titicut Follies, Manoeuvre,* or *Meat,* in which the spectator's relation to the filmic text is of crucial importance.

All four films continue the "American theme" initiated in the early documentaries, although they proceed differently. Wiseman has said that he picks specific institutions to film because their bounded, definable space helps prevent the films from losing focus, from becoming "too diffuse." He adds that such a definition of an institution is not to be taken literally but as a "working definition." In these four films, however, Wiseman eschews his earlier methods of encouraging a reading of a particular institution as a social microcosm, preferring instead to consider American culture itself as an institution. The idea of "cultural spoors" thus ceases to have any significant meaning, since these institutions are, in effect, "the larger beast," hegemonic American culture. Although *Model* and *The Store* do concentrate their examination on particular institutions—on the Zoli agency and the Neiman Marcus flagship store in Dallas, respectively—they both explicitly relate their own work of documentation to the larger cultural business of image creation and consumption.

The films fall neatly into two distinct pairs, connected thematically and stylistically as well as chronologically. *Canal Zone* and *Sinai Field Mission* belong to a tradition in American literature that begins with *The Contrast* (Royall Tyler, 1787), the first American play. The tradition that established the convention of pitting the homespun wit of a New Englander against a foppish Englishman extends to the more modern "ugly American" inflection. In a sense, these two films are similar to Henry James's "international theme." In novels like *The American* (1877) James throws American culture and manners into greater relief by placing its representatives within established European society. Similarly, *Canal Zone* and *Sinai Field Mission* examine American culture by transposing it, by documenting how Americans live, work, and play when abroad. *Model* and *The Store* adapt a different strategy, the first focusing on advertising and the second on conspicuous consumption, both of which to a large extent define American capitalism. Hence these two films are closer to novels like *The Bostonians* (1886)—the word itself commodified in *The Store* as a brand of shoe—wherein aspects of American culture clash internally. Here Wiseman contrasts the idealized imagery of advertising and consumption with the imperfections of the real world.

Canal Zone begins predictably enough, by presenting the operational processes of the Panama Canal. In the lengthy, carefully composed opening sequence, we are shown what is involved in moving a ship through the canal locks, and we are quickly inundated with facts offered by an official canal tourguide: the amount of water in each lock, the length of time it takes to flood a lock with water, the weight of the lock mechanisms, the toll schedules, and so on. As we soon discover, however, this is not the film's real focus, for it quickly shifts its attention, devoting most of its nearly three hour running time to aspects of daily life in the Zone. The title of the film is thus quite precise, for the canal itself is only fleetingly glimpsed throughout the remainder of the film.

As suggested by the many shots of people looking through binoculars and high-powered lenses at the beginning, the film moves from a superficial view, represented by the tourguide's pre-scripted account of statistics about the canal, to a more revealing examination of life in the Zone, magnifying what is already there in order to be seen more clearly. Like the marriage counselor's method within the film, *Canal Zone* seeks to "structure an environment in which you can learn something that you already know but experience it more intently." So it might be said that the film shows two types of apparatuses—the physical machinery of the canal and the intangible machinery of American ideology in the Zone.

Sinai Field Mission, about the group of Americans who operate a buffer zone monitoring station in the Sinai between Egypt and Israel, works similarly. It begins by showing aspects of the monitoring process, although here the viewer is more puzzled than in the opening of *Canal Zone* since the operation of the Sinai Field Mission (SFM) is likely more unfamiliar than that of the Panama Canal. Soon some Israeli officials visit the mission compound, and Mr. Roberts, the deputy director of SFM, serves an analogous function to the canal tourguide by explaining in detail to them, and so to us, the mandate and function of SFM. After this, though, the film goes on to show us a more penetrating view of what life is like for these transplanted Americans inside the compound, returning only occasionally to the ostensible work of the mission.

The Canal Zone, according to Paul Theroux, is "an American suburb in apotheosis, the triumph of banality."[2] Hence the Zone we see in the film seems, at first glance, an American town like so many others. As in the classic "city symphony" documentaries, we see many shots of people at leisure. They jog, ride bikes and skateboards; they play tennis, volleyball, bingo, soccer, water polo; they fish, swim, and lounge on the beach. *Canal Zone*'s emphasis on the games these people play relates it to *Manoeuvre*, the imperialist connection suggested by the sudden appearance of American paratroopers on manoeuvres in Panama near the end of the film. *Canal Zone* shows almost nothing of indigenous Panamanian culture, except for a brief glimpse of local street art and a Panamanian sandlot baseball game (if, indeed, this can properly be called indigenous culture). American culture, by contrast, is everywhere: familiar rituals and ceremonies, television shows (Abbott and Costello and Kentucky Fried Chicken commercials are showing on TV in the waiting room at the Mental Health Clinic, Panamanians staring blankly at the screen), pop music on local radio, current movies (including the revenge movie *Walking Tall, Part Two* [Earl Bellamy, 1975], its presence here suggesting a connection between personal vigilantism and Monroe Doctrine politics).

James Wolcott faults *Canal Zone* for a lack of specificity, saying that it could have been filmed in Iowa or Georgia;[3] but this is less a failure than the precise point of the film. Just as the woman who takes the Thematic Appreciation Test (TAT) obviously reads her own marital problems into the pictures she is shown, so Americans in the Zone have imported their own social customs and values into another environment and culture.

Canal Zone's method is politically loaded. The film concentrates on bourgeois Americans and relegates the impoverished Panamanians to the margins, just as they have been marginalized economically and socially by the Zonians. Yet they appear with regular frequency, like periodic thorns in the viewer's conscience. For example, Panamanian workers are shown pricing food and stocking the shelves of a supermarket where the Zonians shop, and it is they who clean up at the Balboa High School graduation ceremony. They work as garbage pickers, field hands, or skeet pullers for Americans. A shot of a Panamanian man doing menial grounds-keeping work as a big American car drives past forcefully emphasizes the disparity of wealth between the two groups. These occasional "cameo appearances" by Panamanians remind the viewer of the position of privilege held by the film's "major characters," the Americans.

Just as the Panamanian people are distinct from the Zonians, so the Zone is distinctly separate from the country that surrounds it. The film's view is consistent with Theroux's description of the Zonians' perception of Panama as a "big stupid clumsy world of squinting cannibals [that] begins where the Zone ends—it is right

(*Canal Zone*) Indigenous culture is marginalized, as in this shot of a Panamanian worker tending the grounds of Balboa High School.

there, across the Fourth of July Highway, the predatory world of hungry unwashed people gibbering in Spanish."[4] Wiseman shows us a public service announcement on Zonian television advising women viewers to keep their car windows closed when stopped at a red light. Elsewhere, reminiscent of Theroux's anecdote about the librarian who had worked in the Zone for forty years but cannot speak one sentence in Spanish,[5] we see in the film a weekly Spanish lesson television show that, incredibly, is only one minute in length.

The xenophobic garrison mentality of the Zone (in a way, not unlike the besieged welfare center in *Welfare*) is made explicit in the physical appearance of the compound in *Sinai Field Mission*. The place is designed like a fort, several squat buildings huddled together and surrounded by fences and surveillance equipment. Wiseman often films vehicles entering or departing from the compound by showing the gates closing behind them, almost as if the frame itself were narrowing (a similar effect is achieved with the elevator doors in *The Store*), emphasizing this sense of confinement or entrapment and cleverly alluding to the geography of the place

(*Sinai Field Mission*) American culture looms large, as in the hootenanny sequence.

itself (the Mitla and Giddi passes, through which all traffic must flow, are described by Roberts as "bottlenecks"). Frequent announcements broadcast over the loudspeakers and the periodic whirring of helicopter blades on the soundtrack recall *M*A*S*H* (Robert Altman, 1970), a film that shares Wiseman's vision of Americans abroad trying to maintain a neutral humanism. (The paging of "Mr. Roberts" over the loudspeaker system offers another resonant reference: John Ford and Mervyn LeRoy's 1955 war comedy *Mr. Roberts*, where the eponymous hero is played by that icon of Americana, Henry Fonda.)

As the Zonians block out the indigenous realities of Panama, so the Americans in *Sinai Field Mission* seem closed to Middle Eastern culture. One man watching a belly dancer on television is about as close to local culture as the Americans get in the film. Some of the SFM staff play video games, suggesting that, as far as these people are concerned, the belly dancer and the blips on the game screen are both simply images to be consumed. One man talks of his "R and R" trip to Cairo, averring that everyone should go, yet when asked about his trip, he says he stayed drunk the whole time he was there. These innocents abroad think they can "do" Egypt in "five or six days," the way Godard's characters run through the Louvre in *Bande a Parte* (1964). Three Americans from SFM actually do travel into the desert to an old Bedouin burial ground, where they betray their ignorance of local culture. "Is this Mecca?" one of the two women asks, while the other wants to inscribe their names, the graffiti of insensitive tourists on holy ground. This is as far from the mission as Wiseman's camera ever goes. As in *Canal Zone*, indigenous culture is largely relegated to the periphery, a reflection of the attitude of the Americans in the film.

Sinai Field Mission, too, shows Americans devoted to leisure. We see people play an astonishing variety of games, as well as bike, jog, and exercise on various pieces of gym equipment. Wiseman emphasizes this play aspect of life at SFM, just as Roberts, in his explanation of the function and mandate of the mission, uses an extended metaphor of sport (they are the "referees" who can "stop the action" by calling "infractions"). As in *Canal Zone*, Americans fill the spaces they inhabit with their own frivolous luxuries, even to the point of imagining complex political realities in terms of their own leisurely lifestyle. Again as in *Canal Zone*, American popular culture proliferates in the SFM compound. Wiseman shows a Fourth of July celebration, including a hootenanny where several of the staff sing "That Good Old Mountain Dew," an American flag prominently hung behind them. Their feeling of homesickness is made explicit when a trio sings "we're seven thousand miles away from home," eliciting an appreciative round of applause.

Other songs heard in the film include Willie Nelson's "Time of the Preacher" and Glen Campbell's "Southern Nights," both tunes particularly appropriate, since E-Systems, the private contracting company that is responsible for the operational and technical aspects of SFM, is based in Texas. As in *Meat*, western icons abound. Two of the code words used during radio communications are "Alamo" and "Red River." There is a barbecue, a favorite Texas pastime, although here, ironically, it is held indoors. In one sequence, the men play football (one of them wears a Texas Longhorns jersey) and drink beer from a cowboy boot: "This is how a Texan drinks," someone shouts. They sing "The Eyes of Texas Are Upon You" ("That goes for Israel and Egypt," a voice interjects) and make reference to "T for Texas" ("Blue Yodel No. 1"), a song recorded by both Jimmie Rodgers and Bob Wills and the Texas Playboys.

Canal Zone especially emphasizes the rituals and ceremonies of daily life. In Wolcott's words, the film is "A Macy's Day parade of ceremonies."[6] The Americans seem to cling to ceremony and tradition as a way of preserving their national identity the way the priest clings to patriarchy in his antifeminist sermon. There is a particular emphasis on the flag. In ceremonies such as the observance of Law Day (a judge praises their new flag because it "doesn't have any spots"), the presentation of new flags to the VFW by the Zonian Women's Auxiliary (according to the army colonel who officially receives the flags, the ceremony is "a reaffirmation of our great pledge to our country and our allegiance to a great nation"), and the planting of small flags on the gravestones, this icon is repeatedly called upon. Other rituals include a Boy Scouts award dinner, where a fife and drum corp in revolutionary minuteman garb play "Yanke Doodle Dandy"; a funeral service where a man recites Lincoln's Gettysburg Address; and a graduation ceremony at Balboa High School, as awful as the one in *Basic Training*, complete with a turgid valedictorian speech full of platitudes about friendship and loyalty ("Life in America under God is a positive experience").

In a sense, the America of the Canal Zone is like the grotesque middle America depicted in the cult movie *A Boy and His Dog* (L. Q. Jones, 1975), released just two years before Wiseman's film. In this ironic postapocalyptic tale, radioactive contamination has forced most survivors underground, to "Topeka," a self-contained replica of a midwestern town. Desperately attempting to preserve American culture, the community's residents cling to familiar social rituals. In this sunless world they paint their cheeks a rosy hue, broadcast a continuous stream of middle-class homilies over the loudspeaker system, listen to marching bands, and indulge in pie-baking contests. Life in the Zone, described by one reviewer as "Middle America *in vitro*,"[7] is similarly dominated by the rituals and social conventions of bourgeois America as a desperate attempt to maintain its traditional values. Such small ceremonies mean a great deal and make the participants feel part of the larger social order, as the colonel says when accepting the old American flags for disposal. The film's heavy emphasis on such scenes makes the Zone seem, in Frank Rich's words, "a nightmare version of America itself."[8]

As they do to the people of Topeka, ceremony and ritual have become so important to the Zonians because they are a society in crisis, a result of America's eroding imperialist power. (It is one of the film's ironies, after all, that it was made in the bicentennial year). The community of the Zone is plagued by financial cutbacks and morale problems, feeling abandoned by the government that established it back in 1903. Governor Harold Parfitt refers to the current negotiations of the controversial treaty that will turn the canal over to Panama by the year 2000 as "a trauma." At the civic council meeting, we hear that there is a "mini-exodus" of people back home because "a feeling of desperate hopelessness has spread throughout the United States community." In the words of the youth officer, "we're worried about are we going to be here next year and are we going to have a revolution." The strained endurance of Zonian society manifests itself in such problems as failing marriages and child abuse—the rate of which is "about three times above the national average" in the Zone. *Canal Zone*'s closing shots of gravestones, a marked contrast to the opening shots of birds flying in the sky above the canal, constitute a strong editorial comment. In fact, this may be one of the most overtly political moments in all of Wiseman's cinema, as much a criticism of antitreaty sentiment and Big Stick foreign policy as it is a comment on the bourgeois rituals of Zonian life.

Wiseman's sense of irony in the film often amplifies the social problems of the Zone. He includes, for example, a cutaway shot of a local cinema marquee showing *One Flew Over the Cuckoo's Nest*— "a nightmare version of America," indeed. Some of the Zonians are upset because they are not allowed to use the American military facilities, while their own are open for use by military personnel. They complain that the situation is "inequitable" and that (similar to the view of some of the staff in *Sinai Field Mission* about the Finnish detachment of UN forces) they are, in effect, "secondclass citizens"—an ironic complaint given the Zone's imperialist context. Perhaps the largest irony of all is that as the Zonians celebrate their country's bicentennial throughout the film, marking their own revolution as a colony, they feel threatened that Panama is on the verge of doing the same. The film's wry tone, then, is generated essentially as a result of the fact that otherwise common American activities—what Peter Sourian calls the "extraordinarily ordinary"[9]—are shown occurring in an alien environment.

There are similar indications of tensions below the surface in the *Sinai Field Mission* community. We discover that there have been several instances of property damage in the compound by SFM personnel, and that the vandalism is getting worse. Several scenes take place in the compound bar ("I have to have my happy hour drink," one woman says), and in the party scene the men seem surprisingly drunk and rowdy, a stark contrast to the discipline of the Ghanian troops seen at several points in the film. In one shot, a forklift, fully loaded with cartons of liquor, moves dramatically toward the camera, its importance unmistakably emphasized by the forward movement within the frame. In another, a handtruck stacked with cases of Heinekin beer is wheeled into a storeroom, and later we see that the PX is stocked with alcohol and tobacco products. As in many of Douglas Sirk's melodramas, such images suggest problems beneath the veneer of bourgeois society.

Not surprisingly, both the Panama Canal and the Sinai Field Mission are viewed by the Americans themselves essentially as business ventures; after all, as Calvin Coolidge had said, the business of America is business. The governor of the Zone, who also serves as president of the Canal Zone Company, thinks of the canal as an "enterprise," speaking in terms of capital expenditures, equipment depreciation, and investment potential. His assessment of Vietnam was that it was good for canal business, and in the ham radio scene the navy man from Maryland identifies himself as being "in the torpedo business." Gov. Parfitt ominously refers to the company as "the combine," the same phrase Chief Bromden uses for the military-industrial complex in *One Flew Over the Cuckoo's Nest,* and it is shortly after this that Wiseman inserts the marquee shot advertising that film. Similarly, SFM is composed of one hundred and sixty-three people, "twenty-three United States government types and one hundred and forty E-Systems people." However, according to Mr. Thorne, the retiring director of SFM, the two groups have grown closer, to the point that "the two aren't really distinct anymore."

That culture is our business, in Marshall McLuhan's phrase, is also clearly shown in both *Model* and *The Store*. The Zipporah catalogue's concise description of *Model* as presenting "a view of the intersections of fashion, business, advertising, photography, television, and fantasy" summarizes its concerns rather well. *The Store*, which Wiseman acknowledges developed as an outgrowth of his work on *Model*,[10] shows the selling of the goods for which the imagery of advertising stirs desire and, moreover, how capitalism and consumerism have shaped our perception and consciousness. John Berger writes that all advertising is geared toward "a single proposal": "to buying something more."[11] In the film's first sequence inside Neiman-Marcus, a staff meeting of department heads, the vice-president echoes Berger in his emphatic declaration that "we're at Neiman-Marcus for one reason, and one reason only"—sales. This, he adds, is their "one purpose in life." Thus holidays are defined in terms of retailing. Washington's Birthday, for the store president, is "a very meaningful event, particularly in coats," while Christmas, according to the company buyer who conducts the physical exercises for the sales staff, is nothing more than a "particularly intense shopping season." Here there is none of the Hollywood fantasy of benign capitalism, as in, say, *The Devil and Miss Jones* (Sam Wood, 1941) or *Miracle on 34th Street* (George Seaton, 1947). On the contrary, business is competition—in the president's words, a matter of taking "a share of the market away by virtue of having customers come to our store instead of going across the square."

The beginnings of *Model* and *The Store* are indicative of the expanded conception of the institution that informs them. Both begin with exterior shots, not of particular buildings but of the Manhattan and Dallas skylines, respectively. *Model*'s first establishing shot, shown even before the exterior of the Zoli Agency, the locus of the film, is a portion of the Manhattan skyline carefully framed so that the World Trade Center is prominent. (The building has become an icon of America and capitalism, having replaced the Empire State building in John Guillerman's 1976 remake of *King Kong*.) Not coincidentally, during the shooting of the Toyota advertisement, we see models posing against this same part of the skyline. Wiseman returns to the same view in the film's closing image at night, as if to say that the institution of "the culture industry" works around the clock.

In both films Wiseman again uses images of the city streets—buses and store windows and the myriad details of daily activity—not merely as transition shots but also as meaningful commentary. In *The Store* there is a clear contrast between the ambient noise and activity of the street and the quiet Muzak and orderly aisles of merchandise inside Neiman-Marcus. In *Model* the bustle of the real world is contrasted with the constructed hyperreality ("artificially arranged scenes," as Georges Mèliés had described his films) of advertising imagery. Before the filming of the exterior shots for a pantyhose commercial, the city streets are deliberately swept clean, and the director fusses over the position of the sun for "natural" lighting. One photographer's observation in *Model* of "how little we are in touch with the rest of the country" is shown to be more true than he realizes. Andy Warhol, certainly a voice of authority on such matters, tells a film crew that models are the only ones who look good in the clothes they model, and even they normally do not wear them. Consumer imagery in both *Model* and *The Store* are as separate from daily life as the transplanted American societies are from local culture in *Canal Zone* and *Sinai Field Mission*. The startling disjunction between these two worlds—what one of the models interviewed calls "the dividing line between reality and illusion"—emphasizes the extent to which advertising is ideological fantasy.

At first, this aspect of *Model* may seem obvious, even cliché. Thus Wolcott ungenerously refers to one of the film's cutaways, contrasting advertising imagery and daily life, as "a device worthy of John Schlesinger at his most facilely sour."[12] Yet this aspect of the film's structure is crucial and is in fact more complex than the simple contrast it initially appears to be. For example, at different times in the film, street shots include an ambulance and a fire engine coming into the frame. Here both the aleatory nature of reality and the ineluctability of mortality reassert themselves, intruding into advertising's fantasy of timeless perfection. Further, if real life and advertising are distinctly separate, they are also intimately connected, both economically and socially. The emphasis on bridges in these shots—there are at least three, as

(*Model*) The cultural importance of advertising is emphasized in the mise-en-scène of street shots.

well as the Roosevelt Island tramway—suggests such connections, and customer flow in Neiman-Marcus is explicitly referred to in *The Store* as "traffic" during one of the staff meetings.

Our first specific view of New York in *Model* is of a city square, where a band is playing. Behind the musicians and the people on the street loom giant billboards advertising Calvin Klein jeans and Brut cologne. These images at once introduce the film's subject and, through the placement and scale of the ad, suggest the extent to which advertising has infiltrated and dominates daily existence. These shots show us how, as Berger has written, "in the cities in which we live, all of us see hundreds of publicity images every day of our lives. No other kind of image confronts us so frequently." (One particular street shot clearly recalls the composition of the final shot in *Hospital* and its implications of a society inured to the realities of its own functioning.) However, if we are so accustomed to the proliferation of advertising images that, as Berger says, "we scarcely notice their total impact,"[13] in *Model,* because we see ads everywhere—on billboards and bus shelters, on the fronts and sides of busses, and on vans and trucks in almost all the street shots—we become unavoidably conscious of them.

Unlike the untidy bustle in the real world, in the imagery of fashion and advertising, as Romeo's photographer boasts, "everything's perfect." In this art that is "too precise in every part,"[14] even the slightest disorder brings no delight. Twice in *Model* photographic sessions are delayed as wayward hair ("just one little hair that's coming right across") is removed. Advertisers are modern versions of Hawthorne's "The Artist of the Beautiful," beating all nature.[15] The director of the Picone commercial insists not only that commercials are an art but that advertising is "probably the most difficult art form there is." (Humorously, Wiseman inserts shots of the Museum of Modern Art and the Guggenheim Museum at different points in the sequence.) Whereas in movies things can be stretched out in time, the director reasons, "here your concentration is on the tenths of seconds. And the discipline becomes that much more extraordinary." In *The Store* the fur salesman boasts that a particular sable coat is "a true work of art." The music played by the band during the film's opening street sequence is, as Dan Armstrong points out, "the elegant rondo from Mauret's 'Symphonic Fanfares,' the musical theme of public television's 'Masterpiece Theater.'"[16] This is another ironic joke (especially given Wiseman's attitude toward American public television) in the context of advertising's conception of itself as art.

In a sense, the enclosed, idealized worlds of advertising and exclusive retailing are similar to the psychically self-contained American existence in the Canal Zone and the Sinai Field Mission. In the Zone, it is the canal itself that challenges nature. The canal is, in effect, a massive concrete instance of ideology turning culture into nature—"the greatest liberty ever taken with nature," in the words of Lord Bryce. As the ham radio operator points out, the Canal Zone is the only place where he can put out to sea and have his family with him at the same time. The film contains several shots showing the attempt to tame or tether the forces of nature, mundane instances of what the canal represents on a grander scale: a truck spraying chemicals on a lawn, a bull tied by two ropes, a deckhand on a ship golfing with a ball tied to a rope. We see dredging machines lifting rock and silt from the canal, an apparently Sisyphian process challenging the land's natural state, which Wiseman clearly emphasizes in long takes and lengthy pans. If, as Rev. Kennedy remarks in the opening of the Law Day celebration, "all true law is but a participation in and a reflection of Thy divine authority . . . [that is] revealed to us in the amazingly ordered and unswerving laws of nature," then the canal itself is a "crime," a defilement of nature, similar to the tanks in *Manoeuvre*. Ultimately, the canal's "unnaturalness" serves as a metaphor for the unnatural balance of power held by the colonialist Americans in the Zone.

In *Sinai Field Mission* the landscape clearly dominates, a vast, imperturbable space oblivious to the petty battles that occur on its darkling plains. Several shots of abandoned trucks and wrecked jeeps, like empty husks in the desert, set an ominous tone, similar to the images of social and ecological protest in Godfrey Reggio's *Powaqqaatsi* (1988). The images seem to say, along with Percy Shelley's Ozymandias, "Look on my works, ye Mighty, and despair!" In this film Wiseman's typical corridor shots are replaced by shots of flat, expansive vistas. In them, the desert possesses a looming presence, which Wiseman emphasizes by long shots and pans, as if the Sinai were his Monument Valley. In the beginning, a SFM car driving in the desert is dwarfed by the landscape, like the Overland Stage in the famous long shots in Ford's *Stagecoach* (1939). Wiseman's camera zooms out to make the SFM car even smaller in the frame. At one point we see a somewhat ludicrous image of one of the men vacuuming a rug outdoors as, all around, in Shelley's words, "the lone and level sands stretch far away." The film's final images show the Ghanaian battalion of the UN Expeditionary Force marching out of the frame, momentarily leaving the landscape for us to contemplate.

The point is twofold. First, it puts into a larger perspective the American culture that so many Americans unquestioningly assume as global manifest destiny; second, it shows that the mandate of the mission, as laudable as it may be (as with many of the other institutions Wiseman has examined), has become skewed by technology. In the disagreement between the SFM staff and the Israeli colonel, the officer insists he is talking about human beings, not paper and procedures. Wiseman follows his remark with an ironic cut to the ever-present surveillance equipment of the compound. The theme is made explicit in the debate between two of the SFM

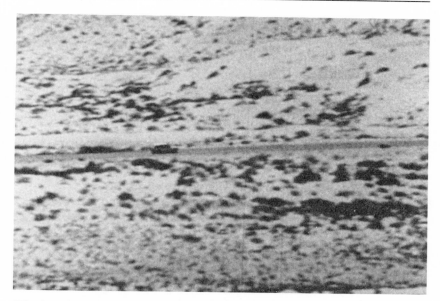

(*Sinai Field Mission*) The Sinai Field Mission vehicle is dwarfed by the landscape.

staff concerning procedure during a medical emergency in the Israeli base. Paul wants to go strictly by the book, but George argues that "meanwhile the guy is bleeding to death." As in *Welfare* and *Hospital*, it is an argument of "technicalities versus need." Wiseman shoots the disagreement between the two men so that they are seen through a barred window in the state department building, the frame within a frame and the bars suggesting the extent to which such humanistic impulses are trapped within the bureaucracy engendered by technological capability.

This theme continues in *Model*, which explores the profession of modeling as the institution that has formalized how people are violated, reduced in importance by labels and stereotypes (a frequent concern in Wiseman's documentaries). The film shows that the discourse of fashion is concerned with surface "looks," with commodification of emotion and desire through imagery. One male model, for example, is told that he has that "Warren Beatty quality" (actor as image) and a female model is informed that she has all the qualities for the sophisticated "Avon kind of look" (product as image). Models are asked by photographers for a "harder look" or "more punky" quality, for looks of sophistication, bitchiness, youth, and shyness ("kind of like, ya know, aw, shucks"). Another male model is told to give "that really nice macho . . . a very typical masculine thing," while in an improvisatory scene yet another is coached to "think young executive rather than guy standing on street corner." Even in *The Store,* a female department head being photographed dislikes her image because "it looks so business," wanting instead "to look like a soft, feminine, non-career lady." Despite Zoli's protest that people ignorant of the modeling business stereotype models, this is, as we see, precisely what the business itself does in its creation of ideal imagery.

So in response to a photographer's complaint that today's younger models have no technique, that they simply strike predetermined poses because "they don't know anything . . . there's no thinking process going on," his more experienced subject proudly claims, "I don't think." Apollonia, the model who provides the legs for the Picone stocking commercial (also the star of *Seraphita's Diary*), is told not to think too much since the leg poses she must strike are "very mechanical." In the next sequence, three models are told to pose as if they were mannequins in Bloomingdale's window. The attitude is literalized by the models during the evening affair. They act as living mannequins, displaying fashions and lounging in poses against a wall. During the shooting of the exterior part of the Picone commercial, a model is referred to twice as "doll" by the director; in another photo session a spotlight shines directly on a model's face, draining it of definition, making it look like a mannequin or an unfinished pod replacement from *Invasion of the Body Snatchers.* The models, in short, are like Bob Walters in High School—only bodies doing a job.

Dan Armstrong's comment that Zoli's agency is "a kind of fashion model's meat market" and Wolcott's description of the reception with the live models against the wall as reminiscent of "sides of beef on a meat rack" acknowledge the ironic connections between *Model* and *Meat.*[17] Indeed, Wiseman invites a comparison between them, for in *Model* he shows how models are "treated like cattle." The first shots inside Zoli's, showing telephone calls to place models in jobs, is reminiscent of the salesmen taking telephone orders in *Meat.* Near the beginning of the film we are shown interviews with several aspiring models, a weeding out process analogous to the feedlot procedure at the Monfort Plant. The models are "packaged" as types, like the uniform cuts of beef wrapped for delivery at the end of *Meat*. One client, for instance, wants an "all-American apple pie" girl for a network pilot on models entitled *All Those Beautiful Girls*. Such categories are the fashion equivalents of the "light heifferettes" and "tri-tips" of meat packing. Sometimes the process changes the models to the extent that, like the animals that enter the packing plant, one can hardly recognize the final product. "What happened to the girl who came in here?" a photographer asks a model after she has had her makeup applied.

As well, the models are frequently treated as sexual objects—as "meat." Thus the photo sessions themselves are full of sexual overtones, both in the posing of the models and in the way photographers and models relate. In the shoot with Romeo (the name itself telling), the female photographer provides a continuous monologue of encouragement rife with sexual innuendo ("So tight. Oh, that's real nice," she purrs), somewhat a reversal of the famous scene with David Hemmings and Verushka in Antonioni's *Blow-Up* (1966). In *The Store* a female customer being photographed in a similarly flirtatious way reveals the extent to which the sexual enticement of fashion imagery has infiltrated the less exotic world of commercial portrait photography. What Wilson Bryan Key had called "subliminal seduction" has now become rather overt.

In *Model,* Wiseman echoes this treatment of the models as images in several ways. First, he initially shows them in the form of magazine cover photos on the wall of the agency before filming them directly. During the interviews, their "actual presence" is intercut with images of them from their portfolios (see p. 190). The camera frequently fragments the models' bodies, just as Apollonia's legs are used to construct a geometrical pattern described as "a peacock effect." When they apply makeup, for example, only parts of their bodies are shown. In one big close-up, lotion is applied to a model's neck, the tight framing accenting its gentle curves, like an abstract sculpture. As images, the models are not whole bodies, they possess no interior meaning, but rather function as cultural signifiers, forms on which we drape the fabric of our dreams. Hence gesture, so important in films like *Essene* and *Deaf and Blind* (in all of Wiseman's other films gesture serves as a sign of personal expression), is reduced merely to posture in *Model*. The models' poses, as in the case of Romeo, are frequently quite unnatural, remote from authentic body language.

In *The Store*, Wiseman continues this theme in his ironic use of mannequins. Everywhere there are store dummies—like the zombies that congregate at the shopping mall in George Romero's *Dawn of the Dead* (1978). The conceit constitutes one of the film's several on-going jokes, seen everywhere from the sales floor to a basement store room to the sewing room. At several points Wiseman presents brief shots of sales staff or customers in stationary positions, mannequins also visible in the frame, so that we are momentarily puzzled as to which of these bodies is "real." In one quick shot, for example, we are unsure whether we are seeing a person touching a ceiling or a mannequin in a pose. In another shot a man walks from the center toward the left of the frame, and the mirror that divides the image, not immediately noticeable to the viewer, "splits" him so that his reflected image walks in the opposite direction. In this very way the desire for consumer goods created by advertising pulls at us, making us discontent with ourselves. In this shot, it is difficult to determine which is the real man and which the image. In the film, as in postmodern culture, sometimes we are not really sure. *The Store*, along with *Meat* and *Model*, form a trilogy that explores how we have achieved for ourselves "the packaged soul" that Vance Packard predicted back in 1957.[18]

Both *Model* and *The Store* feature many close-ups of faces and hands with makeup and nail polish, images of masks rather than authentic selves, faces to meet the faces that they meet. Indeed, Wiseman devotes considerable time to stripping away the seductive appeal of advertising imagery by revealing the processes of its creation. In contrast to the world of Zoli's, where a prospective model's portfolio is tautologically assessed as being good "because it works," Wiseman shows us how these images work to be good. Like the scene in *Not a Love Story* (Bonnie Sherr Klein, 1981) where nude photographer Suze Randall carefully poses stripper Linda Lee Tracey and adds a few drops of "pussy juice" to her vulva, in *Model*'s photo sessions we repeatedly see how carefully advertising imagery composes desire. The thirty-second Evan Picone pantyhose commercial takes almost twenty-five minutes of screen time, showing how tedious and meticulous the work involved in making images appear natural and spontaneous actually is. During the exterior shots for the ad, the soundtrack is invaded by the loud noise of nearby construction work, a comment on the fact that what we are seeing is the construction of an image.

Model and *The Store* are political, like *Canal Zone* and *Sinai Field Mission,* in that they show how politics is reduced by the culture industry to nothing more than image and style. Politics becomes merely one of many possible "styles" from which models may choose or, as one photographer notes, only a phase one goes through. As John Berger writes, in the world of advertising and consumer culture, politics is drained of political content.[19] During one photo session in *Model,* a woman and girl pose on bicycles with a picture of Mao Tse-Tung hanging on the wall behind them, merely another part of the set's bric-a-brac. And the vice-president of Neiman-Marcus, in all seriousness, equates the importance of one's first experience inside the store with the day Kennedy was assassinated. The implications of the "Lindsay Style" cover of *Life* in *Hospital* and Governor Vanderhoof's superficial campaigning in *Meat* here reach their inevitable conclusion in the media saturation of the global village.

In the fantasy world of advertising, politics is superfluous since, as McLuhan notes, it offers a utopian vision that "aims at the goal of a programmed harmony among all human impulses and aspirations and endeavors."[20] So in *Model,* interestingly, unlike most of Wiseman's other films, there appears to be no gender or racial discrimination. Of course the images of the ads tend to feature women in visually inferior ways—*"men act* and *women appear,"* writes Berger[21]—but in the production of these ads it is also true that both sexes are reduced to observed object, to image. At one point we watch what at first seems to be a feminist demonstration, with women shouting and carrying placards. Then an offscreen voice is heard giving directions, telling the women to look happy rather than angry, and we realize that this is not an actual demonstration, not another of the film's many candid street shots, but a set-up for a commercial. The same is true of racial issues. In the film, black and white men and women pose together (although all of the photographers shown are white), and both races are featured on the covers of fashion magazines. So when we briefly see

(*Model*) The feminist demonstration as simulacrum reveals advertising's recuperation of politics.

a street demonstration by the National Black Human Rights Co-
alition, we are forced to wonder whether this is another case of advertising co-optation or the real thing. Significantly, the film
never tells us.

It is no coincidence that Andy Warhol makes (appropriately) a
"cameo appearance" in *Model,* being interviewed for a documentary on modeling. His own work in pop art has demonstrated that
in contemporary media culture, everything is image. Brillo soap
pads and Campbell's Soup cans are no different from images of
Marilyn Monroe or Liz Taylor once they became "stars." In a staff
meeting in *The Store* about the new baked goods department, what
is stressed is not the food itself, but the right image, "an international European attitude food shop." One of the models being
filmed in the same segment of the documentary with Warhol says,
"I didn't shave today because . . . maybe they want real." Reality
itself becomes another possible image, like the Middle Eastern
belly dancer in *Sinai Field Mission.*

Everyone, in fact, is now a spectacle for visual consumption. In
addition to the models leaning against the wall like mannequins or

living sculptures in *Model*, there are roving models who roam through Neiman-Marcus in *The Store* advertising sales in other departments. In one shot in the film, notes Armstrong, "a young black man dances, transistor radio in hand, in front of a department store window, a star watching himself in his own movie."[22] There are also people dressed as chickens, elves, and clowns—their clothes just slightly more obvious as costumes than those of the customers and salesclerks. The giant chicken who delivers Margaret Murphy's birthday message ("Margaret Murphy, come on down") was likely hired by her co-workers, who make it, like the singing telegram from Mona to Robert in *Model*, a public spectacle despite her obvious embarrassment. However, Wiseman's method makes us question the status of profilmic events in the culture of the simulacrum.

Hence the importance in these films of the fashion show. *Model* is, in a sense, a two-hour fashion show, and fashion shows happen elsewhere in *The Store*, as well as in *Canal Zone*. During his fashion presentation in *The Store*, the vice-president defines style as "the perfection of a point of view," which is, in turn, "what society is saying we should look like, live like, act like, be like, what we're trying to be." The film concludes with a lengthy, giddy display of new dresses, the excess of which rivals the Ecclesiastical Fashion Show in Fellini's *Roma* (1971). One reviewer describes it as a parade of "caucasian models, Watusi-tall and anorexic, their lips stung closed, as if they'd been eating alum, slouch[ing] past like Bryn Mawr girls."[23] Here all is beautiful, an ethereal display of the ideal; no one has a "leg problem," like the unfortunate girls in the fashion arts class in *High School*. The superficiality of the spectacle is reinforced by the balloons that float into and almost fill the screen, like the "gems" that pile up in the famous credit sequence of Sirk's *Imitation of Life* (1958). The musical accompaniment provides an ironic commentary: "Who Could Ask For Anything More?" is a rhetorical question in advertising's proffered world of plenitude.

In her analysis of advertising and consumerism, Judith Williamson observes that people and goods become interchangeable (both Warren Beatty and Avon are "looks"), and that products come to replace feelings rather than simply to signify them.[24] So in *The Store*, emotions are attributed to the goods (as in *Missile*, where weapons are said to have "life" and to "recognize" launch commands). We hear, for instance, of "intimate apparel" and "the Romance bra." According to the jewelry salesman, a setting with too much gold is said to take "a little bit of life away from the diamond." At the same time, people themselves become products, just as Neiman-Marcus as an institution, including its employees, becomes a product to be sold. The store's appeal is built largely on its cultivated image as an elite retail establishment, an image that employees, like customers, are constantly sold. In *Model* aspiring models are encouraged to fill their portfolios with "lots of smiles"; in *The Store* salesclerks begin their day by exercising their smile muscles—part of the store's image. During a buyer's meeting, employees are told how wonderful they must be to work there ("If you're with Neiman-Marcus, there's got to be something really incredibly special about you"). So, too, at the film's concluding reception for Stanley Marcus, Lady Bird Johnson and Art Buchwald sit at the head table, their "special" presences functioning as signs attesting to the power and geniality of Mr. Marcus himself. And just as Neiman-Marcus sells itself to its employees, so the store's employees sell themselves to Neiman-Marcus. In her interview for an executive position, the hopeful salesclerk Sabrina tells the personnel director both how wonderful the company is and how much she deserves the promotion. Sabrina offers a seemingly well-rehearsed sales pitch for herself, a perfect demonstration of Williamson's claim that "one of the most alienating aspects of advertising and consumerism [is that] we are both product and consumer; we consume, buy the product, yet we *are* the product."[25]

Exploring in a visual medium the cultural construction of visual images (in a sense, advertising is also a "natural history of the way we live"), Wiseman also logically deconstructs his own work in *Model* and *The Store* through a consistent self-reflexivity. These are Wiseman's most overtly Brechtian films, and like Godard, in them he is more interested in the illusion of reality than in the reality of the illusion. In this sense, the title of *Model* expresses a significant double entendre, suggesting not only the film's ostensible subject but also a blueprint for a kind of documentary cinema that seeks to situate itself outside the dominant tradition of unproblematic observational empiricism.

(*Model*) Devices of production are layed bare during the making of the Toyota commercial.

Most obviously, *Model* is filled with cameras, more so than any of Wiseman's other films (most of which contain someone with a camera). The ubiquitous presence of cameras, light reflectors, boom mikes, and other cinematographic and photographic equipment in the film makes the viewer aware of the apparatus and methods of its own production. There are numerous fashion photo sessions, a tourist taking pictures of the production of a commercial, and the documentary being shot with Warhol and the two male models. Another of the film's self-reflexive strategies is to present images within images, as in the opening montage of magazine cover photos. All of the prospective models' portfolio shots are shown as images, their edges clearly visible rather than filling the entire frame. Similarly, in the improvised busstop seduction scene for the Brut commercial, we see auditions both "live" and on a video monitor, the difference inviting us to compare the two kinds of images.

If Wiseman's own film, like advertising and all other films, is a construction, then what we are seeing is of course not an objective

(*Model*) The models are first shown as images, emphasizing the constructed quality of advertising imagery.

document but a personal statement. *Model*, like any documentary, is a thesis, one of many possible films ("one's man's truth," as Leacock puts it or, in Wiseman's terms, a "report on what I've found"). The film acknowledges itself as a subjectively constructed text in the opening shots of a band in the city square playing a version of "Strike Up the Band" (a reference to *Titicut Follies*, which begins with the same song). The inclusion of the song functions like a signature, announcing the filmmaker's own shaping presence, just as, in a more humorous vein, Wiseman does the same thing in *The Store* by including some Christmas carolers in Neiman-Marcus singing "Wise men, Wise men."

Wiseman exposes the artifice common to all visual images yet seeks to distinguish his practice from both the illusionist mode of advertising and the claimed objectivity in most observational film imagery. As Armstrong notes, "Wiseman uses his own camera differently in *Model*, not to conceal but to reveal."[26] For example, when some of the aspiring models are told in their interviews that their portfolios look good and that Zoli will take a look, they attempt to respond "professionally," which is to say, without excessive enthusiasm. Wiseman's camera captures the smiles that beam from their photos but which they now try to repress in the corners of their mouths. More significantly, just as Wiseman includes shots of the production apparatus, so his frame is "wider," more inclusive, than any of the others. During the making of the Toyota advertisement, for example, we see the camera being loaded, a helicopter providing a wind effect, the shooting of several takes, and the lighting being arranged with mirrors (see p. 189). Prior to the shoot we also see the male model shaving and the female model with curlers in her hair, images that demythologize their "natural" beauty. Similarly, during the making of the documentary-within-the-documentary, Wiseman includes the interviewer's questions, which, as the models are told, will be omitted from the film's soundtrack. Most of this sequence is shot through the bathroom mirror, showing us the image of an image, although we are not aware of this until near the end. Wiseman not only shows us both the person being filmed and the person filming, but by pulling his camera back, he also reveals that the model in the shower is not nude but wearing underwear, thus dispelling the other documentary's illusion.

Similar in effect is Wiseman's use of mirrors in *The Store*. Armstrong points out how in *Model* Wiseman composes sequences in mirrors so that the viewer has to work to distinguish between "real" and "imaginary" space. This use of mirrors is particularly appropriate to a film about the construction of images for, as Berger notes, the mirror is an emblem of the body as sight/site of voyeuristic pleasure.[27] Mirrors are everywhere in *The Store,* always available so that customers can view themselves as images when they try on the products for sale. Sometimes customers are shown first as mirror reflections trying on clothes, a suggestion of the extent to which people are defined by their possessions (as in the famous opening of Max Ophuls's *Madame De . . .* [1953] where the nameless female protagonist is shown only as a mirror reflection surrounded by her feminine accessories). Other shots, as previously mentioned, are formally divided by mirrors, suggesting the alienating split in consciousness that Williamson identifies as a consequence of advertising's activation of desire. In some of the exterior shots Wiseman films people on the street in such a way that both consumer goods and their own reflections are visible in

(*The Store*) The frequent use of mirrors problematizes the distinction between image and reality, reflecting the appeal of advertising.

the storefront windows. In others, we see the reflections of people going by, images of images. In one scene in the jewelry department, mirror reflections of the customer share the frame with the "real" salesperson.

By continually incorporating mirrors into his mise-en-scène, Wiseman often creates effects in *The Store* similar to those in *Model*. Part of the opening street sequence, for example, is a reflection of the street in the store window, although we do not recognize it as such until a bus pulls away in the frame. Similarly, in some of the "split screen" shots created with mirrors, it is difficult, at least initially, to determine what is reflection and what is "real." The presence of the mirrors serves as a reminder to viewers, preventing them from maintaining the imaginary relationship to the film based on what Jacques Lacan calls the mirror phase of psychic development.

Such trompe l'oeil effects are aided by Wiseman's use of black and white film stock in *Model*. The black and white cinematography, according to Wiseman, is "more abstract," "more stylized," than color, and so detracts from the images' denotative content.

Thus, in another way, the viewer is encouraged to perceive the film as a series of images. The absence of color in the film, given its subject, is something of a subversive joke, since it drains the advertising imagery of much of its visual appeal.

The Store, which is in color (it was Wiseman's first documentary in color, preceded only by the fictional *Seraphita's Diary*), works differently. The film's rich color, reminiscent of the garish, hyperreal technicolor of so many classic musicals, helps to keep the viewer aware of the appeal of the goods at Neiman-Marcus and advertising's ability to arouse our desire for them. The first words we hear in the film, "it's too orange," uttered by a shopper about some makeup in the cosmetics department, signals the film's self-awareness of its color. Indeed, such lush imagery is one of the primary elements of advertising's persuasive power.

During an executive meeting the staff of Neiman-Marcus testify to this power. One executive cites the particularly effective series of stylish Chanel television commercials made by British director Ridley Scott (already a hot director with *Alien* [1979] and *Blade Runner* [1982]). With advertising, the vice-president concludes, "you can do anything" because everybody is "vulnerable" to it. The film suggests our passive receptivity to consumerism in the frequently inserted shots of people being moved by escalators, the high angle from which Wiseman usually films them as forceful a statement about the vacuity of contemporary consciousness as Standish Lawder's escalator film, *Necrology* (1970).

In his study of consumerism in popular culture, Jeffrey Shrank found that 90 percent of American adults believed themselves "personally immune" to the seductive sway of advertising, yet the same group accounted for 90 percent of the purchases of advertised products. People who believe themselves to be immune to advertising ("a group to which, no doubt, you, the reader, and I, the writer, belong," Shrank wryly adds) "will not take defensive action."[28] Wiseman's reflexive style in *Model* and *The Store* calls our ability to determine the "status" of images into question, and so we are forced to muster a "defensive action" of active attentiveness.

Wiseman frequently generates perceptual confusion as a result of the uncertainty over the ontological status of images. His methods create an ambiguity about whether some profilmic events (the two political demonstrations) and people (customers near mannequins or mirrors) are "real" or constructed images. Is the man in the street shot simply a man walking quickly, or is he a composed advertising image of "a successful man on the go" ("guy on streetcorner" or "young executive")? Is there any longer a difference? In the Brut ad sequence, the viewer does not know until after the seduction scenario that this is an audition, when Wiseman cuts to the video crew making the commercial. Because of such consistent ambiguity it is virtually impossible to view *Model* and *The Store* from a passive, unengaged position.

Several reviewers were disappointed that *Model* and *The Store* revealed nothing new about American culture.[29] But as in *Canal Zone*, Wiseman is not seeking to tell us something we do not already know. In *Sinai Field Mission* and *Canal Zone*, he presents the familiar with a penetrating look, isolating it for observation (just as the Zonians watch animals in the zoo), and thus defamiliarizing it, in Sklovskij's sense, by removing it from its "usual associations." In *Model* and *The Store*, Wiseman achieves similar ends through reflexivity, by laying bare devices, as well as by defamiliarization. His "wider view" allows us to see more than the narrowly delimited field of vision normally presented in our cultural productions. While it may not be absolutely necessary, as Jay Ruby argues, that in all cases documentary filmmakers be reflexive and self-critical for their work to be politically progressive,[30] Wiseman clearly shows in *Model* and *The Store* that in the documentation of cultural institutions such a method is of crucial importance. The films offer perfect examples of what Ruby calls an "ethnographic trompe l'oeil": "the development of filmic codes and conventions to 'frame' or contextualize the apparent realism of the cinema and cause audiences to 'read' the images as anthropological articulation."[31] All four films examine not only their subjects and their relation to Wiseman's own cinema as a signifying practice but also provide a further understanding of American culture. Wiseman continues to strip our masks from us, even as he concentrates on showing how artfully they are arranged.

NOTES

1. Roland Barthes, *Mythologies*, trans. Annette Lavers (New York: Hill and Wang, 1977), esp. pp. 142–43, 151.

2. Paul Theroux, *The Old Patagonian Express* (New York: Pocket Books, 1980), p. 263.

3. James Wolcott, "Television and Its Discontents: Wiseman's Panamania," *Village Voice*, October 10, 1977, p. 45.

4. Theroux, *The Old Patagonian Express,* p. 242.

5. Ibid., pp. 242–43.

6. Wolcott, "Wiseman's Panamania," p. 45.

7. Louise Sweet, *"Canal Zone," Sight and Sound* 47, no. 1 (Winter 1977–78): 59.

8. Frank Rich, "A Sunny, Nightmare Vision," *Time,* October 10, 1977, p. 103.

9. Peter Sourian, "Television," *The Nation,* October 15, 1977, p. 381.

10. Glenn Rifkin, "Wiseman Looks at Affluent Texans," *New York Times,* December 11, 1983, p. 37.

11. John Berger, *Ways of Seeing* (London: BBC/Penguin, 1972), p. 131.

12. James Wolcott, "Adrift in Cheekbone Heaven," *Village Voice,* September 16, 1981, p. 67.

13. Berger, *Ways of Seeing,* pp. 129–30.

14. Robert Herrick, "Delight in Disorder," in *The Poems of Robert Herrick* (London and New York: Oxford University Press, 1951), p. 29.

15. Nathaniel Hawthorne, "The Artist of the Beautiful," in *Nathaniel Hawthorne: Selected Tales and Sketches,* ed. Hyatt H. Waggoner (New York: Holt, Rinehart and Winston, 1970).

16. Dan Armstrong, "Wiseman's *Model* and the Documentary Project," p. 5.

17. Armstrong, "Wiseman's *Model*," p. 5; Wolcott, "Adrift in Cheekbone Heaven," p. 67.

18. Vance Packard, *The Hidden Persuaders* (New York: Pocket Books, 1958), chap. 21.

19. Berger, *Ways of Seeing,* p. 149.

20. McLuhan, *Understanding Media,* p. 202.

21. Berger, *Ways of Seeing,* p. 47 (emphasis in the original).

22. Armstrong, "Wiseman's *Model*," p. 6.

23. Mary-Lou Weisman, "Neiman-Marcus, The Movie," *New Republic,* December 31, 1983, p. 26.

24. Judith Williamson, *Decoding Advertisements: Ideology and Meaning in Advertising* (London and Boston: Marion Boyars, 1978), pt. 1.

25. Ibid., p. 70.

26. Armstrong, "Wiseman's *Model*," p. 7.

27. Ibid., p. 8; Berger, *Ways of Seeing,* p. 51.

28. Jeffrey Shrank, *Snap, Crackle, and Popular Taste: The Illusion of Free Choice in America* (New York: Delta, 1977), pp. 84–85.

29. John Corry, "TV: *The Store,* a Wiseman Film," *New York Times,* December 14, 1983, p. C34; Karen Rosenberg, "Television: *The Store," The Nation,* December 17, 1983, pp. 642–43; Wolcott, "Adrift in Cheekbone Heaven," p. 67.

30. Jay Ruby, "The Image Mirrored: Reflexivity and the Documentary Film," *Journal of the University Film Association* 29, no. 1 (Fall 1977): 3.

31. Jay Ruby, "Ethnography as *Trompe L'Oeil:* Film and Anthropology," in *A Crack in the Mirror: Perspectives in Anthropology* (Philadelphia: University of Pennsylvania Press, 1982). p. 129.

CHAPTER 7

The Bad and the Beautiful

The Cool World (1963) • *Seraphita's Diary* (1982)

Because Wiseman's documentaries are informed by elements of narrative cinema, no study of his art would be complete without at least a brief consideration of his work in fiction film. Wiseman has insisted that documentary films can be as complex as good novels, and, of course, his telling description of his work as "reality fictions" emphasizes the fictional aspects of their aesthetic construction. "My real interest is in trying to make good movies," he has stated.[1] In interviews Wiseman has often spoken of his wish to make a fiction feature using documentary techniques, citing Pontecorvo's *The Battle of Algiers* as a model.[2] He explains his interest in using documentary techniques in fiction as motivated largely by his view that a documentary "look" invests fiction with greater credibility and social impact, as in the case of Peter Watkins' films. Indeed, Pontecorvo's film has often been mistakenly perceived as a documentary because of its style, even though the film begins with credits and the claim: "Not one foot of newsreel has been used in this reenactment of the battle of Algiers."

Over the years it has been announced periodically that Wiseman has been working on fiction projects. In 1970 an interviewer reported that Wiseman was then at work on a script, to be produced in Hollywood, which the filmmaker described as "an adaptation of a novel about a young man who goes AWOL from the army."[3] In the same year Wiseman told another interviewer that he was writing a script with a grant from the American Film Institute wherein he wanted to use a documentary approach but also employ "a mosaic technique so the film will not have the conventional story line with beginning, middle and end, but will reveal the relationships of the characters to each other."[4] Four years later, on the day after the WNET screening of *Primate*, the *New York Times* reported that Wiseman was preparing to make a fiction film tentatively titled *Yes Yes, No No*. The article quotes Wiseman as saying that he has been working on the script intermittently for two years, and that the story is "a contemporary murder-and-trial drama set in Boston."[5] Benson and Anderson report that Wiseman worked as co-writer on Norman Jewison's *The Thomas Crown Affair* (1968),[6] and he also wrote an early draft of the successful 1980 feature, *The Stunt Man* (directed by Richard Rush), but was uncredited. (Although the final film, according to Wiseman, bears little relation to what he had written, it is tempting to speculate about the connections between *The Stunt Man*'s playful examination of Hollywood illusionism and Wiseman's exposure of the photographic apparatus in *Model*, released the same year. But Wiseman's disclaimer about the relation of the final film to his initial concept and the unavailability of his early screenplay unfortunately prevent one from doing so with any degree of certainty.)

However, the two fiction films Wiseman has produced, despite their separation by almost twenty years, reveal intriguing connections to Wiseman's documentary work. At first glance the two films seem distinctly different. *The Cool World* is an admirable work of gritty social realism, shot on location in black and white, and largely improvised. *Seraphita's Diary*, by contrast, is an experimental drama, carefully constructed in the manner of an interior monologue and photographed almost entirely in an enclosed interior space in bright color. Despite these differences, the two films share a concern with institutional ideology, and although they approach the theme in strikingly different ways, they both demonstrate an interesting use of first person narration and reveal a tension between documentary and fictional material.

In 1960 Wiseman purchased the film rights to Warren Miller's 1959 novel of Harlem gang life, *The Cool World*, for five hundred dollars.[7] He invited New York filmmaker Shirley Clarke, whom he had met as an investor in her previous film, *The Connection* (1960), to direct it, thinking that he lacked the necessary experience to do so himself. Clarke not only directed the film, but also wrote the screenplay in collaboration with Carl Lee, who played Cowboy in both the film and the stage version of *The Connection*. *The Cool World* was completed in time to be shown at the 1963 Venice Film Festival (along with the official American entry, Martin Ritt's *Hud*), where it received generally favorable response as a powerful socially conscious film. Since then, however, the film has been unfairly neglected, both in histories of black American film and in discussions of Wiseman's cinema. Although *The Cool World* precedes *Titicut Follies* by five years, it may be seen to have much in common with Wiseman's subsequent documentary practice.

The film maintains an uneasy but fascinating relationship to Hollywood cinema in its mixture of narrative and documentary elements. This is in large part a result of its use of the conventions of popular cinema, a method, as we have seen, Wiseman frequently employs in his documentaries. In interviews Wiseman has stated his dislike of Hollywood fantasies and the failure of Hollywood movies to confront real social issues.[8] The author of *The Cool World*, Warren Miller, is white but makes a sincere attempt to get at the conditions of inner city ghetto life without condescension. Interestingly, as early as 1949 Miller himself was championing the documentary approach over Hollywood illusionism in films.[9] The book and the film clearly attempt to show some of the problems of contemporary American urban life and, given Wiseman's early optimism about film as an agent for social change, seems a logical choice for Wiseman's first involvement in film.

The story concerns fourteen-year-old black youth Duke Custis (Hampton Clanton) and his struggle to survive in the hostile and violent ghetto environment of Harlem one summer. A member of a street gang named the Royal Pythons, Duke assumes leadership of the gang when the previous president, Blood (Clarence Williams), becomes a junky. He begins to establish a relationship with Luanne (Yolanda Rodriquez), a whore who has taken up residence in the Pythons' apartment. Much of the story concerns Duke's ongoing attempts to raise fifty dollars to buy a gun from Priest (Lee), a local gangster, so that he can make a "rep" for himself during the coming rumble with a rival gang, the Wolves. The gang fight, followed by Duke's arrest, provides *The Cool World's* strong climax.

The film is generally faithful to the novel's narrative and style—indeed, much of the dialogue is retained verbatim—although there are some minor changes in the plot. The book is narrated by Duke in dialect, in the tradition of Mark Twain's *Adventures of Huckleberry Finn,* although a closer parallel is Anthony Burgess's *A Clockwork Orange,* published only three years later.

Duke's story occurred in the past (made apparent by remarks like "but at this time I tellin you about")[10] and is being recounted in some present but as yet unexplained situation. The reader cannot help but wonder about the circumstances of the narration and who it is addressing. Only at the end of the novel, in the final two-page chapter entitled "Where I Am," is it revealed that Duke has been sent to reform school where he is being successfully rehabilitated, and that, in the narrative's present, he has recounted these events to a therapist, Doc Levine. This hardened boy from the violent ghetto, as we discover in the book's only serious lapse into sentimentality, is learning to read and write and now even enjoys tending the institution's flower beds. (*A Clockwork Orange* provides an ironic echo of this ending in the last sentence of the penultimate chapter, Alex's declaration that "I was cured all right.")[11] Immediately before this comforting conclusion, Duke is hauled away by police after the rumble with the Wolves.

The film, however, wisely ends with Duke's arrest, the patrol car whisking him off into the Harlem night. This ending is clearly more appropriate to the tone of both novel and film. It also justifies the cinema's tendency to narrate in the present tense, since there is nothing in the movie to suggest that this story has been, as it were, recollected in tranquility. Also, in refusing to provide narrative closure, the film does not pretend to resolve the problems of poverty, racism, and juvenile delinquency, anticipating the way Wiseman's documentaries frequently end by presenting the viewer either directly or implicitly with unresolved questions and issues.

In its choice of subject *The Cool World* may be seen to have developed from the postwar movies of Hollywood directors like Elia Kazan who, inspired by Italian neorealism, looked at urban and working class milieus. In particular it recalls Sidney Meyers' independent film *The Quiet One* (1948), also a fictional account of a troubled black youth shot on location in Harlem. Stylistically, though, *The Cool World* resembles observational cinema more than it does the classic narrative style. Rather than effacing its pres-

ence, the camera frequently calls attention to itself by its unortho-
dox (direct style) movement, especially in some dialogue scenes
done with a panning camera rather than conventional shot/reac-
tion shot figures. In one shot the camera follows the boys onto a
school bus, the lens aperture adjusting for the extreme difference
in available light (reminiscent of the famous shot following JFK in
Primary). The film was photographed by Baird Bryant entirely on
location in Harlem, often with available lighting, a hand-held
camera, muddy sound, and (with the exception of Carl Lee and
Clarence Williams) nonprofessional actors. (Gloria Foster, who
played Duke's mother, starred the following year in Michael
Roemer and Robert Young's independent production, *Nothing But
a Man* [1964]). According to Wiseman, none of the kids in the film
had any prior professional acting experience.[12] Clarke's method
of directing the actors was to outline a scene, and then allow them
to improvise.[13] There is, consequently, a strong emphasis on the
authenticity of the dialogue, an attempt to duplicate the slang
and rhythms of black urban speech. (The only false note is the
consistent use of the word "motherin' " as a euphemism for swear-
ing.) Lee is listed in the credits for dialogue (according to Lauren
Rabinovitz, he was denied credit as co-director),[14] a clear ac-
knowledgement of the importance given to language in the film.
Even though a few sequences seem to have been postsynced, in
its use of improvised street talk, of *parole* rather than *langue*,
the film recalls Louis Marcorelles's claim about the centrality of
real speech in direct cinema,[15] a dominant feature of Wiseman's
documentaries.

The Cool World also makes use of found symbolism, an expressive device of observational cinema that Wiseman uses so well in
his documentary work. Once when Duke leaves his tenement, for
example, there follows a shot of a dog trotting freely in a street—a
clear metaphor of Duke's "unleashed," rebellious personality. Several signs in the film resonate with meaning, like the cinema marquee glimpsed while Duke sells reefers on the street. The marquee
reads "Adventures of a Angry Young Man," a gramatically incorrect abbreviation for Ritt's *Hemingway's Adventures of a Young Man*
(1962). The mistake is consistent with the ungrammatical speech
of Duke and his friends as well as an appropriate description of his
own story. When Duke and Luanne go to Coney Island, we see a

"Lost Children" sign (like the "Missing Children" sign in *Deaf*, about another group of marginalized youths) just before Luanne disappears. The sign, of course, serves as narrative foreshadowing, but also as editorial comment; in a sense both youths are "lost" even before Luanne literally exits from the narrative.

Much of the credit for the film's authenticity must, of course, be given to director Shirley Clarke, and its style is clearly influenced by her as well. Clarke's work has been consistently informed by a documentary approach (although more recently she has spent much of her time working in experimental video). She had been involved with a number of D. A. Pennebaker's early films, frequently as editor (*Brussels Film Loops*, 1958; *Opening Night in Moscow*, 1959), sometimes as camera operator (*Breaking It Up at the Museum*, 1960). Some of Clarke's own early shorts, *In Paris Parks* (1954), *Bridges-Go-Round* (1958), and *Skyscraper* (1959, on which Willard Van Dyke and Irving Jacoby, as well as Pennebaker, worked), are variations of the city symphony form of documentary. *The Connection*, her first feature, employs a mock cinema verité style; she even includes as characters the two-man documentary film crew supposedly filming the action. *Portrait of Jason* (1967), a two-hour monologue with a frustrated actor, is in its sparse "purity" of technique considered a classic of American cinema verité.

The use of music in *The Cool World* (both the diegetic rhythm and blues and the Mal Waldron score), while as important as the use of found music in Wiseman's documentaries, is probably closer in spirit to Clarke's interest in jazz. *Skyscraper* features a score by jazz composer and arranger Teo Macero; the music for *The Connection* was provided by jazz pianist Freddie Redd; and her most recent feature, *Ornette . . . Made in America* [1978], is an experimental documentary about jazz alto sax innovator Ornette Coleman. Most of the early shorts make use of rapid editing. As Clarke told Rabinovitz in an extensive interview conducted in 1981, there had been no sound, "and the one thing we couldn't do was jazz. So I made them all jazz."[16]

Reviewing *The Cool World* upon its initial release, Andrew Sarris acknowledged its sincerity but disliked Clarke's peripatetic camera, which he described as "visual hysteria blotting out intellectual contemplation." Similarly, both Gordon Hitchens and Dwight MacDonald faulted Clarke for her seemingly uncomfortable combination of fictional and documentary techniques.[17] But rather than being superfluous, the observational style is in fact quite appropriate. First, as suggested above, this style signals an opposition to the smooth flow of the classic Hollywood film, just as the subject is one generally avoided in commercial American cinema (certainly in the early 1960s). Second, it successfully captures the subjective perspective of the narrator, Duke. The film periodically allows us to hear Duke's thoughts (but no one else's) on the soundtrack, clearly marking the film's narration, like that of the novel, as first person. When Duke says, "I gotta keep movin'," the camera visually expresses his feeling; when he scrambles down the street after discovering Priest's body in the Pythons' clubhouse, the restless camera and swish pans visually capture his sudden panic.

The film and the novel emphasize that Duke is not an inexplicable social aberration but that his sensibility is to a large extent shaped by his environment. Hence the network of references to popular culture, and the film's use of genre conventions in particular. Duke's street name, of course, is itself inspired by the iconographical individualist hero established by John Wayne, largely in his western roles. The gun Duke wants to obtain is a Colt, a weapon of central importance to the western genre. (In the book one gangmember identifies the Colt as the firearm used at "Cussers Last Stan." Also, Duke explains at length his admiration for the western hero of a movie he had seen entitled *The Baron of New Mexico,* probably misremembering Samuel Fuller's *The Baron of Arizona* [1949].) When Duke and Luanne go to Coney Island, he has a mock shootout with a mechanical gunfighter in an arcade; the machine's prerecorded voice echoes the word "draw" six times on the soundtrack, an expressionist use of sound that emphasizes the importance of western myth to Duke. For him, as for several of the people in Wiseman's documentaries (the acting coach in *Model,* the officer introducing the training films in *Basic Training*), the perception of reality is informed to a significant extent by popular cinema.

"Stand up and shoot like a man," reads a sign on the mechanical gunslinger. Duke's obsession with being a "man," as he understands it, connects with Wiseman's exploration of gender definition, particularly aggressive masculinity (seen most emphatically in *High School* and *Basic Training*). Duke's fantasy of what people

(*The Cool World*): Genre iconography is invoked throughout the film, in Priest's gangster costume (Carl Lee, left) . . .

will say about him—"There goes Duke Custis. He's a cold killer"— is explicitly echoed by Howard Gilbert, the young black man arrested in *Law and Order,* who boasts "I'm a killer." The pervasive presence of guns in American society and their totemic appeal is also seen in *Juvenile Court* and even *Deaf,* where the children are fascinated more by the deputy's gun than anything else when they visit the county judicial building. Duke's overpowering desire to possess the gun is for him a way of defining his manhood. His thoughts about the Colt, "all black and oiled, just waiting to go," is infused with phallic aggression: "Man, a piece is the key. It's a screwdriver. You get yourself a piece, why, then, everything opens up for you." The close-up of Miss Dewpont's purse with the gun in it visually expresses the sexual potency the youth associates with the weapon.

Priest's black suit and white tie constitute familiar attire in the gangster film. His white moll, Miss Dewpont (Marilyn Cox), is a stock character of the genre. Hardy (Claude Cave), the black youth who plans to escape the neighborhood by playing basketball at an Ivy League college, and Douglas, Blood's freedom-rider

. . . and in the "showdown" between Duke (Hampton Clampton) and the mechanical gunfighter. Luanne (Yolanda Rodriguez) looks on.

brother, are like the gangster film "Pat O'Brien" figure—representing "ballots not bullets." Blood's high-pitched, nervous laughter clearly recalls Richard Widmark's Tommy Udo in *Kiss of Death* (Henry Hathaway, 1947). The shot of one of the Pythons leaving the gang's apartment and pausing at the entrance of the tenement building, shrugging his shoulders, and then being flanked by fellow gangmembers before descending the steps, is strikingly reminiscent of James Cagney's trademark body language in *Public Enemy* (William Wellman, 1931) and other gangster movies, employing the genre's conventional triangular deployment of gangsters within the frame. Duke's fantasy of acquiring the gun and being "at the top of the heap" recapitulates the desire of virtually every American movie gangster (particularly as depicted in the famous conclusion of Raoul Walsh's *White Heat* [1949], when Cagney yells out "Top of the World, Ma," before immolating himself atop a huge gas tank). The overly stylized and choreographed scene in which the Wolves intimidate Hardy in the schoolyard recalls *West Side Story* (Robert Wise, 1961), while the later fight there on the jungle gym (a sly metaphor) appears to prefigure the stylized combat in *The Warriors* (Walter Hill, 1979). (Clarke had been a dancer and choreographer before becoming a filmmaker, and was heavily influenced by the dance films of Maya Deren).

Most of these references allude to dominant, white popular culture. In Richard Wright's novel *Native Son* (1940), when the impressionable and confused black youth Bigger Thomas goes to the movies, he sees lobby cards advertising two films: "One, *The Gay Woman,* was pictured on the posters in images of white men and white women lolling on beaches, swimming, and dancing in night clubs; the other, *Trader Horn,* was shown on the posters in terms of black men and black women dancing against a wild background of barbaric jungle."[18] Bigger, like Duke, is overwhelmed by the dominant white culture around him, presenting impossible alternatives as role models. On the one hand, he is offered a lifestyle of the rich and famous that he can never attain, and on the other, a debasing racist stereotype. In *The Cool World,* black popular culture emerges only occasionally, as when gospel music plays or we see a poster advertising a James Brown show at the Apollo Theatre. By contrast, white popular culture appears everywhere (as it does in *Canal Zone*), in the smiling face of a white woman on a large Canada Dry billboard, in the Mr. Freezee caricature, in the white doll held by black hands in one of the street shots. Duke, like Bigger, is attracted to but excluded from the fantasies of white culture, and both express their rage at cultural marginalization through violence.

In his influential 1962 article, "Notes on the New American Cinema," Jonas Mekas explicitly sets the work of several independent filmmakers, including Clarke, against the " 'official' (Hollywood) cinema."[19] *The Cool World* sets itself apart by the unusual observational context in which it deploys genre conventions, a split that embodies aesthetically what W. E. B. Du Bois referred to as the "twoness" of the black American experience.[20] This twoness, as Addison Gayle points out, was necessarily reflected in artistic production: "The black artist of the past worked with the white public in mind. The guidelines by which he measured his production was its acceptance or rejection by white people."[21] Further, according to Henry Louis Gates, Jr., black writing is marked by a revision of—or "signifying" upon—texts in the Western tradition. It is precisely in this play upon white texts, he argues, that black texts articulate their difference.[22] *The Cool World,* with its stylistic mix, is, like black writing and jazz, what Gates would call a "mulatto text." Thus, what Sarris sees as Clarke's inability to blend "the materials of stylized melodrama into the network of realistic cross-references"[23] is actually a tension essential to the film's "counter-cinema" strategy and meaning.

Racial tensions surface throughout the narrative of *The Cool World,* beginning immediately in the opening scene with a Black Muslim's speech on the street about the white man being the devil. The accompanying montage of street shots shows that the only whites to be seen in the neighborhood are cops; there is no doubt as to who wields institutionalized power here. (When the police arrest Duke at the end, they grab him saying, "Get up, you little black bastard.") The glaring presence of Miss Dewpont, the only important white character in the film, and Priest's abusive treatment of her are inevitably charged with racial implications. As in *Law and Order, Primate, Welfare,* and other Wiseman documentaries, race is a burning issue informing all social relations.

Just as the film acknowledges a cultural split between black and mainstream America, so it emphasizes the physical separateness of Harlem (as the American community is isolated from the rest of Panama in *Canal Zone*). This sense of the ghetto as an oppressive, enclosed space is immediately established in the opening montage of Harlem street life. Other montage sequences, remarkably similar to Wiseman's street shots in his documentaries, appear regularly throughout the film. They frequently separate major sequences in the narrative, as they often do the major parts, what Nichols calls the "tesserae," of Wiseman's mosaics. The tracking shots of Harlem streets with their rows of tenement houses near the beginning of the film is strikingly similar to the openings of *High School* and *Law and Order,* early Wiseman documentaries separated from *The Cool World* by only a few years. The physically and emotionally sick people who endlessly file into New York's Metropolitan Hospital in *Hospital* might very well come from this neighborhood; the woman who has her purse snatched by Duke is, in a sense, the woman who is the victim of the same crime in *Law and Order.* The film's treatment of Harlem as both a distinct physical space and *weltanshauung* invites one to view the ghetto itself as an institution, the way institutions in Wiseman's later films become

defined as much by constraints of ideology as by physical boundaries. Wiseman himself has made the connection, noting that "a
hospital or a high school is as much a ghetto as central Harlem."[24]

The film not only explores life in the urban ghetto as a distinct
world but establishes at the outset that this environment exists in
the context of, adjacent to, affluent America and capitalism. The
poverty of Harlem—Harrington's "Other America," as mentioned in *High School*—starkly contrasts with but is not inseparable
from Wall Street or Central Park South, the route the school bus
takes downtown. In a sense, Harlem is revealed as a gap between
American ideology and its practice. References to business, profit,
and purchasing power recur throughout the film. Priest, a gangster *cum* entrepreneur, like the Canal Zone Company refuses to do
business on credit. As Duke is taken away in the patrol car at the
end of the film, we hear a radio news broadcast; a report of gang
warfare in Harlem comes between items about "a communist
stronghold" (presumably in Southeast Asia) and lobbying to require the first astronauts on the moon to plant an American flag.
Duke's fate is sandwiched between the forces of American capitalist imperialism, like that of the Panamanians in *Canal Zone*.

The first major sequence of *The Cool World*, the school trip
downtown, deserves particular mention in this context because it
is crucial to the film and also suggestive in the context of Wiseman's documentary work. In her review of the film, Harriet Polt
cited this sequence as one of its major flaws, describing it as "too
blatantly ironic" and "extraneous to the body of the film";[25] in fact,
however, quite the opposite is true. On the last day of school, before summer vacation, Duke's class is taken south by bus along
Fifth Avenue to Wall Street in lower Manhattan. Most obviously,
the trip demonstrates how very much these boys are out of place
outside of Harlem. It is much like the scene where working-class
boys are taken on a cricket trip to Mill Hill, a school for wealthy
children, in *We Are the Lambeth Boys* (Karel Reisz, 1959). ("It ain't
the Waldorf, but it'll do," says Priest's henchman, later surveying
the Pythons' apartment.) The sequence further establishes the
sense of the ghetto as a bounded space, one that the boys may
leave but from which they can never really escape. Their alienation is shown when they pause at the statue of Alexander Hamil-
ton—"standing on the very ground where George Washington,

the founder of this country, once actually was," the teacher observes—but are not the least interested or impressed. As they leave the site, the teacher reminds the boys to take a copy of a pamphlet entitled "Own a Share of America," after which there is an abrupt cut to Duke back in Harlem stealing a purse. The editing here serves as a comment on the disenfranchisement of these poor black youths (the black men in both *Basic Training* and *Welfare* who say they have no country are called to mind), and anticipates the ironic use of editing Wiseman employs in his documentaries.

Additionally, the school trip sequence, coming at the beginning of the film, brings Duke and his friends out of their element into what is probably a more familiar, less threatening environment for white viewers. As Donald Bogle notes, Harlem is a place largely unfamiliar to white viewers, even to most of the liberals among them.[26] This initial situation is then reversed; white viewers are placed in a similar position to the boys on the bus, as they are then taken on an excursion into the ghetto. David Eames observes that Wiseman himself would not be interested in a guided tour, that he prefers instead to get inside the institutions he shoots rather than perceive them from a distance.[27] Thus the appearance of the Japanese tourists with their inevitable cameras in *Meat* counterpoints Wiseman's more probing camera, just as *Canal Zone* opens with a voice-over explanation of the canal's operations by an official tour guide before it penetrates the ideology masked by the cascade of official statistics. *The Cool World* works in a similar way. The shallow tour offered to the black youths is contrasted to the film's more thorough examination, below the physical surface, through the first-person narration. The film seeks to immerse the viewer in the Harlem environment, just as Wiseman would later claim that with *Titicut Follies* he "wanted to put the audience for the film in the state hospital."[28]

Upon the film's release, Wiseman declared "I intend to make sure that *The Cool World* is not exploited as just another picture about juvenile delinquency."[29] The subject had been popular in the 1930s, in such movies as *Wild Boys of the Road* (William Wellman, 1933), *Dead End* (William Wyler, 1937), and *Angels with Dirty Faces* (Michael Curtiz, 1938), and reemerged in the postwar youth culture of the 1950s in such films as *The Wild One* (Laslo Benedek,

1954), *Blackboard Jungle* (Richard Brooks, 1955), and *Rebel without a Cause* (Nicholas Ray, 1955). But the issue was trivialized in short order by the flood of formula teen exploitation quickies released by American International Pictures, independent producers Albert Zugsmith and Sam Katzman, and *The Delicate Delinquent* (Don McGuire, 1957) with Jerry Lewis.[30] By the early 1960s Gidget and the Annette Funicello/Frankie Avalon cycle of beach movies were upon us. It is in this context that *The Cool World* stands out as a healthy antidote. Nobody is reformed by film's end, unlike, say, the Sidney Poitier character in *Blackboard Jungle*. In Hollywood it is possible that the kids in *Angels Wash Their Faces* (Ray Enright, 1939) become the likeable Bowery Boys and even go on to save America from a Fifth Column spy ring. The Royal Pythons might wash their faces, but the blackness of their skin will never come off. The honest attempt of *The Cool World* to deal with contemporary social issues in an uncompromising manner thus marks Wiseman's first attempt to analyze the gaps and contradictions of America's institutions, what becomes his ongoing documentary project.

It is possible, then, to see *The Cool World* as the first work in Wiseman's institutional series. It is not insignificant that he distributes the film along with his documentaries through his own company, Zipporah Films. However, my purpose here is not to reclaim a neglected film for classic auteurism, nor to co-opt what some might claim is an example of black film for a white filmmaker or for liberal, white criticism. Rather, such a reading foregrounds and seeks to make sense of the tensions and cracks that exist in the film on both the thematic and stylistic levels. The questions raised by the issues of genre and authorship in this collaboration of three different artists (Wiseman, Clarke and Lee; two male, one female; two white, one black) reflect the more important tensions in the film that may be understood as articulating part of the black experience in America.

Seraphita's Diary, although very different from *The Cool World* and perhaps not nearly as successful aesthetically, also works against the conventions of Hollywood movies. Indeed, its very subject is a condemnation of the cult of glamor that Hollywood both generates and thrives upon. The film begins (quite the opposite from the disclaimer in *The Battle of Algiers*) with an insert title informing us that it "is adapted from the diaries and letters of the fashion model Seraphita who disappeared under mysterious circumstances on August 12, 1980." Seraphita is a beautiful woman struggling to be recognized for herself rather than as an image of beauty. The various men in her life—the producer, the elegant Lambert, the "Banana Republic President," among others—respond to her essentially in terms of her physical pulchritude. Mr. Juice tells her that "once you are famous you are public property," like the models in *Model*, Monroe and Liz for Warhol, or Warhol for Wiseman. The photographer William even refers to her as a "thing." She gets letters from a young "fan" (comically dressed as a sports "fan" and wielding a baseball bat between his legs like a phallus) that praise her for her "perfection."

Seraphita keeps a diary, she says, because it is "somebody really to talk to." She feels trapped by her own physical beauty, dreaming of a world with no mirrors. The narrative is framed by showing an old man picking up and putting down Seraphita's diary; she never gets to speak directly, her voice remaining contained or trapped within the imagination of the implied male reader/viewer. What the viewer sees, then, is the male's image of Seraphita's discussion—perhaps the only justifiable feminist narrative construction for a male artist.

The film's most obvious connections are to *Model* and *The Store*, the two films that bracket *Seraphita's Diary* chronologically. Its star, Apollonia Van Ravenstein, is one of the models who appears in the former film (it is she who provides the legs for the pantyhose commercial's "peacock effect"). Some of the dialogue in the film alludes to or even repeats lines from *Model*. For example, Patricia's remark, "that dimple blows me away every time," is also said of the male model with "the Warren Beatty quality." In the film's tour-de-force centerpiece, the fashion photography sequence, William speaks to Seraphita with the same kind of sexually coaxing monologue used by the photographers in *Model*, and his instructions to her are, again as in *Model*, put in terms of looks ("sexy and sultry," "that wide-eyed look"). Sometimes his prompting literally duplicates the words of encouragement given to the models in the earlier film ("a little bit more bitchy," "a little bit more innocent"), and in one instance ("now wet your lips again") also recalls the scene in the photography studio in *The Store*. Dolls and mannequins are scattered throughout the film, a self-conscious visual reference to both documentaries. In one scene, Seraphita carries a doll, an appropriate embodiment of her "statuesque" beauty. (In the Picone commercial in *Model* the director more than once refers to the model as "doll.") Later, the producer speaks to the doll lying on the bed as if it were Seraphita herself. During the fashion photography sequence, the hair stylist makes up a dressmaker's dummy with no head, all the while talking to it as if to Seraphita.

As such imagery might suggest, *Seraphita's Diary* continues, although in a radically different way, the deconstructionist project of *Model* and *The Store*. Interestingly, this film, the only fiction film directed by Wiseman to date, works quite differently from either *The Cool World* or *The Battle of Algiers* (the film he often claimed would be his fictional model), for rather than seeking to encourage the suspension of disbelief, it consistently acknowledges itself as artifice. The diaries and letters are read by Apollonia, who performs all the roles, so that the viewer is denied the possibility of easy entry into the narrative through the mobilization of character "identification." And while she wears different makeup and clothes for each character, Apollonia makes no attempt to submerge her own identity within these various roles. She is clearly acting and doing so in a manner that, judged by conventional standards of realist narrative film, is rather poor. Apollonia is somewhat wooden on the screen, and her noticeable accent never entirely disappears (except perhaps when in the role of Gwendy, the superficial makeup person, who she manages to portray with deadly satiric accuracy). But what would normally be perceived as a failure in this regard is in the context of the film paradoxically an asset, for it serves to undermine the creation of what E. M. Forster calls "round" (as opposed to "flat") characters.

Indeed, it is not only the characters that are flat in the film. As in what Brian Henderson labels the "non-bourgeois" camera style of Godard's *Weekend* (1967),[31] *Seraphita's Diary* flattens out virtually every aspect of illusionist pleasure typical of the Hollywood film. With the exception of the brief narrative frame, the action (what little there is of it) is spatially restricted to a small apartment and shot with a camera that is for the most part stationary. The film is,

(*Seraphita's Diary*) Seraphita (Apollonia) "in role" as William, the photographer.

in effect, an instance of minimalist cinema. A dance, for example, is rendered essentially as an assemblage of signifiers—Apollonia's body moving rhythmically, music playing, disco lights flashing. The film makes no pretense of realism, no attempt to disguise the fact that there is no one else in the "discotheque." Later, imagining herself in a scenario inspired by her reading of Gabriel Garcia Marquez's *One Hundred Years of Solitude* (1967), Seraphita is shown in animal-like poses, wearing sunglasses and sticking out her tongue, accompanied by drum music and jungle sounds—a parody through excess of the conventional signifiers of steamy ("Latino") sensuality. (One of the film's final credits, humorously, is for "hair, makeup, and animals.") Similarly, the scene where Seraphita recalls a traumatic experience as a child in Amsterdam is presented simply in a darkened shot, her face lit from below by a flashlight, a rudimentary signifier of horror or terror in the classic narrative cinema.

The one time the film opts for visual excess, for spectacle rather than simplification, occurs toward the end of the photography sequence when Seraphita begins to model the latest fashions. But

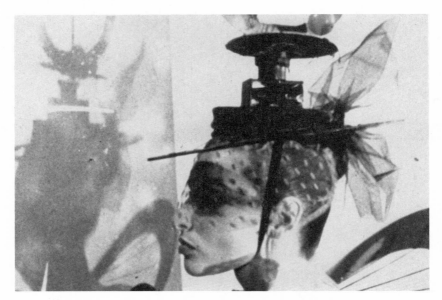

(*Seraphita's Diary*) Seraphita's excessive costuming deflates the appeal of fashion.

this sequence ultimately distances the viewer in a similar way because it grows so excessive that it is impossible to take seriously. Seraphita appears in a series of costumes that begins more or less realistically but becomes increasingly ludicrous. We see her in a ridiculous grasslike outfit (described by Emma as "a perfect blend of Southwestern, Navaho, and English influences"), an outfit that makes her head look like an eight ball or a lamp base, and another "screwy" costume that suggests a corkscrew. Some of the ensembles, particularly the headpieces (the film gives five credits for costuming), match the uninhibited excess typical of Shirley Russell's or Danilo Donati's designs. A rubber chicken hanging from a wire (perhaps a reference to the surreal silliness of *Hellzapoppin'* [H. C. Potter, 1941]?) provides an ironic comment on the whole affair.

The film's "non-bourgeois" style is, finally, a grand joke, and perfectly suited to the subject of fashion and beauty since it presents them as superficial images. Seraphita wants to be loved for herself but is instead a victim of fashion as examined in *Model.* Echoing the sentiment of *Essene* and the *Deaf and Blind* series, she defines true friendship as getting out of oneself and really understanding another, but her physical beauty functions as an obstacle and she remains an enigma. Her friends perceive her in terms of what she means to them rather than what she is for herself. One friend says that she was generous with her money, another says exactly the opposite. Like Charles Foster Kane, she was a different person to different people. "You just feel sucked dry," Seraphita remarks about having tried to live up to everyone's image of her. Ultimately she disappears, like Anna in Michelangelo Antonioni's *L'Avventura* (1960), because she already has been erased by society's disregard of her as a person.

While Seraphita feels no one truly perceives her for herself, she is at the same time tired of her inauthenticity, of performing "the way that they expect you to perform." The viewer is prevented as much as possible from voyeuristically viewing Seraphita as a sexual object. Instead, we are forced to attend to her complaint rather than recuperate it visually. Among the first images of Seraphita we see are shots of her in curlers putting on eye makeup—images that, as in *Model,* reveal the work involved in looking beautiful. In these shots she holds a hand mirror, her eye reflected in it. She looks back at us looking at her, the relay of gazes undermining our typically privileged position as invisible spectator. Toward the end of the film we see her taking a beauty treatment, wearing cold cream and cucumbers on her eyes—a "masque" (pun intended). At one point Seraphita presents herself as a parody version of Rita Hayworth in *Gilda* (Charles Vidor, 1946), underscoring her presence on the screen as an image of potential sexual pleasure. All the while flashes from William's camera accompany her performance, a further reminder that we are looking at a sight displayed for our pleasure. Thus, when one of Apollonia's breasts works free and becomes visible as her strapless dress slips, the sight is hardly erotic; rather, her body is demystified by the camera's steady, unblinking, gaze.

Seraphita's Diary may be seen, too, as a meditation on the signifying power of visual imagery, particularly documentary imagery, a theme explored frequently in Wiseman's other work. Seraphita herself is like an inkblot for other people, in a sense similar to Wiseman's documentaries at the level of reception. In the film Wiseman uses an interview structure, as in a conventional news documentary, to allow Seraphita to speak directly. However, she is shown interviewing herself (just as she writes in her diary to have "somebody really to talk to"). The stylistic conventions of the documentary interview are employed to convey an interior monologue or stream of consciousness. This content would seem unsuited to a documentary style, yet this is, in a sense, exactly the way Wiseman's documentaries, his personal "reports," function. The testimonials from Seraphita's friends at the end would appear to enhance the film's documentary authority, much as the interviews with the "witnesses" do for Warren Beatty's otherwise conventional historical drama, *Reds* (1981). But the friends' comments are undercut by the costumes they wear, some of them as bizarre as the outfits Seraphita models earlier. These apparently documentary talking head shots, then, address the essential question in observational cinema of whether or not people "act" in front of the camera. One of the film's points, as demonstrated everywhere in Wiseman's documentary work, is that this distinction is largely false, for the presentation of the self in everyday life, to borrow Erving Goffman's phrase, is already a social and ideological construction. We are all models, the only difference being that some of us are more professional than others.

Like *The Cool World*, *Seraphita's Diary* employs documentary elements in the service of fiction. The reference to *One Hundred Years of Solitude* is especially significant, for Marquez's technique of "magic realism," like Wiseman's sense of reality fiction, is a combination of fictional and documentary elements. Whereas the documentary quality of *The Cool World* works in part to enhance the suspension of disbelief in its fiction, the fictional aspects of *Seraphita's Diary* challenge the authority of its status as documentation. Ironically, while Wiseman's keen observational style invests the profilmic reality of his documentaries with meaning, making the world rich with signification, his approach to fiction in *Seraphita's Diary* is to drain the diegesis of the kind of superficial significance normally encouraged by narrative cinema.

Certainly *Seraphita's Diary* was not what Wiseman's admirers—nor, for that matter, his detractors—expected. Perhaps this accounts for both its critical and commercial failure, although its single-minded pursuit of illusionist deconstruction undoubtedly was a significant factor as well. The film played only at one local Cambridge cinema, the Beacon Hill, for three weeks, then quietly closed "with the muted sputter of a Roman candle that goes off without going up."[32] But it is clearly a personal film (this is the only one of Wiseman's films with "handwritten" credits), addressing several of the issues he also explores in his documentaries. In fact, for this film Wiseman assigned the responsibility of recording the sound, a job which he has done himself on all of his documentaries, to someone else because he wanted to concentrate his attention fully on the task of directing. Seraphita remarks about her diary that she wishes to write things simply, "and not try to phrase them well." Similarly, the film's minimalist style is a simple kind of *écriture* in comparison to the polished prose of classic narrative cinema. *Seraphita's Diary,* despite its stylistic one-dimensionality, shows not only that Wiseman remains an independent filmmaker stubbornly working outside the commercial mainstream, but that, just as he condemns the easy stereotyping of people in his documentaries, he refuses to be pigeonholed as a certain kind of filmmaker.

NOTES

1. Stephen Mamber, "The New Documentaries of Frederick Wiseman," *Cinema* 6, no. 1 (n.d.): 39.

2. See, for example, John Graham, "How Far Can You Go: A Conversation with Fred Wiseman," *Contempora* 1, no. 4 (October/November 1970): 33; and Ira Halberstadt, "An Interview with Fred Wiseman," *Filmmakers Newsletter* 7, no. 4 (February 1974): 25.

3. Donald McWilliams, "Frederick Wiseman," *Film Quarterly* 24, no. 1 (Fall 1970): 26.

4. Janet Handelman, "An Interview with Frederick Wiseman," *Film Library Quarterly* 3, no. 3 (1970): 9.

5. A. H. Weiler, "Wiseman to Make 'Yes Yes, No No,' First Fiction Film," *New York Times,* December 6, 1974, p. 78.

6. Thomas W. Benson and Carolyn Anderson, *Reality Fictions: The Films of Frederick Wiseman* (Carbondale and Edwardsville: Southern Illinois University Press, 1989), p. 32.

7. Ibid., p. 11; and Christina Robb, "Focus on Life," *Boston Globe Magazine,* January 23, 1983, p. 27.

8. See, for example, Beatrice Berg, " 'I Was Fed Up with Hollywood Fantasies,' " *New York Times,* February 1, 1970, sec. 2, pp. 25–26.

9. See Warren Miller, "Progress in Documentary," in Lewis Jacobs, ed., *The Documentary Tradition: From Nanook to Woodstock,* 2d ed. (New York: Norton, 1979), pp. 247–50.

10. Warren Miller, *The Cool World* (New York: Crest, 1965), p. 26.

11. Anthony Burgess, *A Clockwork Orange* (London: Heinemann, 1962), p. 184.

12. Quoted in Anon., "The Talk of the Town," *New Yorker,* September 14, 1963, p. 34.

13. Ibid., p. 34; Gordon Hitchens, "*The Cool World*," *Film Comment* 2, no. 2 (1964): 52.

14. Lauren Rabinovitz, *Points of Resistance: Women, Power and Politics in the New York Avant-Garde Cinema, 1943–71* (Urbana: University of Illinois Press, 1990).

15. Louis Marcorelles, *Living Cinema: New Directions in Contemporary Filmmaking,* trans. Isabel Quigly (London: George Allen & Unwin, 1973).

16. Rabinovitz, *Points of Resistance.*

17. Andrew Sarris, "*The Cool World*," *Village Voice,* April 23, 1964, rptd. in Sarris, *Confessions of a Cultist: Notes on the Cinema 1955–1969* (New York: Simon and Schuster, 1970), pp. 135–36; Hitchens, "*The Cool World*," p. 53; and Dwight MacDonald, "*The Cool World*," *Dwight MacDonald on Movies* (Englewood Cliffs, N.J.: Prentice-Hall, 1969) pp. 323–27.

18. Richard Wright, *Native Son* (New York: Harper & Row, 1966), p. 33.

19. Jonas Mekas, "Notes on the New American Cinema," *Film Culture,* no. 24 (Spring 1962): 6–16.

20. See Thomas Cripps, *Black Film as Genre* (Bloomington and London: Indiana University Press, 1979), p. 5.

21. Addison Gayle, ed., *The Black Aesthetic* (Garden City, N.Y.: Doubleday, 1971), p. xxi.

22. See Henry Louis Gates, Jr., *The Signifying Monkey: A Theory of Afro-American Literary Criticism* (New York and Oxford: Oxford University Press, 1988).

23. Sarris, "*The Cool World*," p. 136.

24. Berg, "'I Was Fed Up With Hollywood Fantasies,'" p. 25.

25. Harriet Polt, "*The Cool World*," *Film Quarterly* 17, no. 2 (Winter 1963): 34.

26. Donald Bogle, *Toms, Coons, Mulattoes, Mammies, & Bucks* (New York: Bantam, 1974), p. 284.

27. David Eames, "Watching Wiseman Watch," *New York Times Magazine,* October 2, 1977, p. 99.

28. Quoted in Benson and Anderson, *Reality Fictions,* p. 39.

29. Quoted in Anon., "Talk of the Town," *New Yorker,* September 14, 1963, p. 35.

30. For details on many of these movies see Richard Staehling, "From *Rock Around the Clock* to *The Trip:* The Truth about Teen Movies," in Todd McCarthy and Charles Flynn, eds., *Kings of the Bs* (New York: Dutton,

1975), pp. 220–51; and Thomas Doherty, *Teenagers and Teenpics: The Juvenilization of American Movies in the 1950s* (Boston: Unwin Hyman, 1988).

31. See Brian Henderson, "Towards a Non-bourgeois Camera Style," *Film Quarterly* 24, no. 2 (Winter 1970–71): 2–14.

32. Robb, "Focus on Life," p. 15.

CHAPTER 8

And the Ship Sails On

Near Death (1989)

At the time of this writing, Wiseman's two newest films, *Near Death* (1989) and *Central Park* (1990), were recently broadcast on PBS within a few months of each other. *Central Park* examines how that rectangle of public space in the middle of Manhattan, while apparently natural, is in actuality a hypperreal space carefully designed, gardened, and otherwise maintained like any other part of the city. The park's illusion of natural space is expressed by Wiseman's parody of *Woodstock* (Michael Wadleigh, 1970) within the film, complete with an execrable Jimi Hendrix imitation! The labyrinth of roads and walkways periodically shown winding through the park testifies to the incursions of culture upon nature. Early in the film, we are shown what is in effect a "cutaway" view of masonry work being done within a pedestrian tunnel while above all seems "natural." The park, ironically, is shown to be simply one more social institution that Wiseman has turned his camera upon.

Given this emphasis, the film might most profitably be discussed with documentaries like *Canal Zone, Primate,* and *Racetrack,* which are in large part concerned with culture's ideological recuperation of nature. Because of the constraints of time and space, however, a close reading of *Central Park* will have to await subsequent analysis. Any critic attempting a comprehensive treatment of Wiseman's oeuvre inevitably will be frustrated by his productivity, a consistent output that manifests no sign of abating. Indeed, the task is rather like that of the Canal Zone company, with its endless, Sisyphian dredging of the canal. Already he is at work editing his next film, *Aspen.*

Nevertheless, it would seem fitting to conclude this book by briefly considering *Near Death,* not only because it may be one of Wiseman's greatest achievements but also because it so powerfully gathers together many of the concerns examined in his previous films. *Near Death* combines the humanist ethic of *Essene* and the *Deaf and Blind* series with the institutional and technological structures that, as seen in so many of the other documentaries, threaten it. Shot in the intensive care unit of Boston's Beth Israel Hospital, the concerns of *Near Death* are, in fact, similar to those of *Central Park* in the sense that the film reveals the extent to which, as Arthur Kleinman puts it, "death is no longer regarded as a natural event."[1]

If Wiseman's previous films have documented "a natural history of the way we live," in *Near Death* he examines aspects of the way we die. Actually, the whispers of mortality have frequently hovered on the margins of Wiseman's cinema, from the images of Malinowski's fate in *Titicut Follies* (echoed in *Near Death* by the lengthy close-up of Mr. Gavin's intubated face) to the somber, startling invocation of Vietnam in *Basic Training* to the suddenly flaccid carcasses and useless eyes of the animals in *Meat* to the grisly business of *Missile.* (Indeed, many writers connect the modern avoidance and technologizing of death as a reaction to the threat of an impersonal, meaningless extinction made possible by our ability to wage nuclear war.) Now, though, Wiseman confronts death squarely for the first time. Like such monumental documentaries as *Our Hitler* (Hans Jurgen Syberberg, 1977) *Shoah,* and Wiseman's own *Deaf and Blind* series, *Near Death* is "less a viewing experience than a total immersion."[2]

In the course of its gripping six-hour running time, we become familiar with the patients, their families, and the medical staff, the multiple perspective steeping us in medical and ethical dilemmas. Throughout the film, death is foregrounded, neither romanticized nor avoided. ("This is you. It's sad and it's frustrating and it's anger-provoking, but your lungs are about as bad as they can get," a nurse bluntly tells a patient early on.) Death is as omnipresent for the viewer as it is for those whom Wiseman's camera records.

At the beginning of the film we are shown a scene of CPR in progress, the patient failing to respond, and another patient, Mrs. Weiner, expiring. "Okay, she's dead. 7:53," the nurse announces in a matter-of-fact tone, seeming simultaneously professional and in different. After a nurse explains that one patient's family wants to be called only if the father dies, Wiseman follows with one of his typical transitional shots, a janitor mopping a floor. But dealing with death is seldom so tidy, especially, as *Near Death* goes on to show, given the technological capacity to prolong life so central to modern medical treatment. The body of Mr. Cabra, the youngest of the patients presented, is wheeled down the freight elevator and along a hallway to the morgue, a meager pile of his belongings on his chest, a powerful image of our passage through life. The body is shown as physically, palpably present, requiring the effort of four people—one of the nurses wipes her brow from the strain—to put it in a morgue drawer ("place body feet first"). In the postautopsy sequence, the internal organs are arranged neatly on a tray like an artful collage; the discrepancy between this simple sum of bodily parts and the person to whom they once belonged (when does "he" become "the cadaver"? one is encouraged to ask) forces the viewer to contemplate the meaning of death.

Toward the end of *Hospital* we see a woman who has suffered a severe heart attack. The attending physician attempts to get the woman's medical history from her daughter, who responds with confusion and suspicion, delaying emergency treatment. Perhaps she is simply in shock at the possible loss of her mother, but because she does not cope well with her mother's imminent death, she hinders rather than helps the medical staff in their efforts. Similarly, one of the doctors remarks at the beginning of *Near Death,* presumably to a patient's spouse but of course to the film's audience as well, "I know this is a very difficult topic for you." Indeed, Mr. Gavin's wife wants to avoid discussing the likely possibility of her husband's death because, as she says, "it's a touchy subject." Later, another doctor observes (commenting as much on the rationale for the film's structure as on his own situation) that if people fail to hear what's being said to them the first time because it is so frightening, then they have to be told over and over, honestly, so that eventually they will understand. Indeed, only after several lengthy discussions about the fate of her husband and the choices shemust make does Mrs. Sperazza ask what the respirator actually does. Dr. Taylor, with impressive patience, repeats the explanation yet again.

Once more we are reminded of the ending of *Hospital,* a sequence of such crucial importance in Wiseman's cinema. If we avoid confronting death, Wiseman sheds light on its dark dominion. According to Wiseman, "ordinary people don't have enough information to deal with the choices that high-tech medicine presents. . . . Yet more than half of us will die in a hospital. So in a sense, *Near Death* could be regarded as a rehearsal."[3] Certainly the high cost of dying is a central part of American life, begging for scrutiny. According to Dr. Weiss in *Near Death,* a full two-thirds of one's entire health care costs in the United States are incurred during the final twenty-one days of life. Yet, as several writers on death and dying have noted, the subject is a difficult one to address because of its taboo nature.[4] Hence *Near Death* may be, to return to Bill Nichols' description, Wiseman's most "tactless" work.

The film follows the developments of four patients in intensive care, all of whom are kept alive with life-support technology. These are presented in succession, although there is the occasional overlap, as when Mrs. Factor's situation is briefly discussed in the section devoted to the case of Mr. Cabra. Preceding these specifically detailed case studies is an "overture" sequence that establishes a sense of place and, as already suggested, the looming presence of death; it also introduces the ethical complexities that inevitably arise in intensive care treatment. In each of the four case studies, Wiseman alternates sequences featuring the patient (either with medical staff or family members) with sequences featuring the medical staff discussing the patient among themselves. Each case is punctuated by brief montages of exterior shots (periodically recalling the last shot of *Hospital*) that alternate between night and day. On the simplest level, these provide an awareness of passing time—such awareness, of course, being crucial to a work dealing with the stark fact of mortality. Dr. Weiss tells Mrs. Factor, "you've got as much time as you want," but even in the best of circumstances this is hardly the case. Indeed, several shots of medical personnel talking in the film are framed so that clocks can be seen on the wall behind them; time's winged chariot, as it were, is always at our backs.

The film's structure expresses several tensions—between interior and exterior, day and night, staff and patients—embodying

on a formal level a double focus that further reflects the ambiva-
lence that makes coping with death so difficult, identified explicitly by Dr. Weiss as a split between intellectual and emotional
response. This split is further thematized in the film as a tension
between technology and humanity. In this sense, *Near Death*
clearly builds upon Wiseman's previous work. The intensive care
unit, with its battery of machines, is yet another impersonal institution (frequent shots of computer screens monitoring vital functions suggest this view) that moves its clients through a process,
the outcome almost entirely predetermined. The distinctive, periodic exterior shots of the hospital and local traffic, as well as Dr.
Weiss's discussion of the hospital budget and state health care leg-
islation, serve to establish the hospital ward as another cultural
spoor (death, in Avery D. Weisman's words, is "an extended per-
sonification of the suffering we have endured").[5] As in so many of
the other films, the merit of the process is called into question. As
Dr. Weiss puts it: "More technology for unclear benefit."

Beth Israel's intensive care unit is one of the most technologically sophisticated hospital units in the country.[6] Wiseman emphasizes the overwhelming presence of this technology in several
montages of the equipment at work. As explained in one of the
ethics meetings shown in the film, this technology is used largely
to maintain life in order to give families time to accept the likely
possibility of death. Indeed, the very first comment in the film by
a doctor concerns instructions to change a patient's respiratory
"settings" so that it "doesn't look like he's breathing so hard" because it is disconcerting to the family. In several cases the technological interventions ("these powerful medications that can only be
given here in the intensive care unit") are said to do little more
than prolong the inevitable. "It's like a peashooter against an
atomic blast," is Dr. Weiss's vivid metaphor. Dr. Schulman's comment to Mrs. Cabra about her husband, "there may be very little
that we can do," echoes the refrain of the police in *Law and Order*.

But this sophisticated technology creates ethical problems by, in
effect, confusing the boundary between life and death (as the
boundary between nature and culture is blurred in *Central Park*).
Dr. Weiss, grasping for words, explains that moral dilemmas result
because there is no longer a satisfactory definition for "terminally
ill." In one of the ethics meeting, a nurse identifies the difficulties

wrought by the increased sophistication of medical care. Because technology now can keep a patient's heart beating even though that person is technically dead ("dead but alive"), the consequence is confusion for the family. The alternatives of, as one doctor puts it, "life in an institution with a tube in your throat on a machine" or dying tomorrow inevitably raise the question posed by Elisabeth Kubler-Ross and others as to whether medicine is to be a humanitarian profession that reduces suffering or an impersonal science for prolonging life.[7]

Opposing the cold comfort of machinery and the resultant ethical complexity is simple human contact—what Kubler-Ross calls empathy.[8] As far as the film shows, the primary function and concern of the doctors becomes giving comfort. They constantly speak of "making people comfortable" and of "maximizing comfort." This extends even to the physicians and nurses themselves, who, as Dr. Weiss puts it, must "feel comfortable" with their choices. In fact, we see the doctors involved in virtually no medical procedures at all in the film. Rather, they are more like counselors, gradually moving patients and their families toward the acceptance of death and serving as a sounding board for grief and pain. Mrs. Sperazza says that Dr. Taylor is "not only the doctor, he's my friend." Perhaps much of the actual medical treatment was omitted from the film because we have seen this already in *Hospital,* but its relative absence suggests that despite sophisticated technology it is human contact that is of paramount importance ("I'm a human being, not a computer," asserts one nurse).

Throughout the film there are shots of hands touching people, as in the *Deaf and Blind* films. Doctors, patients and relatives frequently touch each other as they talk. Dr. Schulman touches Mrs. Cabra's hand when she cries, and as the Cabra family goes off together to consider their choices, their arms are entwined in mutual support. When a nurse discusses with Mrs. Sperazza her husband's condition, she touches the distraught woman's leg; a friend, seated on her other side, also touches her (reminiscent of some shots of prayer and contact in *Essene*). Sperazza himself is asked at different times by a nurse, his wife, and his son to respond with a squeeze of the hand, while Mrs. Factor is so weak that she can communicate only through feeble hand gestures. One of the most genuinely moving moments in all of Wiseman's cinema is the shot of Dr. Factor gently stroking and kissing his wife's hand as he intones "more healing time" over and over again. Throughout the film, then, touching becomes the physical emblem of the fact that, as one patient says, "we need each other to survive," whether it be the difficulties or the end of life.

Wiseman underscores the importance of these gestures of contact in several ways. Sometimes images are carefully composed so that they are positioned in the middle of the frame, clearly the center of visual attention. This is the case, when, after a lengthy and frank discussion with Mr. Torres about the state of his lungs, Nurse Burke signals her move to leave by touching his hand. Wiseman also uses editing to emphasize these gestures. For example, he moves to a close-up of Mrs. Sperazza holding her husband's hand ("Here I am, honey") when she tries to soothe him and again when Dr. Taylor does the same to comfort her. Wiseman also emphasizes empathy through changes in focus. When Dr. Taylor speaks with Mr. Gavin's family, the camera refocuses from Mrs. Gavin in the left foreground of the frame to her husband in bed in the right background and back to her again, underscoring their bond and the shared responsibility of their decision.

The importance of human contact is further emphasized in the film by the expression of its opposite, isolation. When a nurse says that Mrs. Weiner cannot hear anything, the camera reverse zooms, moves away from the patient to show the terrible distance between people (as it does again later when a nurse speaks with Bernice Factor). When Gavin's doctor departs, the camera zooms in to a brief, tight close-up of the dying man's face; despite the solicitude of others, he, like everyone, inevitably must face his mortality himself. At one point Mr. Torres also realizes this, telling a nurse: "This isn't your body."

When Dr. Taylor seeks to solicit Mr. Gavin's own view of his situation ("Could you share with me your thoughts?" he asks), the two men are divided diagonally within the frame by the bed rail. This works as a graphic representation of Gavin's understanding: "I'm on a borderline. I could pass away or I could survive." Elsewhere, two doctors use similar metaphors, referring to patients "walking a tightrope" and being "on the edge." At one point Gavin is framed so that he is partially obscured by a drawn curtain, another image of his borderline status. Similarly, when Dr. Kurland talks to Mrs. Factor—apparently, this is the first frank discussion anyone has had with her about the likely possibility of her death— his hand rests on the bed rail in the center of the frame. The touches of the doctors and families, who are of course powerless to prevent death, are capable of making death easier to cope with by providing a reassuring anchor to the world of the living.

Of course, the bed rail motif represents not only that borderline between life and death, but also the barriers that separate people. On one level, this barrier is the very technology employed in the service of prolonging life—an irony suggested, for example, by the image of Torres's face under an oxygen mask, his voice muf- fled by it. But it is also the psychological barrier of avoidance, of people not wanting to deal with the death of a loved one, as Mrs. Sperazza says of her son. Several times Dr. Taylor refers to the fail- ure of families to talk openly and frankly as "a barrier"—the iden- tical word used by thanatologist Avery Weisman in the same context.[9] Bernice Factor is "disgusted and frustrated" because nei- ther the medical staff nor her husband has as yet spoken openly with her. Her husband, although identified as a doctor of some kind, refuses to acknowledge her likely death; he is described as being uncooperative with the medical staff and not "free-flowing with his feelings." Another patient's death is said to be unfortu- nate because of the "unresolved issues" still hanging between the members of the family. These barriers are precisely imaged by the shot of Mr. Cabra, his mouth taped closed, family members on ei- ther side of his bed behind the handrails; people may be close, but not necessarily intimate.

During one of the nurses' ethics meetings, when it is remarked that nobody is comfortable with the decision to terminate treat- ment, several voices speak at once, the babble confirming the truth of the statement. The striking shot of a large window reflect- ing brilliant white with an immobile elderly person on either side can be read as either a gentle Ernst Lubitsch-like image of death or a horrifying Melvillian notion of the "dumb blankness" that be- speaks death's emptiness.[10] During one of the rounds discussions, as the staff discuss whether intensive care treatment would have mattered in Gavin's case, the camera roams around the group as if, like everyone involved, seeking a proper perspective. Wiseman himself has quipped, "I'm against death, but I don't know any remedy for it."[11] The joke, like much of the humor in his other films, is in part a defense against the unpleasant reality his camera records. But in the film itself Wiseman noticeably restrains his own sense of humor. Instead he leaves humor's therapeutic power to those he films, like Mrs. Sperazza, who consoles her husband by reminding him that he wanted to lose weight anyway. Wiseman in *Near Death* maintains "a gentle neutrality of quiet dignity, seeking to learn, to understand, to participate."[12]

Interestingly, this reticent, even respectful, tone complicates the viewer's reactions to the film. This, in addition to its subject, makes *Near Death* as challenging a viewing experience as any of Wiseman's other documentaries. The viewer is presented with the same emotional/intellectual split as the people involved, much like the experience offered by *Primate*. Doctors and nurses acknowledge that there is a transference of anger against the abstract implacability of human mortality to the more concrete target of the medical staff. A nurse explains that in one case a family viewed her as having killed their mother since "I was the most visible person." "Who else is there to be angry at?" asks Dr. Weiss elsewhere; "It's a lot healthier to be angry at the doctors."

The medical staff are likely to strike the viewer as callous at first. The rough shaving of Sperazza by a nurse—his eyes suddenly, and for the first time in the film, open wide in an angry glare when his face is cut—recalls the treatment of Jim in *Titicut Follies*. But such powerful images of staff mistreatment in *Near Death* are rare; rather, it is the language of the staff that frequently seems to betray indifference toward the fate of patients. At the very beginning of the film, Wiseman encourages an initial antipathy toward the doctors and nurses by showing a doctor remarking that a patient "may not fly" when extubated, as if the patient were merely a machine. Later, Dr. Weiss wonders if Dr. Factor should "call it a day" and agree not to reintubate his wife; another choice is "whether to get trached or just to bag it." Like the withdrawal that characterizes the workers in *Welfare*, the doctors employ euphemisms to describe a situation: "We shy away from the word 'experiment' 'cause it sounds like we're treating you like a guinea pig," Gavin is told. Attacks are "episodes of pain"; reconsidering the possibility of meaningful survival is "reassessing goals," and so on.

Most importantly, the word *death* is virtually never used between medical staff and patients and their families. In one meeting a nurse is emphatic in her claim that it is better to give families the news directly, though this does not seem to happen in practice. Mrs. Factor is not told explicitly that she will probably die if she is extubated for a long while, despite the fact that she is characterized as a strong woman, the dominant member of her family. More pointedly, staff members decide that they may have to keep her husband out of the room if he continues to behave in an uncooperative manner and "decide how things are going to be handled in terms of care." "Well," Dr. Weiss remarks with apparent flippancy, "you know what Freud said, neurosis is no excuse for bad manners."

Because of such comments and behavior, the staff seems somewhat dishonest if not devious in its indirect strategy of coaxing patients and families against sustained dependence on the respirator. According to Kleinman, one of the distinctive features of Beth Israel's intensive care ward is the physician's emphasis on bringing patients and families into the "decision-making process."[13] Dr. Weiss explains in the film, "everything here is sort of built on the Quaker concept of consensus," but he adds that difficulty arises when "one of those elements is out of synch." Doctors continually ask patients and families whether they would want to go back on the machine if it becomes necessary, and while it is commendable that the doctors continually seek this consultation, it sometimes appears as if they are badgering people into submission. For example, the fact that Mrs. Cabra's personal physician gets her to agree to withhold CPR should her husband's heart fail again is assessed as "some small victory." In a sense, the choice these patients and families are offered is merely "the guise of real choice,"[14] little more than a gentler version of the double-bind confronting the students in *High School*. One wants to protest that these doctors— "endowed with magic and mystery"[15]—are abusing their position.

As the film goes on, however, the spectator's initial response is inevitably modified, as various members of the hospital staff wrestle with the ethical questions involved. These lengthy discussions can themselves be understood as a method of either avoidance or coping,[16] the latter likely to make one feel more sympathetic toward them. We see that they are only human after all, trapped in an extremely difficult position. Certainly, they seem quite aware of their professional personas and the consequent crucial influence they have in the decision-making process. Also, the more we see, the more likely we are to think, as Weisman asserts, that to insist upon full disclosure is "as dogmatic and inexcusable" as avoiding discussion.[17] The constant talk by doctors in the film, their refusal to express hopelessness to families even when they admit it privately, is explicitly said by Kubler-Ross to be of great support at a time when people feel particularly helpless.[18] So Dr. Taylor comes to seem the embodiment of patience, particularly when he gently repeats basic information about the respirator to Mrs. Sperazza or tactfully waits until Mrs. Gavin is ready to identify the inevitable decision she must make. Dr. Weiss observes that there are few situations in life that require a more careful rhetoric; the initial humorous impression he creates because of his manic logorrhea is inevitably modified. Perhaps his annoying habit of almost never finishing a sentence before he begins another is his way of coping with the emotional strain of working in intensive care? ("Well, you know I mean I am quite nihilistic about you know what you what actually happens," he stammers at one point.) In short, the film encourages the viewer to oscillate between conflicting views of Dr. Weiss and, by extension, of the entire medical staff, much the same way we look at Hickman in *Basic Training*.

Similarly, in each case the doctor is shown to embody the paradox of being both "a healer and someone equally baffled by inexorable death."[19] So patients and doctors alike resort to faith rather than science as a response to death's unfathomable finality. Dr. Weiss himself clings to hope; at one point he asserts that they should extubate a patient, "leave it in God's hands, and see what happens." Mrs. Gavin and Mrs. Sperazza ("I don't know what else to do, just hope and say a prayer for him," admits the former) also submit to fate. The doctor depicts life as an inscrutable Shakespearian scenario in which we are destined to play only bit roles: "She was called, and we're minor actors." Doctors, too, we learn, suffer from a sickness unto death; our response to them is softened, as toward the police in *Law and Order*.

Finally, the film raises several crucial questions. What constitutes an appropriate death? When should technological intervention cease? Is euthanasia morally justifiable? With whom does responsibility for such decisions rest? These are crucial, consuming questions for the staff, the patients, the families, and the spectator. Of course, the issues surrounding the quality of death really concern the quality of life, what Weisman calls "the practical significance of mortality." He declares: "If we can discover more significant and more acceptable ways of facing death, then perhaps we will also find a method of accentuating the values and goals of life."[20] A shot of a nurse's image reflected in the window over the Boston cityscape suggests the importance for living of the way we deal with death. The life-affirming implications of thanatology are asserted by the film's opening shots of scullers on a river; like sperm, they move upstream, the bright cityscape on the horizon connoting vibrant and teeming life. Dr. Weiss is fully aware of the limits of his work ("If you wanted to give people quality of life, you could like be a furniture salesman or something—it's easy to fix things that are fixable") but he perseveres at what he terms a Sisyphian task anyway, since sometimes patients do recover. Wiseman periodically inserts into the film brief shots of Dr. Factor sitting, keeping silent vigil over his wife. Our sympathy is evoked for this man who cannot accept the death that everyone else agrees is inevitable. Yet in a title at the end of the film we learn that Mrs. Factor survived and is living at home with her husband.

As Susan Sontag has written: "All photographs are *memento mori*. To take a photograph is to participate in another person's (or thing's) mortality, vulnerability, mutability. Precisely by slicing out this moment and freezing it, all the photographs testify to time's relentless melt."[21] *Near Death* is no exception. Life inevitably shines through the paraphernalia of death (humorously, in the form of the nurse who comically sneezes, wipes her hand on her lab coat, and then scratches her armpit during one of the rounds discussions). The film's cinematographic content itself is a symbolic challenge to death. Since it is the patients and their families who command attention, not the technology that surrounds them, certainly Wiseman's footage is a testament to their affirmation of life, which will remain long after they have shuffled off their mortal coils.

In *Near Death,* the difficulty of making an informed decision about whether to withdraw life support but being required to do so nevertheless is emblematic of Wiseman's entire approach to

documentary. The ethical questions raised by filming actual people and situations, transforming them into aesthetic objects,[22] are
surely answered by Wiseman's distinctive method. In Wiseman's
films, as I have argued throughout this book, it is the complexity
of the aesthetic experience that is emphasized over the simplicity
of the Griersonian pronouncement. Whereas Grierson felt it necessary to add a voice-over to Flaherty's images of a potter at work
in *Industrial Britain* (1933), an exhortation to "look at these
hands," Wiseman shows hands yet requires the viewer to decipher
their significance. In *Near Death*, then, the barrier or borderline
functions on yet another level as a (cinema) screen between passive
spectatorship and active viewing, a screen that, like the proscenium in the theater, Wiseman has typically sought to eliminate.
Wiseman's documentaries are often seen as homogenous; the
same stark, cinema verité style is used to explore a series of state-
supported institutions and private industries. But, as I hope the
preceding pages have made clear, these films display a wider
range of textual strategies than has generally been acknowledged.
Ultimately, his work counters Richard Blumenberg's claim that
aesthetic criteria in documentary film "separates itself from the
ethical,"[23] for in Wiseman's cinema the two are inseparable. On
both levels, Wiseman's films are truly voyages of discovery.

NOTES

1. Arthur Kleinman, "Do Not Go Gentle," *New Republic*, February 5,
1990, p. 28.
2. Janet Maslin, "Frederick Wiseman's *Near Death*," *New York Times*,
October 7, 1989, p. 11.
3. Quoted in Harry F. Waters, "A Stiff Dose of Intensive Care," *Newsweek*, January 22, 1990, p. 52.
4. See, for example, Elisabeth Kubler-Ross, *On Death and Dying* (New
York: Macmillan, 1973); and Avery D. Weisman, *On Dying and Denying: A
Psychiatric Study of Terminality* (New York: Behavioral Publications, 1972).
5. Weisman, *On Dying and Denying*, p. 220.
6. Kleinman, "Do Not Go Gentle," p. 29.
7. Kubler-Ross, *On Death and Dying*, p. 10.
8. Ibid., p. 33.
9. Weisman, *On Dying and Denying*, p. 18.

10. Herman Melville, *Moby Dick: or, The Whale,* ed. Harrison Hayford and Hershell Parker (New York: Norton, 1967), p. 169.

11. Quoted in David Livingstone, "A Heart-Wrenching Reminder of Our Own Mortality," (Toronto) *Globe and Mail Broadcast Week,* January 27, 1990, p. 9.

12. Avery Weisman, *The Realization of Death* (New York and London: Jason Aronson, 1974), p. 7.

13. Kleinman, "Do Not Go Gentle," p. 29.

14. Ibid. See also the exchange between Susan M. Wolf, "*Near Death—In the Moment of Decision,*" *New England Journal of Medicine* 322, no. 3 (June 18, 1990): 208–09; and Wiseman, *et. al.,* "Letter to the Editor," *New England Journal of Medicine* 322, no. 22 (May 31, 1990):1605–06.

15. Weisman, *On Dying and Denying,* p. 200.

16. Kubler-Ross, *On Death and Dying,* p. 7.

17. Weisman, *On Dying and Denying,* p. 18.

18. Ibid., p. 26.

19. Ibid., pp. 200–01.

20. Weisman, *On Dying and Denying,* p. 4. See also his *Realization of Death,* pp. 4, 16.

21. Susan Sontag, *On Photography* (New York: Delta, 1978), p. 15.

22. Larry Gross, John Stuart Katz, and Jay Ruby, eds., *Image Ethics: The Moral Rights of Subjects in Photographs, Film, and Television* (New York: Oxford University Press, 1988), p. 21.

23. Richard M. Blumenberg, "Documentary Films and the Problem of Truth," *Journal of the University Film Association* 29, no. 1 (Fall 1977): 21.

Filmography

The Cool World (1964; b&w, 104 min.)
screenplay by Shirley Clarke and Carl Lee
adapted from the novel by Warren Miller and the play by Warren
    Miller and Robert Rossen
photographed by Baird Bryant
sound recorded by David Jones
music by Mal Waldron
produced by Frederick Wiseman
directed and edited by Shirley Clarke

Titicut Follies (1967; b&w, 83 min.)
photographed by John Marshall
sound recorded by Frederick Wiseman
produced, edited, and directed by Frederick Wiseman
awards:
First Prize, Best Documentary, Mannheim Film Festival, 1967
Critics Prize, Festival dei Popoli, Florence, 1967
Best Film Dealing With the Human Condition, Festival dei Popoli,
    1967

High School (1968; b&w, 75 min.)
photographed by Richard Leiterman
sound recorded by Frederick Wiseman
produced, edited, and directed by Frederick Wiseman

Law and Order (1969; b&w, 81 min.)
photographed by William Brayne
sound recorded by Frederick Wiseman
produced, edited, and directed by Frederick Wiseman
awards:

Emmy, Best Documentary, 1969
Award for Exceptional Merit, Philadelphia International Film Festival, 1971

Hospital (1970: b&w, 84 min.)
photographed by William Brayne
sound recorded by Frederick Wiseman
produced, edited, and directed by Frederick Wiseman
awards:
Emmy, Best Documentary, 1970
Emmy, Best Director, 1970
Catholic Film Workers Award, Mannheim Film Festival, 1970
Dupont Award, Columbia University School of Journalism, For Excellence in Broadcast Journalism, 1970
Red Ribbon, American Film Festival, 1972

Basic Training (1971; b&w, 89 min.)
photographed by William Brayne
sound recorded by Frederick Wiseman
produced, edited, and directed by Frederick Wiseman
awards:
Award for Exceptional Merit, Philadelphia International Film Festival, 1971

Essene (1972; b&w, 89 min.)
photographed by William Brayne
sound recorded by Frederick Wiseman
produced, edited, and directed by Frederick Wiseman
awards:
Gabriel Award, Catholic Broadcasters Association, 1972

Juvenile Court (1973; b&w, 144 min.)
photographed by William Brayne
sound recorded by Frederick Wiseman
produced, edited, and directed by Frederick Wiseman
awards:
Silver Phoenix, Atlanta International Film Festival, 1974
CINE Golden Eagle, Council of International Nontheatrical Events, Washington, D.C., 1974
Dupont Award, Columbia University School of Journalism, For Excellence in Broadcast Journalism, 1974
Emmy nomination, Best News Documentary, 1974

Primate (1974; b&w, 105 min.)
photographed by William Brayne
sound recorded by Frederick Wiseman
produced, edited, and directed by Frederick Wiseman

Welfare (1975; b&w, 167 min.)
photographed by William Brayne
sound recorded by Frederick Wiseman
produced, edited, and directed by Frederick Wiseman
awards:
Gold Medal, Special Jury Award, Virgin Islands International Film
    Festival, 1975
Best Documentary, Athens International Film Festival, 1976
Ohio State Award for Excellence in Broadcasting, 1977

Meat (1976; b&w, 113 min.)
photographed by William Brayne
sound recorded by Frederick Wiseman
produced, edited, and directed by Frederick Wiseman

Canal Zone (1977, b&w, 174 min.)
photographed by William Brayne
sound recorded by Frederick Wiseman
produced, edited, and directed by Frederick Wiseman
awards:
Golden Athena Prize for Best Feature, Athens International Film
    Festival, 1978

Sinai Field Mission (1978; b&w, 127 min.)
photographed by William Brayne
sound recorded by Frederick Wiseman
produced, edited, and directed by Frederick Wiseman

Manoeuvre (1979; b&w, 115 min.)
photographed by John Davey
sound recorded by Frederick Wiseman
produced, edited, and directed by Frederick Wiseman
awards:
CINE Golden Eagle Certificate, 1980
Best Documentary, Festival Internacional de Cinema, Portugal, 1980

Model (1980; b&w, 129 min.)
photographed by John Davey
sound recorded by Frederick Wiseman
produced, edited, and directed by Frederick Wiseman
awards:
CINE Golden Eagle Certificate, 1981

Seraphita's Diary (1982; color, 89 min.)
screenplay by Frederick Wiseman
photographed by John Davey
sound recorded by David John
adapted, produced, edited, and directed by Frederick Wiseman
awards:
Honorary Mention, Festival dei Popoli, 1983
Gold Special Jury Award, Houston Film Festival, 1983

The Store (1983; color, 118 min.)
photographed by John Davey
sound recorded by Frederick Wiseman
produced, edited, and directed by Frederick Wiseman

Racetrack (1985; b&w, 114 min.)
photographed by John Davey
sound recorded by Frederick Wiseman
produced, edited, and directed by Frederick Wiseman

Blind (1986; color, 132 min.)
photographed by John Davey
sound recorded by Frederick Wiseman
produced, edited, and directed by Frederick Wiseman
awards:
Honorary Mention, American Film and Video Festival, 1987

Deaf (1986; color, 164 min.)
photographed by John Davey
sound recorded by Frederick Wiseman
produced, edited, and directed by Frederick Wiseman

Adjustment and Work (1986; color, 120 min.)
photographed by John Davey
sound recorded by Frederick Wiseman
produced, edited, and directed by Frederick Wiseman

Multi-Handicapped (1986; color, 126 min.)
photographed by John Davey
sound recorded by Frederick Wiseman
produced, edited, and directed by Frederick Wiseman

Missile (1987; color, 115 min.)
photographed by John Davey
sound recorded by Frederick Wiseman
produced, edited, and directed by Frederick Wiseman

Near Death (1989; b&w, 358 min.)
photographed by John Davey
sound recorded by Frederick Wiseman
produced, edited, and directed by Frederick Wiseman
awards:
L'Age d'Or Prize, Royal Film Archive, Belgium, 1989
International Critics' Prize, Berlin Film Festival, 1990
Media Award, Retirement Research Foundation, 1990
Broadcast Media Award, American Association of Critical Care
    Nurses, 1990
DuPont Award, Columbia University School of Journalism, For Ex-
    cellence in Broadcast Journalism, 1991

Central Park (1990; color, 176 min.)
photographed by John Davey
sound recorded by Frederick Wiseman
produced, edited, and directed by Frederick Wiseman
awards:
CINE Golden Eagle Certificate, 1990

Individual Awards

Gold Hugo Award, Chicago International Film Festival, 1972

Personal Achievement Gabriel, Catholic Broadcasters Association, 1975

Great Director Tribute and Award for Continuing Directorial Achievement in the Documentary Field, USA Film Festival, 1984

Virginia Festival of American Film Award for Excellence in Documentary Filmmaking, 1988

Humanitarian Award, Massachusetts Psychological Association, 1990

Career Achievement Award, International Documentary Association, 1990

George Foster Peabody Personal Award, University of Georgia, School of Journalism and Mass Communication, 1990

Retrospective Screenings

Chicago International Film Festival, 1972
National Film Theatre, London, England, 1972
Swedish Film Cinematheque, Stockholm, Sweden, 1975
Danish Cinematheque, Copenhagen, Denmark, 1975
Paris Film Cinematheque, Paris, France, 1975
Norsk Filminstitutt, Oslo, Norway, 1976
Filmex, Los Angeles International Film Festival, 1976
Spanish Film Cinematheque, Madrid and Barcelona, Spain, 1978
Cleveland International Film Festival, 1979
Denver International Film Festival, 1979
Stiftung Deutsche Kinemathek, Berlin, Germany, 1979
Royal Film Archive, Brussels, Belgium, 1980
American Film Institute, 1980
Festival Internacional de Cinema, Lisbon, Portugal, 1980
Danske Filmskole, Copenhagen, Denmark, 1982
Svenska Filminstitutet/Cinemateket, Stockholm, Sweden, 1982
Durban Film Festival, Durban, South Africa, 1983
U.S.A. Film Festival, Dallas, Texas, 1984

Select Bibliography

Allen, Jeanne. "Self-Reflexivity and the Documentary Film." *Cine-Tracts*, no. 1 (Summer 1977): 37–43.

Allen, Robert C. "Case Study: The Beginnings of American Cinema Verité." In *Film History: Theory and Practice*, ed. Robert C. Allen and Douglas Gomery, 213–41. New York: Knopf, 1985.

Ames, Elizabeth. "Fred Wiseman's Candid Camera." *Horizon* 24, no. 9 (September 1974): 62–66.

Anderson, Carolyn. "The Conundrum of Competing Rights in *Titicut Follies*." *Journal of the University Film Association* 33, no. 1 (Winter 1981): 15–22.

———. "The *Titicut Follies* Audience and the Double Bind of Court-Restricted Exhibition." In *Current Research in Film: Audiences, Economics, and Law* 3, ed. Bruce A. Austin, 189–214. Norwood, N.J.: Ablex, 1987.

———, and Thomas W. Benson. "Direct Cinema and the Myth of Informed Consent: The Case of *Titicut Follies*." In *Image Ethics: The Moral Rights of Subjects in Photography, Film, and Television*, ed. Larry Gross, John Katz, and Jay Ruby. New York: Oxford University Press, 1988.

Anderson, John W. "Representation and the Ethnographic Film." *Film Criticism* 4, no. 1 (1979): 89–100.

Andrew, J. Dudley. *The Major Film Theories.* New York: Oxford University Press, 1976.

Anon. "Talk of the Town." *New Yorker,* October 24, 1988, pp. 31–32. [*Missile*]

———. "Talk of the Town." *New Yorker,* October 5, 1981, 41. [*Model*]

———. "Talk of the Town: New Producer" *New Yorker,* September 14, 1963, pp. 33–35.

———. "Viewpoints: Shooting the Institution." *Time,* December 9, 1974, pp. 95, 98.

Arlen, Michael. "Frederick Wiseman's 'Kino Pravda.'" *New Yorker,* April 21, 1980, pp. 91–101.

————. "The Air." *New Yorker,* November 25, 1974, pp. 149–55. [*Primate*]

Armes, Roy. *Film and Reality.* Baltimore: Pelican, 1974.

Armstrong, Dan. "Wiseman's Cinema of the Absurd: *Welfare,* or 'Waiting for the Dole.'" *Film Criticism* 12, no. 3 (Spring 1988): 3–19.

————. "Wiseman's *Model* and the Documentary Project: Towards a Radical Film Practice." *Film Quarterly* 37, no. 2 (Winter 1983–84): 2–10; rptd. in *New Challenges for Documentary,* ed. Alan Rosenthal, 180–90. Berkeley: University of California Press, 1988.

————. "Wiseman's Realm of Transgression: *Titicut Follies,* the Symbolic Father, and the Spectacle of Confinement." *Cinema Journal* 29, no. 1 (Fall 1989): 20–35.

Arnold, Gary. "Frederick Wiseman's 'Primates.'" *Washington Post,* December 5, 1974, pp. B1, B15.

————. "*Law and Order.*" *Washington Post,* March 7, 1970, p. C6.

————. "Wiseman's *Welfare:* Compelling Case Study." *Washington Post,* September 24, 1975, pp. C1–2.

Atkins, Thomas R. "American Institutions: The Films of Frederick Wiseman." *Sight and Sound* 43, no. 4 (Autumn 1974): 232–35.

————, ed. *Frederick Wiseman.* New York: Simon & Schuster, 1976.

Barnouw, Erik. *Documentary: A History of the Nonfiction Film.* New York: Oxford University Press, 1974.

Barr, Charles. "Cinemascope Before and After." *Film Quarterly* 16, no. 4 (1963): 4–24; rptd. in *Film Theory and Criticism,* ed. Gerald Mast and Marshall Cohen, 120–46. New York: Oxford University Press, 1974.

Barsam, Richard M. "American Direct Cinema: The Re-Presentation of Reality." *Persistence of Vision* 3/4 (Summer 1986): 131–56.

————. *Nonfiction Film: A Critical History.* New York: Dutton, 1973.

————. "Nonfiction Film: The Realist Impulse," in *Film Theory and Criticism,* ed. Gerald Mast and Marshall Cohen, 2d ed., 580–93. New York: Oxford University Press, 1979.

————, ed. *Nonfiction Film: Theory and Criticism.* New York: Dutton, 1976.

Barthes, Roland. *Mythologies,* ed. and trans. Annette Lavers. New York: Hill and Wang, 1977.

————. *S/Z,* trans. Richard Howard. New York: Hill and Wang, 1974.

Basinger, Jeanine. *The World War II Combat Film: Anatomy of Genre.* New York: Columbia University Press, 1986.

Bassoff, Betty Zippin. "*Welfare.*" *Social Work* 20, no. 6 (November 1975): 498.

Bazin, André. *What Is Cinema?,* 2 vols., ed. and trans. Hugh Gray. Berkeley: University of California Press, 1971.

Benson, Thomas W. "The Rhetorical Structure of Frederick Wiseman's *High School.*" *Communications Monographs* 47 (1980): 233–61.

————, and Carolyn Anderson. *Reality Fictions: The Films of Frederick Wise-*

man. Carbondale and Edwardsville: Southern Illinois University Press, 1989.

———. "The Rhetorical Structure of Frederick Wiseman's *Model.*" *Journal of Film and Video* 36, no. 4 (Fall 1984): 30–40.

Berg, Beatrice. "'I Was Fed Up with Hollywood Fantasies.'" *New York Times,* February 1, 1970, sec. 2, pp. 25–26.

Berger, John. *Ways of Seeing.* London: BBC/Penguin, 1972.

Berliner, Don. "TV Mailbag." *New York Times,* March 1, 1970, sec. 2, pp. 21–22.

Biro, Yvette. *Profane Mythology: The Savage Mind of the Cinema,* trans. Imre Goldstein. Bloomington: Indiana University Press, 1982.

Blue, James. "One Man's Truth: An Interview with Richard Leacock." *Film Comment* 3, no. 2 (Spring 1965): 15–22; rptd. in *The Documentary Tradition,* ed Lewis Jacobs, 2d ed., 406–19. New York: Norton, 1979.

———. "Thoughts on Cinéma Vérité and a Discussion with the Masyles Brothers." *Film Comment* 2 (Fall 1965): 22–30.

Bluem, A. William. *Documentary in American Television.* New York: Hastings House, 1972.

Bluestone, George. "The Intimate Television Documentary." *Television Quarterly* 4 (Spring 1965): 49–54.

Blumenberg, Richard M. "Documentary Film and the Problem of 'Truth.'" *Journal of the University Film Association* 29, no. 1 (Fall 1977): 19–22.

Bordwell, David, and Kristin Thompson. *Film Art: An Introduction,* 2 ed. New York: Knopf, 1986.

———, Janet Staiger, and Kristin Thompson. *The Classical Hollywood Cinema.* New York: Columbia University Press, 1985.

Bourne, Geoffrey H. "Yerkes Director Calls Foul." *New York Times,* December 15, 1974, p. 33.

Boyd, Malcolm. *"Essene." New York Times,* November 12, 1973, p. 17.

Boyum, Joy Gould. "Watching Real Life Problems." *Wall Street Journal,* October 1, 1973, p.3. *[Juvenile Court]*

Bradlow, Paul. "Two . . . But Not of a Kind." *Film Comment* 5, no. 3 (1968): 60–61. *[Titicut Follies]*

Branigan, Edward. *Point of View in the Cinema: A Theory of Narration and Subjectivity in Classical Film.* New York: Mouton, 1984.

Breitrose, Henry. "On the Search for the Real Nitty-Gritty: Some Problems and Possibilities in Cinéma Vérité." *Film Quarterly* 17 (Summer 1964): 36–40.

Bromwich, David. "Documentary Now." *Dissent,* October 1971, pp. 507–12.

Brown, Les. "Scientist Angrily Cancels TV Discussion of *Primate.*" *New York Times,* December 7, 1974, p. 59.

Browne, Nick. "The Spectator-in-the-Text: The Rhetoric of *Stagecoach*." *Film Quarterly* 29, no. 2 (Winter 1975–76): 26–38.

Burch, Noel. *Theory of Film Practice*, trans. Helen R. Lane. New York: Praeger, 1973.

Cameron, Ian, and Mark Shivas. "Cinéma Vérité: New Methods, New Approach." *Movie* 8 (April 1963): 12–27.

Campbell, J. Louis III. " 'All Men Are Created Equal': Waiting for Godot in the Culture of Inequality." *Communications Monographs* 55 (1988): 143–61.

————, and Richard Buttny. "Rhetorical Coherence: An Exploration into Thomas Farrell's Theory of the Synchrony of Rhetoric and Conversation." *Communication Quarterly* 36, no. 4 (Fall 1988): 262–75.

Canby, Vincent. "The Screen: *Titicut Follies* Observes Life in a Modern Bedlam." *New York Times,* October 4, 1967, p. 38.

Carroll, Noel. "From Real to Reel: Entangled in Nonfiction Film." *Philosophic Exchange* 14 (1983): 24–45.

Cass, James. *"High School." Saturday Review,* April 19, 1969, p. 57.

Clandfield, David. *Canadian Film.* Toronto: Oxford University Press, 1987.

Coleman, John. "Long Look." *New Statesman,* November 1975, pp. 589–90. [*Welfare*]

Coles, Robert. "Senses and Sensibility." *New Republic,* August 29, 1988, pp. 58–60.

————. "Stripped Bare at the Follies." *New Republic,* January 20, 1968, pp. 18, 28–30.

Combs, Richard. *"Model." Monthly Film Bulletin* 48, no. 567 (April 1981): 73.

Corry, John. "TV: *The Store*, a Wiseman Film." *New York Times,* December 14, 1983, p. C34.

————. "Wiseman Examines Racetracks." *New York Times,* June 4, 1986, p. C26.

Crain, Jane Larkin. "TV Vérité." *Commentary* 56, no. 6 (December 1973): 70–75.

Crowther, Bosley. "Screen: Fighting to the Top in Harlem." *New York Times,* April 21, 1964, p. 42.

Cunningham, Stuart. "The Look and its Revocation: Wiseman's *Primate*." *Australian Journal of Screen Theory,* nos. 11–12 (1982): 86–95.

Curry, Timothy Jon. "Frederick Wiseman: Sociological Filmmaker?" *Contemporary Sociology* 14, no. 1 (January 1985): 35–39.

Davidson, David. "Direct Cinema and Modernism: The Long Journey to *Grey Gardens*." *Journal of the University Film Association* 33, no. 1 (Winter 1981): 3–13.

Denby, David. "Documenting America." *Atlantic,* March 1970, pp. 139–42; rptd. in *The Documentary Tradition,* ed. Lewis Jacobs, 2d ed., 447–82. New York: Hopkinson and Blake, 1972; and in *Nonfiction Film: Theory and Criticism,* ed. Richard Barsam, 310–14. New York: Dutton, 1976.

―――. "The Real Thing." *New York Review,* November 8, 1990, pp. 24–27.

―――. "Taps." *New York,* October 4, 1971, p. 69. [*Basic Training*]

DeVries, Hillary. "Fred Wiseman's Unblinking Camera Watches How Society Works." *Christian Science Monitor,* May 1, 1984, pp. 25–27.

Dowd, Nancy Ellen. "Popular Conventions." *Film Quarterly* 22, no. 3 (Spring 1969): 28–31. [*Titicut Follies*]

Eames, David. "Watching Wiseman Watch." *New York Times Magazine,* October 2, 1977, pp. 96–102, 104, 108.

Eaton, Mick, ed. *Anthropology—Reality—Cinema: The Films of Jean Rouch.* London: British Film Institute, 1979.

Ellis, Jack C. "Changing of the Guard: From the Grierson Documentary to Free Cinema." *Quarterly Review of Film Studies* 7, no. 1 (Winter 1982): 232–35.

Ellsworth, Liz. *Frederick Wiseman: A Guide to References and Sources.* Boston: G. K. Hall, 1979.

Faucher, Charles A. "The Kids of *High School.*" *Media and Methods* 6, no. 1 (September 1969): 54–55.

Featherstone, Joseph. *"High School." New Republic,* June 21, 1969, pp. 28–30.

Feldman, Seth, ed. *Take Two.* Toronto: Irwin, 1984.

―――. "Documentary Performance." *Canadian Drama* 5, no. 1 (Spring 1979): 11–25.

―――, and Joyce Nelson, eds. *Canadian Film Reader.* Toronto: Peter Martin Associates, 1977.

Feldman, Sylvia. "The Wiseman Documentary." *Human Behavior* 5 (February 1976): 64–69.

Friedenberg, Edgar Z. "Ship of Fools: The Films of Frederick Wiseman." *New York Review of Books,* October 21, 1971, pp. 19–22.

Fuller, Richard. " 'Survive, Survive, Survive': Frederick Wiseman's New Documentary *Basic Training.*" *The Film Journal* 1, nos. 3–4 (Fall/Winter 1972): 74–79; rptd. in *Frederick Wiseman,* ed. Thomas R. Atkins, 103–12. New York: Simon & Schuster, 1976.

Gates, Henry Louis, Jr. *The Signifying Monkey: A Theory of Afro-American Literary Criticism.* New York: Oxford University Press, 1988.

Gay, Ken. "Documentary." *Films and Filming* 18, no. 10 (July 1972): 78.

―――. *"Primate." Films and Filming* 21, no. 6 (March 1975): 37–38.

Gayle, Addison, ed. *The Black Aesthetic.* Garden City, N.Y.: Doubleday, 1971.

Geduld, Harry M. "Garbage Cans and Institutions: The Films of Frederick Wiseman." *The Humanist* 31, no. 5 (September/October 1971): 36–37.

Gill, Brendan. "The Current Cinema." *New Yorker,* October 28, 1967; pp. 166–67.

Goodman, Walter. "Hands That Could Launch the Missiles." *New York Times,* August 31, 1988, p. C22.

Graham, John, and George Garett. "How Far Can You Go: A Conversation with Fred Wiseman." *Contempora* 1, no. 4 (October/November 1970): 30–33; rptd. as "There Are No Simple Solutions." *The Film Journal* 1, no. 1 (Spring 1971): 43–47; and in *Frederick Wiseman,* ed. Thomas R. Atkins, 33–45. New York: Simon & Schuster, 1976.

Grierson, John. *Grierson on Documentary,* rev. ed., ed. H. Forsyth Hardy. Berkeley: University of California Press, 1966.

Gronbeck, Bruce. "Celluloid Rhetoric: On Genres of Documentary." *Form and Genre: Shaping Rhetorical Action,* ed. Karlyn Kohrs Campbell and Kathleen Hall Jamieson, 139–61. Falls Church, Va.: The Speech Communication Association, n.d.

Gross, Larry, John Stuart Katz, and Jay Ruby, eds. *Image Ethics: The Moral Rights of Subjects in Photographs, Film, and Television.* New York: Oxford University Press, 1988.

Halberstadt, Ira. "An Interview with Fred Wiseman." *Filmmakers Newsletter* 7, no. 4 (February 1974): 19–25; rptd. in *Nonfiction Film: Theory and Criticism,* ed. Richard M. Barsam, 296–309. New York: Dutton, 1976.

Handelman, Janet. "An Interview with Frederick Wiseman." *Film Library Quarterly* 3, no. 3 (1970): 5–9.

Harpole, Charles H. "What Is the 'Documentary Film'?" *Filmmaker's Newsletter* 6 (April 1973): 25–27.

Hatch, Robert. "Films." *The Nation,* April 27, 1964, pp. 447–48. [*The Cool World*]

———. "Films." *The Nation,* October 30, 1967, p. 445–46. [*Titicut Follies*]

Hecht, Candra. "Total Institutions on Celluloid." *Society* 9 (April 1972): 44–48.

Heider, Karl G. *Ethnographic Film.* Austin: University of Texas Press, 1976.

Henderson, Brian. "The Long Take." *Film Comment* 7, no. 2 (Summer 1971): 6–11; rptd. in *Movies and Methods,* ed. Bill Nichols, 388–400. Berkeley: University of California Press, 1976.

————. "Toward a Non-bourgeois Camera Style." *Film Quarterly* 24, no. 2 (Winter 1970/71): pp. 2–14; rptd. in *Movies and Methods,* ed. Bill Nichols, 422–38. Berkeley: University of California Press, 1976.

————. "Two Types of Film Theory." *Film Quarterly* 24, no. 3 (Spring 1971): 33–42.

Hichens, Gordon. *"The Cool World." Film Comment* 2, no. 2 (1964): 52–53.

Issari, M. Ali, and Doris A. Paul. *What is Cinema Verité.* Metuchen, N.J.: Scarecrow Press, 1979.

Jacobs, Lewis, ed. *The Documentary Tradition,* 2d. ed. New York: Oxford University Press, 1979.

Janis, Eugenia, and Wendy MacNeil, eds. *Photography within the Humanities.* Danbury, N.H.: Addison House, 1977.

Janssen, Peter A. "The Last Bell." *Newsweek,* May 19, 1969, p. 102. [*High School*]

Kael, Pauline. "The Current Cinema." *New Yorker,* January 31, 1970, pp. 74–76. [*Hospital*]

————. *"High School." New Yorker,* October 18, 1969, pp. 199–204; rptd. in *Frederick Wiseman,* ed. Thomas R. Atkins, 95–101. New York: Simon & Schuster, 1976.

Kawin, Bruce. *Mindscreen: Bergman, Godard, and First-Person Film.* Princeton, N.J.: Princeton University Press, 1978.

Kleinman, Arthur. "The American Medical Way of Death: Do Not Go Gentle." *New Republic,* February 5, 1990, pp. 28–29. [*Near Death*]

Knight, Arthur. "Cinéma Vérité and Film Truth." *Saturday Review,* September 9, 1967, p. 44.

Kracauer, Siegfried. *Theory of Film: The Redemption of Physical Reality.* New York: Oxford University Press, 1960.

Kraemer, Chuck. "Fred Wiseman's *Primate* Makes Monkeys of Scientists." *New York Times,* December 1, 1974, sec. 2, pp. 1, 31.

Kuhn, Annette. "The Camera I: Observations on Documentary." *Screen* 19, no. 2 (1978/79): 71–83.

Leacock, Richard. "For an Uncontrolled Cinema." *Film Culture* 22–23 (Summer 1961); rptd. in *Film Culture Reader,* ed. P. Adams Sitney, 76–78. New York and Washington: Praeger, 1970.

Le Péron, Serge. "Cinema Independant Americain: Fred Wiseman." *Cahiers du cinéma* 303 (September 1979): 41–49.

————. "Wiseman ou le cinema Americain vu de dos." *Cahiers du cinéma* 330 (December 1981): 43–49.

Levin, G. Roy. *Documentary Explorations: 15 Interviews with Film-makers.* Garden City, N.Y.: Anchor/Doubleday, 1971.

Lewis, Caroline. *"Essene." Monthly Film Bulletin* 41 (September 1974): 198.

———. *"High School." Monthly Film Bulletin* 41 (August 1974): 177.

———. *"Juvenile Court." Monthly Film Bulletin* 41 (June 1974): 129.

———. *"Welfare." Monthly Film Bulletin* 43 (March 1976): 65.

Lewis, Jon. "The Shifting Camera Point of View and Model of Language in Frederick Wiseman's *High School." Quarterly Review of Film Studies* 7, no. 1 (Winter 1982): 69–77.

Lovell, Alan, and Jim Hillier. *Studies in Documentary.* New York: Viking. 1972.

Macdonald, Dwight. *"The Cool World." Dwight Macdonald on Movies.* Englewood Cliffs, N.J.: Prentice-Hall, 1969.

MacDougall, David. "Beyond Observational Cinema," in *Principles of Visual Anthropology,* ed. Paul Hockings, 109–24. The Hague: Mouton, 1975; rptd. in *Movies and Methods,* vol. 2. ed. Bill Nichols, 274–86. Berkeley: University of California Press, 1985.

———. "Prospects of the Ethnographic Film." *Film Quarterly* 23, no. 2 (Winter 1969/70): 16–30.

McLuhan, Marshall. *Understanding Media: The Extensions of Man.* New York: Signet, 1964.

McWilliams, Donald E. "Frederick Wiseman." *Film Quarterly* 24, no. 1 (Fall 1970): 17–26.

Mamber, Stephen. *Cinema Verite in America: Studies in Uncontrolled Documentary.* Cambridge: MIT Press, 1973.

———. "Cinéma Vérité and Social Concerns." *Film Comment* 9, no. 6 (November/December 1973): 8–15.

———. "High School." *Film Quarterly* 23, no. 3 (Spring 1970): 48–51.

———. "The New Documentaries of Frederick Wiseman." *Cinema* (L. A.) 6, no. 1 (n.d.): 33–40.

———. "One Man's *Meat." New Republic,* December 4, 1976, pp. 21–22.

Marcorelles, Louis. *Living Cinema: New Directions in Contemporary Filmmaking.* New York: Praeger, 1973.

Maslin, Janet. "Frederick Wiseman's *Near Death." New York Times,* October 7, 1979, pp. 11, 13.

May, John R., and Michael Bird, eds. *Religion in Film.* Knoxville: University of Tennessee Press, 1982.

Meehan, Thomas. "The Documentary Maker." *Saturday Review of the Arts,* December 1972, pp. 12, 14, 18.

Mekas, Jonas. "A Call for a New Generation of Film-makers." *Film Culture* 19 (1959); rptd. in *Film Culture Reader,* ed. P. Adams Sitney, 73–76. New York and Washington: Praeger, 1970.

———. "Notes on the New American Cinema." *Film Culture* 24 (Spring 1962): 6–16; rptd. in *Film Culture Reader,* ed. P. Adams Sitney, 87–107. New York and Washington: Praeger, 1970.

Meyer, Karl E. "Television: Report from Purgatory." *Saturday Review,* September 20, 1975, p. 52.

Miller, Warren. *The Cool World.* New York: Crest Books, 1965.

Morgenstern, Joseph. "It Don't Make Sense." *Newsweek,* February 9, 1970, pp. 85–86. [*Hospital*]

———. "Probing the Kafkaesque World of Welfare." *New York Times,* September 21, 1975, sec. 2, pp. 1, 25.

Nichols, Bill. "Documentary Theory and Practice." *Screen* 17, no. 4 (Winter 1976–77): 34–38.

———. "Fred Wiseman's Documentaries: Theory and Structure." *Film Quarterly* 31, no. 3 (Spring 1978): 15–28.

———. *Ideology and the Image.* Bloomington: Indiana University Press, 1981.

———. "The Voice of Documentary." *Film Quarterly* 36, no. 3 (Spring 1983): 17–30; rptd. in *Movies and Methods,* ed. Bill Nichols, vol. 2, 258–73. Berkeley: University of California Press, 1985; and in *New Challenges for Documentary,* ed. Alan Rosenthal, 48–63. Berkeley: University of California Press, 1988.

Nicholson, Philip, and Elizabeth Nicholson. "Meet Lawyer-Filmmaker Frederick Wiseman." *American Bar Association Journal* 61, no. 3 (1975): 328–32.

O'Connor, John J. "TV: *Primate,* A Study by Wiseman." *New York Times,* December 5, 1974, p. 124.

———. "TV: Strong Wiseman Documentary on Monastery." *New York Times,* November 14, 1972, p. 94.

———. "TV: Wiseman Captures the World of Modeling." *New York Times,* September 16, 1981, p. C26.

———. "The Film is About Killing." *New York Times,* October 3, 1971, sec. 2, p. 17. [*Basic Training*]

———. "Wiseman's Latest Film Is Another 'Reality Fiction.' " *New York Times,* November 7, 1976, p. 26. [*Meat*]

———. "Wiseman's *Welfare* is on Channel 13 Tonight." *New York Times,* September 24, 1975, p. 91.

Perez, Michael. *"Hospital." Le Quotidien de Paris,* June 22, 1974, p. 8.

Plantinga, Carl. "Defining Documentary: Fiction, Non-Fiction, and Projected Worlds." *Persistence of Vision* 5 (Spring 1987): 44–54.

Polt, Harriet R. *"The Cool World." Film Quarterly* 17, no. 2 (Winter 1963): 33–35.

Pryluck, Calvin. "Ultimately We Are All Outsiders: The Ethics of Documentary Filming." *Journal of the University Film Association* 28, no. 1 (Winter 1976): 21–29; rptd. in *New Challenges for Documentary,* ed. Alan Rosenthal, 255–68. Berkeley: University of California Press, 1988.

Rayns, Tony. *"Basic Training."* *Monthly Film Bulletin* 41 (November 1974): 246–47.

Rice, Eugene. *"Essene:* A Documentary Film on Benedictine Community Life." *American Benedictine Review* 24, no. 3 (1973): 382.

Rice, Susan. "The Movies: *Hospital."* *Media and Methods* 6, no. 7 (March 1970): 14.

———. "Shirley Clarke: Image and Images." *Take One* 3, no. 2 (November 1970): 20–22.

Rich, Frank. "A Sunny, Nightmare Vision." *Time,* October 10, 1977, p. 103. [*Canal Zone*]

Richardson, Elliot. "Letters: Focusing Again on *Titicut."* *Civil Liberties Review* 1, no. 3 (Summer 1974): 148–49; rptd. in *Frederick Wiseman,* ed. Thomas R. Atkins, 67–69. New York: Simon & Schuster, 1976.

Rifkin, Glenn. "Wiseman Looks at Affluent Texans." *New York Times,* December 11, 1983, pp. 37, 44. [*The Store*]

Robb, Christina. "Focus on Life." *Boston Globe Magazine,* January 23, 1983, pp. 15–17, 26–34.

Robinson, David. "Apes and Essentials." (London) *Times,* January 10, 1975, p. 11. [*Primate*]

Robinson, Donald. "A Slanted, Cruelly Middle-Class-Debunking Film." *Phi Delta Kappan* 51, no. 1 (September 1969): 47. [*High School*]

Rose, Daniel Asa. "Frederick Wiseman Takes His Camera to the Races." *New York Times,* June 1, 1986, pp. 29, 38.

Rosenberg, Karen. *"The Store."* *The Nation,* December 17, 1983, pp. 642–43.

Rosenblatt, Roger. "Frederick Wiseman's *Welfare."* *New Republic,* September 27, 1975, pp. 65–67.

Rosenthal, Alan, ed. *The Documentary Conscience: A Casebook in Film Making.* Berkeley: University of California Press, 1980.

———, ed. *New Challenges for Documentary.* Berkeley: University of California Press, 1988.

———, ed. *The New Documentary in Action: A Casebook in Film Making.* Berkeley: University of California Press, 1972.

Rotha, Paul. *Documentary Film.* New York: Hastings, 1952.

Ruby, Jay. "Ethnography as *Trompe l'Oeil:* Film and Anthropology." In *A Crack in the Mirror: Reflexive Perspectives in Anthropology,* ed. Jay Ruby, 121–31. Philadelphia: University of Pennsylvania Press, 1982.

———. "The Image Mirrored: Reflexivity and the Documentary Film." *Journal of the University Film Association* 29, no. 1 (Fall 1977): 3–11; rptd. in *New Challenges for Documentary,* ed. Alan Rosenthal, 64–77. Berkeley: University of California Press, 1988.

Russell, Cristine. "Science on Film: The *Primate* Controversy." *Bioscience* 25, no. 3 (March 1976): 151–154, 218.

Sarris, Andrew. "Films." *Village Voice*, November 9, 1967, p. 33. [*Titicut Follies*]

———. "*The Cool World*." *Village Voice*, April 23, 1964; rptd. in *Confessions of a Cultist: On the Cinema, 1955–1969*, 135–36. New York: Simon & Schuster, 1971.

Schickel, Richard. "The Sorriest Spectacle." *Life*, December 1, 1967, p. 12 [*Titicut Follies*]; rptd. in *Film 67/68*, ed. Richard Schickel and John Simon, 246–48. New York: Simon & Schuster, 1968; and in *Second Sight: Notes on Some Movies, 1965–1970*, 155–59. New York: Simon & Schuster, 1972; and in *Frederick Wiseman*, ed. Thomas R. Atkins, 91–93. New York: Simon & Schuster, 1976.

———. "A Vérité View of High School." *Life*, September 12, 1969; rptd. in *Film 69/70*, ed. Joseph Morgenstern and Stefan Kanfer, 209–11. New York: Simon and Schuster, 1969; and in *Second Sight: Notes on Some Movies, 1965–1970*, 256–58. New York: Simon & Schuster, 1972.

———. "Where Misery Must Be Confronted." *Life*, February 6, 1970, p. 14. [*Hospital*]

Scott, Nancy. "The Christo Films: *Christo's Valley Curtain* and *Running Fence*." *Quarterly Review of Film Studies* 7, no. 1 (Winter 1982): 61–68.

Sheed, Wilfred. "Films." *Esquire*, March 1968, pp. 52, 55. [*Titicut Follies*]

Sidel, Victor W. "*Hospital* on View." *New England Journal of Medicine* 285, no. 5 (January 29, 1970): 279.

Sitney, P. Adams, ed. *Film Culture Reader*. New York and Washington: Praeger, 1970.

Slavitt, David R. "*Basic Training*." *Contempora* 2, no. 1 (September/February 1972): 10–11.

Sobchack, Vivian C. "*No Lies*: Direct Cinema as Rape." *Journal of the University Film Association* 29, no. 1 (Fall 1977): 13–18; rptd. in *New Challenges for Documentary*, ed. Alan Rosenthal, 332–41. Berkeley: University of California Press, 1988.

Sontag, Susan. "Spiritual Style in the Films of Robert Bresson." *Against Interpretation*, 177–95. New York: Farrar, Strauss & Giroux, 1966.

———. *On Photography*. New York: Delta, 1978.

Sourian, Peter. "Television." *The Nation*, October 15,1977, 181–82. [*Canal Zone*]

Steele, Robert. "*Essene*." *Film News*, September 1973, p. 24.

Stott, William. *Documentary Expression and Thirties America*. New York: Oxford University Press, 1973.

Sullivan, Patrick. *"Essene." Film Quarterly,* 27, no. 1 (Fall 1973): 55–57; rptd. in *Frederick Wiseman,* 113–20. New York: Simon & Schuster, 1976.

————. "Frederick Wiseman's *Primate." New Republic,* January 25, 1975, pp. 30–32.

Sutherland, Allan T. "Wiseman on Polemic." *Sight and Sound* 47, no. 2 (Spring 1978): 82.

Swartz, Susan. "The Real Northeast." *Film Library Quarterly* 6, no. 1 (1972–73): 12–15.

Sweet, Louise. *"Canal Zone." Sight and Sound* 47, no. 1 (Winter 1977–78): 59–60.

Tarratt, Margaret. *"Juvenile Court." Films and Filming* 19, no. 11 (August 20, 1974): 43–44.

————. *"Meat." Films and Filming* 23, no. 9 (June 1977): 42–43.

Taylor, Charles. *"Titicut Follies." Sight and Sound* 57, no. 2 (Spring 1988): 98–103.

Tuch, Roland. "Frederick Wiseman's Cinema of Alienation." *Film Library Quarterly* 11, no. 3 (1978): 9–15, 49. [*Meat*]

Tudor, Andrew. *Theories of Film.* New York: Viking Press, 1974.

Vaughan, Dai. *Television Documentary Usage.* London: British Film Institute, 1976.

Vertov, Dziga. *Kino-Eye: The Writings of Dziga Vertov,* ed. Annette Michelson, trans. Kevin O'Brien. Berkeley: University of California Press, 1984.

Vogel, Amos. *Film as a Subversive Art.* New York: Random House, 1974.

Walker, Jesse. "Film Reviews: *The Cool World." Film Comment* 1/2, no. 2 (Spring 1964): 51–52.

Wakefield, Dan. "American Close-Ups." *Atlantic,* May 1969, pp. 107–8. [*High School*]

Walters, Harry F. "Inside a Shopping Shrine." *Newsweek,* December 19, 1983, p. 81.

————. "Wiseman on Welfare." *Newsweek,* September 29, 1975, pp. 62–63.

Waugh, Thomas, "Beyond Vérité: Emile de Antonio and the New Documentary of the Seventies." *Movies and Methods,* vol. 2, ed. Bill Nichols, 233–58. Berkeley: University of California Press, 1985.

————, ed. *"Show Us Life": Toward a History and Aesthetics of the Committed Documentary.* Metuchen, N. J.: Scarecrow Press, 1984.

Weiler, A. H. "Wiseman to Make 'Yes Yes, No No,' First Fiction Film." *New York Times,* December 6, 1974, p. 78.

Weisman, Mary-Lou. "Neiman-Marcus, the Movie." *New Republic,* December 31, 1983, pp. 25–26.

Westin, Alan. " 'You Start Off with a Bromide': Conversation with Film Maker Frederick Wiseman." *Civil Liberties Review* 1, no. 2 (Winter/ Spring 1974): 52–67; rptd. in *Frederick Wiseman,* ed. Thomas R. Atkins, 47–66. New York: Simon & Schuster, 1976.

Williams, Christopher, ed. *Realism in the Cinema: A Reader.* London: Routledge, 1980.

Wilson, David. *"Meat." Monthly Film Bulletin* 44, no. 520 (May 1977): 102–3.

Winston, Brian. "Before Flaherty, Before Grierson." *Sight and Sound* 57, no. 4 (Autumn 1988): 277–79.

———. "Direct Cinema: The Third Decade." *Sight and Sound* 52, no. 4 (Autumn 1983): 238–43; rptd. in *New Challenges for Documentary,* ed. Alan Rosenthal, 517–29. Berkeley: University of California Press, 1988.

———. "Documentary: I Think We Are in Trouble." *Sight and Sound* 48, no. 1 (Winter 1978–79): 2–7; rptd. in *New Challenges for Documentary,* ed. Alan Rosenthal, 21–33. Berkeley: University of California Press, 1988.

Wiseman, Frederick. "A Filmmaker's Choices." *Christian Science Monitor,* April 25, 1984, p. 30.

———, et al. "Letter to the Editor." *New England Journal of Medicine* 322, no. 22 (May 31, 1990): 1605–06.

———. "Letters: Focusing Again on *Titicut." Civil Liberties Review* 1, no. 3 (Summer 1974): 149–51; rptd. in *Frederick Wiseman,* ed. Thomas R. Atkins, 69–73. New York: Simon & Schuster, 1976.

———. "Reminiscences of a Filmmaker: Fred Wiseman on *Law and Order." Police Chief* 36, no. 9 (September 1969): 32–35.

———. "Wiseman on *Juvenile Court." Journal of the University Film Association* 25, no. 3 (1973); 48–49, 58.

———. "What Public TV Needs: Less Bureaucracy." *New York Times,* November 27, 1988, pp. 35, 42.

Wolcott, James. "Adrift in Cheekbone Heaven." *Village Voice,* September 11, 1981, p. 67. [*Model*]

———. "Blood on the Racks: Wiseman's *Meat." Village Voice,* November 15, 1976, p. 95.

———. "*Welfare* Must Be Seen." *Village Voice,* September 29, 1975, p. 126.

———. "Television and its Discontents: Wiseman's Panamania." *Village Voice,* October 10, 1977, p. 45.

Wolf, Susan M., "*Near Death*—In the Moment of Decision." *New England Journal of Medicine* 322, no. 3 (June 18, 1990): 208–09.

Wollen, Peter. *Signs and Meaning in the Cinema,* rev. ed. Bloomington and London: Indiana University Press, 1972.

Youdelman, Jeffrey. "Narration, Invention, and History: A Documentary Dilemma." *Cineaste* 12, no. 2 (1982): 8–15; rptd. in *New Challenges for Documentary*, ed. Alan Rosenthal, 454–64. Berkeley: University of California Press, 1988.

Zimmerman, Paul D. "Shooting It Like It Is." *Newsweek*, March 17, 1969, pp. 134–35.

Zoglin, Richard. "Let the Music Go Inside of You." *Time*, June 20, 1988, p. 64. [*Deaf and Blind*]

Index

Frame enlargements appear on pages given in **boldface.**

A Note on the Author

BARRY KEITH GRANT, professor of film studies at Brock University, Ontario, Canada, is the editor of *Film Genre Reader* and *Film Study in the Undergraduate Curriculum,* among other volumes.